10 Most Sacred Places in the World

Compiled by
Tisha Durham

Scribbles

Year of Publication 2018

ISBN : 9789387513129

Book Published by

Scribbles

(An Imprint of Alpha Editions)

email - alphaedis@gmail.com

Produced by: PediaPress GmbH
Limburg an der Lahn
Germany
http://pediapress.com/

The content within this book was generated collaboratively by volunteers. Please be advised that nothing found here has necessarily been reviewed by people with the expertise required to provide you with complete, accurate or reliable information. Some information in this book may be misleading or simply wrong. Alpha Editions and PediaPress does not guarantee the validity of the information found here. If you need specific advice (for example, medical, legal, financial, or risk management) please seek a professional who is licensed or knowledgeable in that area.

Sources, licenses and contributors of the articles and images are listed in the section entitled "References". Parts of the books may be licensed under the GNU Free Documentation License. A copy of this license is included in the section entitled "GNU Free Documentation License"

The views and characters expressed in the book are those of the contributors and his/her imagination and do not represent the views of the Publisher.

Contents

Articles   **1**

Mecca and Medina   **1**
    Mecca 1
    Medina 31

St. Peters Basilica   **51**
    St. Peter's Basilica 51

Mahabodhi Temple   **103**
    Mahabodhi Temple 103

Golden Temple   **125**
    Golden Temple 125

Pashupatinath Temple   **141**
    Pashupatinath Temple 141

Mount Kailash   **159**
    Mount Kailash 159

Mount Olympus   **169**
    Mount Olympus 169

Dome of the Rock   **189**
    Dome of the Rock 189

Western Wall   **205**
   Western Wall 205

Karnak Temple   **249**
   Karnak 249

Appendix   **273**
   References 273
   Article Sources and Contributors 286
   Image Sources, Licenses and Contributors 288

Article Licenses   **293**

Index   **295**

Mecca and Medina

Mecca

Mecca مكة المكرمة *Makkah al-Mukarramah* Bakkah	
 Clockwise from top left: Jabal al-Nour, the Kaaba in the Great Mosque of Mecca (prior to the completion of the Abraj Al-Bait), overview of central Mecca, Mina and the modern Jamaraat Bridge	
Nickname(s): *Umm al-Qurā* (أم القرى, "Mother of All Settlements")	
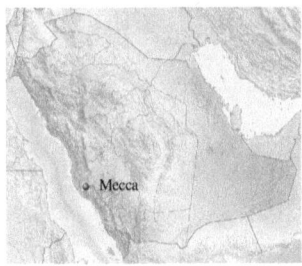 Location of Mecca	
Coordinates: 21°25′N 39°49′E[1] Coordinates: 21°25′N 39°49′E[1]	
Country	Saudi Arabia

Region	Makkah Region
Founded by	Prophet Ismā'īl, son of Abraham (Islamic tradition)
Government	
• Mayor	Osama al-Bar
• Provincial Governor	Khalid bin Faisal Al Saud
Area²	
• City	760 km² (290 sq mi)
• Urban	850 km² (330 sq mi)
• Metro	1,200 km² (500 sq mi)
Elevation	277 m (909 ft)
Population (2010)	
• City	1,675,368
• Density	2,200/km² (5,700/sq mi)
Time zone	AST (UTC+3)
Area code(s)	(+966) 12
Website	www<wbr/>.holymakkah<wbr/>.gov<wbr/>.sa³

Mecca[5] (/ˈmɛkə/) or **Makkah** (Arabic: مكة *Makkah* [ˈmaka]) is a city in the Tihamah plain in Saudi Arabia that is also the capital and administrative headquarters of the Makkah Region. The city is located 70 km (43 mi) inland from

Jeddah in a narrow valley at a height of 277 m (909 ft) above sea level, and 340 kilometres (210 mi) south of Medina. Its resident population in 2012 was roughly 2 million, although visitors more than triple this number every year during the *hajj* ("pilgrimage") period held in the twelfth Muslim lunar month of *Dhu al-Hijjah*.

As the birthplace of Muhammad and the site of Muhammad's first revelation of the Quran (specifically, a cave 3 km (2 mi) from Mecca), Mecca is regarded as the holiest city in the religion of Islam[6] and a pilgrimage to it known as the Hajj is obligatory for all able Muslims. Mecca is home to the Kaaba, by majority description Islam's holiest site, as well as being the direction of Muslim prayer. Mecca was long ruled by Muhammad's descendants, the sharifs, acting either as independent rulers or as vassals to larger polities. It was conquered by Ibn Saud in 1925. In its modern period, Mecca has seen tremendous expansion in size and infrastructure, home to structures such as the Abraj Al Bait, also known as the Makkah Royal Clock Tower Hotel, the world's fourth tallest building and the building with the third largest amount of floor area. During this expansion, Mecca has lost some historical structures and archaeological sites, such as the Ajyad Fortress. Today, more than 15 million Muslims visit Mecca annually, including several million during the few days of the Hajj.[7] As a result, Mecca has become one of the most cosmopolitan cities in the Muslim world,[8] even though non-Muslims are prohibited from entering the city.

Etymology and usage

"Mecca" is the familiar form of the English transliteration for the Arabic name of the city, although the official transliteration used by the Saudi government is *Makkah*, which is closer to the Arabic pronunciation. The word "Mecca" in English has come to be used to refer to any place that draws large numbers of people, and because of this some English speaking Muslims have come to regard the use of this spelling for the city as offensive. The Saudi government adopted *Makkah* as the official spelling in the 1980s, but is not universally known or used worldwide. The full official name is *Makkah al-Mukarramah* or *Makkatu l-Mukarramah* (مكة المكرمة, pronounced [makkah al mukarramah] or [makkatul mukarramah]Wikipedia:Please clarify), which means "Mecca the Honored", but is also loosely translated as "The Holy City of Mecca".

The ancient or early name for the site of Mecca is *Bakkah* (also transliterated Baca, Baka, Bakah, Bakka, Becca, Bekka, etc.). An Arabic language word, its etymology, like that of Mecca, is obscure. Widely believed to be a synonym for Mecca, it is said to be more specifically the early name for the valley located therein, while Muslim scholars generally use it to refer to the sacred area of the city that immediately surrounds and includes the Kaaba.

Potential ancient references

The Greek historian Diodorus Siculus writes about Arabia in his work Bibliotheca historica, describing a holy shrine: "And a temple has been set up there, which is very holy and exceedingly revered by all Arabians".[16] Claims have been made this could be a reference to the Kaaba in Mecca. However, the geographic location Diodorus describes is located in northwest Arabia, around the area of Leuke Kome, closer to Petra and within the former Nabataean Kingdom and Rome's Arabia Petraea.[17,18]

Ptolemy lists the names of 50 cities in Arabia, one going by the name of "Macoraba". There has been speculation this is could be a reference to Mecca. However, due to the lack of a description or any other supporting literature, the claim is seen as contentious.

Islamic view

In the Islamic view, the beginnings of Mecca are attributed to Ishmael's descendants. The Old Testament chapter Psalm 84:3-6, and a mention of a pilgrimage at the Valley of Baca, that Muslims see as referring to the mentioning of Mecca as Bakkah in Quran Surah 3:96.

Some time in the 5th century, the Kaaba was a place of worship for the deities of Arabia's pagan tribes. Mecca's most important pagan deity was Hubal, which had been placed there by the ruling Quraysh tribe[19] and remained until the 7th century.

In the *Sharḥ al-Asāṭīr*, a commentary on the Samaritan midrashic chronology of the Patriarchs, of unknown date but probably composed in the tenth century C.E., it is claimed that Mecca was built by the sons of Nebaioth, the eldest son of Ishmael.[20,21,22]

In the 5th century, the Quraysh took control of Mecca, and became skilled merchants and traders. In the 6th century they joined the lucrative spice trade, since battles elsewhere were diverting trade routes from dangerous sea routes to more secure overland routes. The Byzantine Empire had previously controlled the Red Sea, but piracy had been increasing. Another previous route that ran through the Persian Gulf via the Tigris and Euphrates rivers was also being threatened by exploitations from the Sassanid Empire, and was being disrupted by the Lakhmids, the Ghassanids, and the Roman–Persian Wars. Mecca's prominence as a trading center also surpassed the cities of Petra and Palmyra.[23] The Sassanids however did not always pose a threat to Mecca, as in 575 CE they protected Mecca city from invasion by the Kingdom of Axum, led by its Christian leader Abraha. The tribes of southern Arabia asked the Persian king Khosrau I for aid, in response to which he came south to Arabia with foot-soldiers and a fleet of ships into Mecca. The Persian intervention prevented Christianity from spreading eastward into Arabia, and Mecca and the Islamic prophet Muhammad, who was at the time six years old in the Quraysh tribe, "would not grow up under the cross."

By the middle of the 6th century, there were three major settlements in northern Arabia, all along the south-western coast that borders the Red Sea, in a habitable region between the sea and the great mountains to the east. Although the area around Mecca was completely barren, it was the wealthiest of the three settlements with abundant water via the renowned Zamzam Well and a position at the crossroads of major caravan routes.

The harsh conditions and terrain of the Arabian peninsula meant a near-constant state of conflict between the local tribes, but once a year they would declare a truce and converge upon Mecca in an annual pilgrimage. Up to the 7th century, this journey was intended for religious reasons by the pagan Arabs to pay homage to their shrine, and to drink from the Zamzam Well. However, it was also the time each year that disputes would be arbitrated, debts would be resolved, and trading would occur at Meccan fairs. These annual events gave the tribes a sense of common identity and made Mecca an important focus for the peninsula.[23]

The *Year of the Elephant* is the name in Islamic history for the year approximately equating to 570 CE. According to Islamic tradition, it was in this year that Muhammad was born.[24] The name is derived from an event said to have occurred at Mecca. According to early Islamic historians such as Ibn Ishaq, Abraha the Christian ruler of Yemen, which was subject to the Kingdom of Aksum of Ethiopia, built a great church at Sana'a known as *al-Qullays* in honor of the Aksumite king Negus. It gained widespread fame, even gaining the notice of the Byzantine Empire. Abraha attempted to divert the pilgrimage of Arab people from Kaaba to al-Qullays and appointed a man named Muhammad ibn Khuza'i to Mecca and Tihamah as a king with a message that al-Qullays was both much better than other houses of worship and purer, having not been defiled by the housing of idols. When Muhammad ibn Khuza'i got as far as the land of Kinana, the people of the lowland, knowing what he had come for, sent a man of Hudhayl called 'Urwa bin Hayyad al-Milasi, who shot him with an arrow, killing him. His brother Qays who was with him fled to Abraha and told him the news, which increased his rage and fury and he swore to raid the Kinana tribe and destroy the temple. Ibn Ishaq further states that one of the men of the Quraysh tribe was angered by this, and going to Sana'a, slipped into the church at night and defiled it; it is widely assumed that they did so by defecating in it. Abraha[25,26] marched upon the Kaaba with a large army, which included one or more war elephants, intending to demolish it. When news of the advance of Abraha's army came, the Arab tribes of the Quraysh, Banu

Kinanah, Banu Khuza'a and Banu Hudhayl united in defense of the Kaaba. A man from the Himyarite Kingdom was sent by Abraha to advise them that Abraha only wished to demolish the Kaaba and if they resisted, they would be crushed. Abdul Muttalib told the Meccans to seek refuge in the hills while he with some leading members of the Quraysh remained within the precincts of the Kaaba. Abraha sent a dispatch inviting Abdul-Muttalib to meet with Abraha and discuss matters. When Abdul-Muttalib left the meeting he was heard saying, "The Owner of this House is its Defender, and I am sure he will save it from the attack of the adversaries and will not dishonor the servants of His House." Abraha attacked Mecca However, the lead elephant, known as Mahmud, is said to have stopped at the boundary around Mecca and refused to enter. It has been theorized that an epidemic such as by smallpox could have caused such a failed invasion of Mecca.[27] The reference to the story in Qur'an is rather short. According to the al-Fil sura, the next day, [as Abraha prepared to enter the city], a dark cloud of small birds sent by Allah appeared. The birds carried small rocks in their beaks, and bombarded the Ethiopian forces and smashed them like "eaten straw".

Camel caravans, said to have first been used by Muhammad's great-grandfather, were a major part of Mecca's bustling economy. Alliances were struck between the merchants in Mecca and the local nomadic tribes, who would bring goods – leather, livestock, and metals mined in the local mountains – to Mecca to be loaded on the caravans and carried to cities in Syria and Iraq.[28] Historical accounts also provide some indication that goods from other continents may also have flowed through Mecca. Goods from Africa and the Far East passed through en route to Syria including spices, leather, medicine, cloth, and slaves; in return Mecca received money, weapons, cereals and wine, which in turn were distributed throughout Arabia. The Meccans signed treaties with both the Byzantines and the Bedouins, and negotiated safe passages for caravans, giving them water and pasture rights. Mecca became the center of a loose confederation of client tribes, which included those of the Banu Tamim. Other regional powers such as the Abyssinian, Ghassan, and Lakhm were in decline leaving Meccan trade to be the primary binding force in Arabia in the late 6th century.

Thamudic inscriptions

Some Thamudic inscriptions which were discovered in south Jordan contained names of some individuals such as *"Abd Mekkat"* which means in English "Servant of Mecca".[29]

There were also some other inscriptions which contained personal names such as *"Makky"* which means "The Meccan", but Jawwad Ali from the University of Baghdad suggested that there's also a probability of a tribe named "Mecca".[30]

Figure 3: *Jabal al-Nour is where Muhammad is believed to have received the first revelation of God through the Archangel Gabriel.*

Islamic tradition

According to Islamic tradition, the history of Mecca goes back to Abraham (Ibrahim), who built the Kaaba with the help of his elder son Ishmael in around 2000 BCE when the inhabitants of the site then known as Bakkah had fallen away from the original monotheism of Abraham through the influence of the Amalekites.

Muhammad and conquest of Mecca

Muhammad was born in Mecca in 570, and thus Islam has been inextricably linked with it ever since. He was born in a minor faction, the Hashemites, of the ruling Quraysh tribe. It was in Mecca, in the nearby mountain cave of Hira on Jabal al-Nour, that, according to Islamic tradition, Muhammad began receiving divine revelations from God through the Archangel Gabriel in 610 AD, and advocated his form of Abrahamic monotheism against Meccan paganism. After enduring persecution from the pagan tribes for 13 years, Muhammad emigrated (see Hijra) in 622 with his companions, the *Muhajirun*, to Yathrib (later called Medina). The conflict between the Quraysh and the Muslims, however, continued: The two fought in the Battle of Badr, where the Muslims defeated the Quraysh outside Medina; while the Battle of Uhud ended indecisively. Overall, Meccan efforts to annihilate Islam failed and proved to be costly and unsuccessful. During the Battle of the Trench in 627, the combined armies of Arabia were unable to defeat Muhammad's forces.[23]

In 628, Muhammad and his followers wanted to enter Mecca for pilgrimage, but were blocked by the Quraysh. Subsequently, Muslims and Meccans entered into the Treaty of Hudaybiyyah, whereby the Quraysh promised to cease fighting Muslims and promised that Muslims would be allowed into the city to perform the pilgrimage the following year. It was meant to be a ceasefire for 10 years. However, just two years later, the Quraysh violated the truce by slaughtering a group of Muslims and their allies. Muhammad and his companions, now 10,000 strong, marched into Mecca. However, instead of continuing their fight, the city of Mecca surrendered to Muhammad, who declared peace and amnesty for its inhabitants. The pagan imagery was destroyed by Muhammad's followers and the location Islamized and rededicated to the worship of God. Mecca was declared as the holiest site in Islam ordaining it as the center of Muslim pilgrimage, one of the faith's Five Pillars. Then, Muhammad returned to Medina, after assigning Akib ibn Usaid as governor of the city. His other activities in Arabia led to the unification of the peninsula.

Muhammad died in 632, but with the sense of unity that he had passed on to his Ummah (Islamic nation), Islam began a rapid expansion, and within the next few hundred years stretched from North Africa into Asia and parts of Europe. As the Islamic Empire grew, Mecca continued to attract pilgrims from all across the Muslim world and beyond, as Muslims came to perform the annual Hajj pilgrimage.

Mecca also attracted a year-round population of scholars, pious Muslims who wished to live close to the Kaaba, and local inhabitants who served the pilgrims. Due to the difficulty and expense of the Hajj, pilgrims arrived by boat at Jeddah, and came overland, or joined the annual caravans from Syria or Iraq.

Medieval and pre-modern times

Mecca was never the capital of any of the Islamic states but Muslim rulers did contribute to its upkeep. During the reigns of Umar (634–44 CE) and Uthman ibn Affan (644–56) concerns of flooding caused the caliphs to bring in Christian engineers to build barrages in the low-lying quarters and construct dykes and embankments to protect the area round the Kaaba.[31]

Muhammad's migration to Medina shifted the focus away from Mecca. This focus moved still more when Ali, the fourth caliph, took power choosing Kufa as his capital. The Umayyad Caliphate moved the capital to Damascus in Syria and the Abbasid Caliphate to Baghdad, in modern-day Iraq, which remained

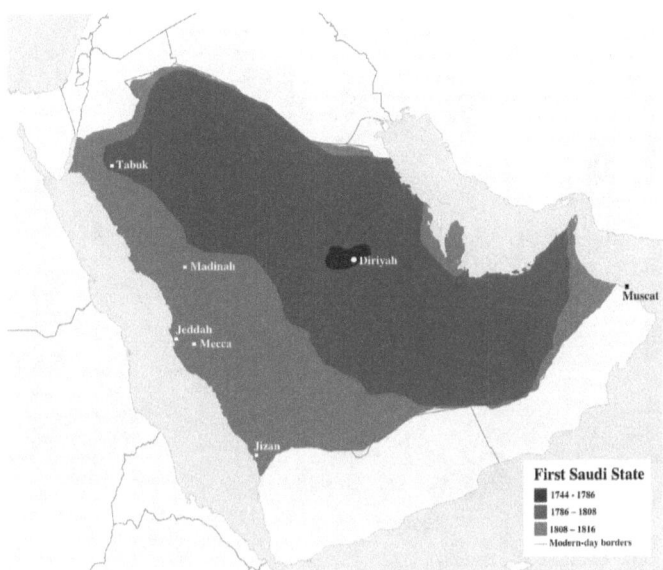

Figure 4: *The First Saudi State*

the center of the Islamic Empire for nearly 500 years. Mecca re-entered Islamic political history during the Second Islamic Civil War, when it was held by Abd Allah ibn al-Zubayr, an early Muslim who opposed the Umayyad caliphs. The city was twice besieged by the Umayyads, in 683 and 692. For some time thereafter the city figured little in politics, remaining a city of devotion and scholarship governed by the Hashemite Sharifs.

In 930, Mecca was attacked and sacked by Qarmatians, a millenarian Ismaili Muslim sect led by Abū-Tāhir Al-Jannābī and centered in eastern Arabia. The Black Death pandemic hit Mecca in 1349.

In 1517, the Sharif, Barakat bin Muhammed, acknowledged the supremacy of the Ottoman Caliph but retained a great degree of local autonomy.

In 1803 the city was captured by the First Saudi State,[32] which held Mecca until 1813. This was a massive blow to the prestige of the (Turkish) Ottoman Empire, which had exercised sovereignty over the holy city since 1517. The Ottomans assigned the task of bringing Mecca back under Ottoman control to their powerful *Khedive* (viceroy) of Egypt, Muhammad Ali Pasha. Muhammad Ali Pasha successfully returned Mecca to Ottoman control in 1813.

In 1818, followers of the Salafi juristic school were again defeated, but some of the Al Saud clan survived and founded the Second Saudi State that lasted until 1891 and led on to the present country of Saudi Arabia.

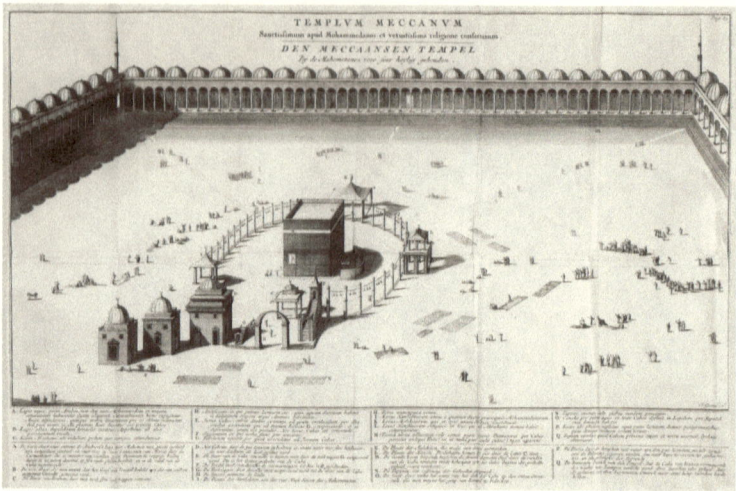

Figure 5: *Mecca in 1718*

Mecca was regularly hit by cholera outbreaks. Between 1830 and 1930 cholera broke out among pilgrims at Mecca 27 times.[33]

Revolt of Sharif of Mecca

In World War I, the Ottoman Empire was at war with Britain and its allies, having sided with Germany. It had successfully repulsed an attack on Istanbul in the Gallipoli Campaign and on Baghdad in the Siege of Kut. The British agent T. E. Lawrence conspired with the Ottoman governor Hussain bin Ali, the Sharif of Mecca. Hussein bin Ali revolted against the Ottoman Empire from Mecca, and it was the first city captured by his forces in the Battle of Mecca (1916). Sharif's revolt proved a turning point of the war on the eastern front. Sharif Hussein declared a new state, the Kingdom of Hejaz, and declared Mecca as the capital of the new kingdom.

News reports in November 1916[34] via contact in Cairo with returning Hajj pilgrims, said that with the Ottoman Turkish authorities gone, Mecca at Hajj 1916 was thankfully free of the previous massive extortion and illegal money-demanding by Turks who were agents of the Ottoman government.

Figure 6: *Mecca ca. 1778*

Figure 7: *Mecca in the late 1880s*

Figure 8: *Mecca in 1910*

Figure 9: *Bird's-eye view of Kaaba crowded with pilgrims in 1910*

Saudi Arabia

Following the 1924 Battle of Mecca, the Sharif of Mecca was overthrown by the Saud family, and Mecca was incorporated into Saudi Arabia.[35]

Under Saudi rule, much of the historic city has been demolished as a result of construction programs – see below.

On 20 November 1979 two hundred armed Islamist dissidents led by Saudi preacher Juhayman al-Otaibi seized the Grand Mosque. They claimed that the Saudi royal family no longer represented pure Islam and that the Masjid al-Haram (The Sacred Mosque) and the Kaaba, must be held by those of true faith. The rebels seized tens of thousands of pilgrims as hostages and barricaded themselves in the mosque. The siege lasted two weeks, and resulted in several hundred deaths and significant damage to the shrine, especially the Safa-Marwa gallery. Pakistani forces carried out the final assault; they were assisted with weapons, logistics and planning by an elite team of French commandos from the French GIGN commando unit.

Destruction of historic buildings

Under Saudi rule, it has been estimated that since 1985 about 95% of Mecca's historic buildings, most over a thousand years old, have been demolished.[36]

Historic sites of religious importance which have been destroyed by the Saudis include five of the renowned "Seven Mosques" initially built by Muhammad's daughter and four of his "greatest Companions": Masjid Abu Bakr, Masjid Salman al-Farsi, Masjid Umar ibn al-Khattab, Masjid Sayyida Fatima bint Rasulullah and Masjid Ali ibn Abu Talib.[37]

It has been reported that there are now fewer than 20 structures remaining in Mecca that date back to the time of Muhammad. Other buildings that have been destroyed include the house of Khadijah, the wife of Muhammad, demolished to make way for public lavatories; the house of Abu Bakr, Muhammad's companion, now the site of the local Hilton hotel; the house of Muhammad's grandson Ali-Oraid and the Mosque of abu-Qubais, now the location of the King's palace in Mecca; Muhammad's birthplace, demolished to make way for a library; and the Ottoman-era Ajyad Fortress, demolished for construction of the Abraj Al Bait Towers.[38]

The reason for much of the destruction of historic buildings has been for the construction of hotels, apartments, parking lots, and other infrastructure facilities for Hajj pilgrims. However, many have been destroyed without any such reason. For example, when the house of Ali-Oraid was discovered, King Fahd himself ordered that it be bulldozed lest it should become a pilgrimage site.

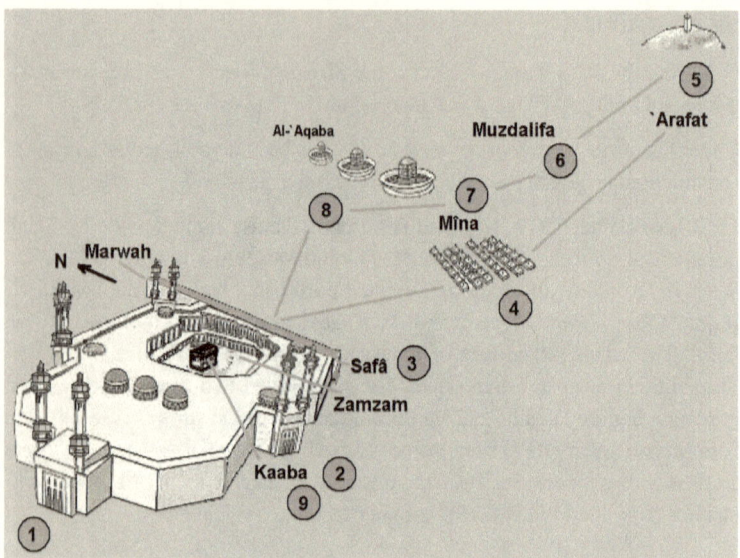

Figure 10: *The Hajj involves pilgrims visiting the Masjid al-Haram, but mainly camping and spending time in the plains of Mina and Arafah.*

Pilgrimage

The pilgrimage to Mecca attracts millions of Muslims from all over the world. There are two pilgrimages: the Hajj and the Umrah.

The Hajj, the 'greater' pilgrimage is performed annually in Mecca and nearby sites. During the Hajj, several million people of varying nationalities worship in unison. Every adult, healthy Muslim who has the financial and physical capacity to travel to Mecca and can make arrangements for the care of his/her dependents during the trip, must perform the Hajj at least once in a lifetime.

Umrah, the lesser pilgrimage, is not obligatory, but is recommended in the Qur'an. Often, they perform the Umrah, the lesser pilgrimage, while visiting the Masjid al-Haram.

Incidents during Pilgrimage

Mecca has been the site of several incidents and failures of crowd control because of the large numbers of people who come to make the Hajj. For example, on 2 July 1990, a pilgrimage to Mecca ended in tragedy when the ventilation system failed in a crowded pedestrian tunnel and 1,426 people were either suffocated or trampled to death in a stampede.[39] On 24 September 2015, 700 pilgrims were killed in a stampede at Mina during the stoning-the-Devil ritual at Jamarat.

Geography

Mecca is at an elevation of 277 m (909 ft) above sea level, and approximately 80 km (50 mi) inland from the Red Sea.[40] Central Mecca lies in a corridor between mountains, which is often called the "Hollow of Mecca." The area contains the valley of Al Taneem, the Valley of Bakkah and the valley of Abqar. This mountainous location has defined the contemporary expansion of the city. The city centers on the Masjid al-Haram area, which is lower than most of the city. The area around the mosque is the old city. The main avenues are *Al-Mudda'ah* and *Sūq al-Layl* to the north of the mosque, and *As-Sūg As-saghīr* to the south. As the Saudis expanded the Grand Mosque in the center of the city, hundreds of houses were replaced by wide avenues and city squares. Traditional homes are built of local rock and are generally two to three stories. The total area of Mecca today is over 1,200 km^2 (460 sq mi).

In pre-modern Mecca, the city used a few chief sources of water. The first were local wells, such as the Zamzam Well, that produced generally brackish water. The second source was the spring of Ayn Zubayda. The sources of this spring are the mountains of Jabal Sa'd (Jabal Sa'd) and Jabal Kabkāb, which are a few kilometers east of Jabal Arafa or about 20 km (12 mi) southeast of Mecca. Water was transported from it using underground channels. A very sporadic third source was rainfall which was stored by the people in small reservoirs or cisterns. The rainfall, scant as it is, also presents the threat of flooding and has been a danger since earliest times. According to Al-Kurdī, there had been 89 historic floods by 1965, including several in the Saudi period. In the last century the most severe flood was in 1942. Since then, dams have been build to ameliorate this problem.

Neighborhoods

- Ajyad
- Al Adl[41]
- Al Faisaliyyah
- Al Gemmezah
- Al Ghassalah
- Al Hindawiyyah
- Al Iskan
- Al Khalediya
- Al Maabda
- Al Muaisem

- Al Nuzha
- Al Rasaifah
- Al Shoqiyah
- Al Shubaikah
- Al Sulaimaniyyah
- Al Tundobawi
- Al Utaibiyyah
- Al Zahir
- Al Zahra
- Aziziyah
- Gazza[42]
- Jabal Al Nour
- Jarwal
- Jurhum
- Mina
- Misfalah
- Shar Mansur
- Suq Al Lail

Climate

Mecca features a hot desert climate. Like most Saudi Arabian cities, Mecca retains warm to hot temperatures even in winter, which can range from 18 °C (64 °F) at night to 30 °C (86 °F) in the afternoon. Summer temperatures are extremely hot and break the 40 °C (104 °F) mark in the afternoon dropping to 30 °C (86 °F) in the evening. Rain usually falls in Mecca in small amounts scattered between November and January.

Climate data for Mecca

Month	Jan	Feb	Mar	Apr	May	Jun	Jul	Aug	Sep	Oct	Nov	Dec	Year
Record high °C (°F)	37.4 (99.3)	38.3 (100.9)	42.4 (108.3)	44.7 (112.5)	49.4 (120.9)	49.6 (121.3)	49.8 (121.6)	49.7 (121.5)	49.4 (120.9)	47.0 (116.6)	41.2 (106.2)	38.4 (101.1)	49.8 (121.6)
Average high °C (°F)	30.5 (86.9)	31.7 (89.1)	34.9 (94.8)	38.7 (101.7)	42.0 (107.6)	43.8 (110.8)	43.0 (109.4)	42.8 (109)	42.8 (109)	40.1 (104.2)	35.2 (95.4)	32.0 (89.6)	38.1 (100.6)
Daily mean °C (°F)	24.0 (75.2)	24.7 (76.5)	27.3 (81.1)	31.0 (87.8)	34.3 (93.7)	35.8 (96.4)	35.9 (96.6)	35.7 (96.3)	35.0 (95)	32.2 (90)	28.4 (83.1)	25.6 (78.1)	30.8 (87.4)
Average low °C (°F)	18.8 (65.8)	19.1 (66.4)	21.1 (70)	24.5 (76.1)	27.6 (81.7)	28.6 (83.5)	29.1 (84.4)	29.5 (85.1)	28.9 (84)	25.9 (78.6)	23.0 (73.4)	20.3 (68.5)	24.7 (76.5)
Record low °C (°F)	11.0 (51.8)	10.0 (50)	13.0 (55.4)	15.6 (60.1)	20.3 (68.5)	22.0 (71.6)	23.4 (74.1)	23.4 (74.1)	22.0 (71.6)	18.0 (64.4)	16.4 (61.5)	12.4 (54.3)	10.0 (50)
Average precipitation mm (inches)	20.8 (0.819)	3.0 (0.118)	5.5 (0.217)	10.3 (0.406)	1.2 (0.047)	0.0 (0)	1.4 (0.055)	5.0 (0.197)	5.4 (0.213)	14.5 (0.571)	22.6 (0.89)	22.1 (0.87)	111.8 (4.402)
Average precipitation days	4.0	0.9	1.8	1.8	0.7	0.0	0.3	1.5	2.0	1.9	3.9	3.6	22.4
Average relative humidity (%)	58	54	48	43	36	33	34	39	45	50	58	59	59
Mean monthly sunshine hours	260.4	245.8	282.1	282.0	303.8	321.0	313.1	297.6	282.0	300.7	264.0	248.0	3,400.5
Mean daily sunshine hours	8.4	8.7	9.1	9.4	9.8	10.7	10.1	9.6	9.4	9.7	8.8	8.0	9.3

Source #1: Jeddah Regional Climate Center
Source #2: Deutscher Wetterdienst (sun, 1986–2000)

Landmarks

Mecca houses the Masjid al-Haram, the largest mosque in the world. The mosque surrounds the Kaaba, which Muslims turn towards while offering daily prayer. This mosque is also commonly known as the *Haram* or *Grand Mosque*.

As mentioned above, because of the Wahhabist hostility to reverence being paid to historic and religious buildings, Mecca has lost most of its heritage in recent years and few buildings from the last 1,500 years have survived Saudi rule.

Expansion of the city is ongoing and includes the construction of 601 m (1,972 ft) tall Abraj Al Bait Towers across the street from the Masjid al-Haram. The towers were the third tallest building in the world when completed in 2012. The construction of the towers involved the demolition of the Ajyad Fortress, which in turn sparked a dispute between Turkey and Saudi Arabia.[43]

The Zamzam Well is home to a celebrated water spring. The Qishla of Mecca was an Ottoman castle facing the Grand Mosque and defending the city from attack. However, the Saudi government removed the structure to give space for hotels and business buildings near to the Grand Mosque.[44] Hira is a cave near Mecca, on the mountain named Jabal Al-Nūr in the Tihamah region of present-day Saudi Arabia. It is notable for being the location where Muhammad received his first revelations from God through the angel Jibreel, also known as Gabriel to Christians.[45]

The Qur'an Gate, located on the Jeddah-Mecca Highway, marks the boundary of the area where non-Muslims are prohibited to enter. It is the entrance to Makkah and the birthplace of Muhammad. The gate was designed in 1979 by an Egyptian architect, Samir Elabd, for the architectural firm IDEA Center. The structure is that of a book, representing the Qur'an, sitting on a rehal, or book stand.[46]

Economy

The Meccan economy has been heavily dependent on the annual pilgrimage. As one academic put it, "[Meccans] have no means of earning a living but by serving the hajjis." Income generated from the Hajj, in fact, not only powers the Meccan economy but has historically had far-reaching effects on the economy of the entire Arabian Peninsula. The income was generated in a number of ways. One method was taxing the pilgrims. Taxes especially increased during the Great Depression, and many of these taxes existed as late as 1972. Another way the Hajj generates income is through services to pilgrims. For example, the Saudi national airline, Saudia, generates 12% of its income from

Figure 11:
The Masjid al-Haram panorama.

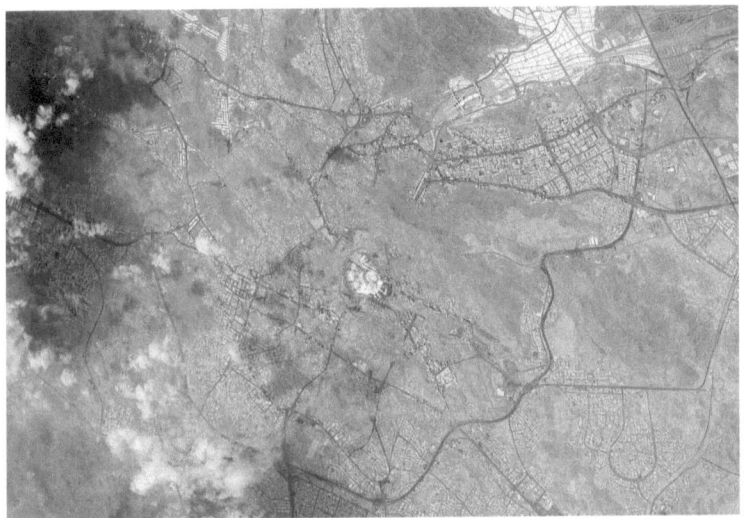

Figure 12: *Mecca as seen from the International Space Station.*

Figure 13: *The Quran Gate*

Figure 14: *Abraj Al Bait.*

the pilgrimage. Fares paid by pilgrims to reach Mecca by land also generate income; as do the hotels and lodging companies that house them.

The city takes in more than $100 million, while the Saudi government spends about $50 million on services for the Hajj. There are some industries and factories in the city, but Mecca no longer plays a major role in Saudi Arabia's economy, which is mainly based on oil exports.[47] The few industries operating in Mecca include textiles, furniture, and utensils. The majority of the economy is service-oriented.

Nevertheless, many industries have been set up in Mecca. Various types of enterprises that have existed since 1970: corrugated iron manufacturing, copper smithies, carpentry shops, upholstering establishments, vegetable oil extraction plants, sweets manufactures, flour mills, bakeries, poultry farms, frozen food importing, photography processing, secretarial establishments, ice factories, bottling plants for soft drinks, barber shops, book shops, travel agencies and banks.

The city has grown substantially in the 20th and 21st centuries, as the convenience and affordability of jet travel has increased the number of pilgrims participating in the Hajj. Thousands of Saudis are employed year-round to oversee the Hajj and staff the hotels and shops that cater to pilgrims; these

Figure 15: *Makkah Azizia district at noon*

workers in turn have increased the demand for housing and services. The city is now ringed by freeways, and contains shopping malls and skyscrapers.

Health care

Health care is provided by the Saudi government free of charge to all pilgrims. There are ten hospitals in Mecca:[48]

- Ajyad Hospital (Arabic: مستشفى أجياد)
- King Faisal Hospital (Arabic: مستشفى الملك فيصل بحي الششه)
- King Abdul Aziz Hospital (Arabic: مستشفى الملك عبدالعزيز بحي الزاهر)
- Al Noor Specialist Hospital (Arabic: مستشفى النور التخصصي)
- Hira Hospital (Arabic: مستشفى حراء)
- Maternity and Children Hospital (Arabic: مستشفى الولادة والأطفال)
- King Abdullah Medical City (Arabic: مدينة الملك عبدالله الطبية)
- Khulais General Hospital (Arabic: مستشفى خليص العام)
- Al Kamel General Hospital (Arabic: مستشفى الكامل العام)
- Ibn Sena Hospital in Bahhrah (Arabic: مستشفى ابن سينا بحداء / بحره)

There are also many walk-in clinics available for both residents and pilgrims.

Figure 16: *The Masjid al-Haram and Kaaba.*

Culture

Mecca's culture has been affected by the large number of pilgrims that arrive annually, and thus boasts a rich cultural heritage.

As a result of the vast numbers of pilgrims coming to the city each year, Mecca has become by far the most diverse city in the Muslim world. In contrast to the rest of Saudi Arabia, and particularly Najd, Mecca has, according to *The New York Times*, become "a striking oasis" of free thought and discussion and, also, of "unlikely liberalism" as "Meccans see themselves as a bulwark against the creeping extremism that has overtaken much Islamic debate".

The first press was brought to Mecca in 1885 by Osman Nuri Pasha, an Ottoman Wāli. During the Hashemite period, it was used to print the city's official gazette, *al-Qibla*. The Saudi regime expanded this press into a larger operation, introducing the new Saudi official gazette *Umm al-Qurā*. Henceforth presses and printing techniques were introduced in the city from around the Middle East, mostly via Jeddah.

Mecca owns its hometown paper, *Al Nadwa*. However, other Saudi and international newspapers are also provided in Mecca such as the *Saudi Gazette*, *Al Madinah*, *Okaz* and *Al-Bilad*. The first three are Mecca's (and other Saudi cities') primary newspapers focusing mainly on issues that affect the city, with over a million readers.

Many television stations serving the city area include Saudi TV1, Saudi TV2, Saudi TV Sports, Al-Ekhbariya, Arab Radio and Television Network and various cable, satellite and other specialty television providers.

In pre-modern Mecca the most common sports were impromptu wrestling and foot races. Football is the most popular sport in Mecca, the city hosting some of the oldest sport clubs in Saudi Arabia such as, Al-Wahda FC (established in 1945). King Abdulaziz Stadium is the largest stadium in Mecca with capacity of 38,000.[49]

Cuisine

As in other Arabian cities Kabsa (a spiced dish of rice and meat) is the most traditional lunch but the Yemeni mandi (a dish of rice and tandoori cooked meat) is also popular. Grilled meat dishes such as shawarma (flat-bread meat sandwich), kofta (meatballs) and kebabWikipedia:Please clarify are widely sold in Mecca. During Ramadan, fava beans in olive oil and samosas are the most popular dishes and are eaten at dusk. These dishes are almost always found in Lebanese, Syrian, and Turkish restaurants.Wikipedia:Citation needed

The mixture of different ethnicities and nationalities amongst Meccan residents has significantly impacted Mecca's traditional cuisine.Wikipedia:Citation needed The city has been described as one of the most cosmopolitan Islamic cities, with an international cuisine.

Traditionally during the month of Ramadan, men (known as Saggas) provided mineral water and fruit juice for Muslims breaking their fast at dusk. Today, Saggas make money providing sweets such as *baklava* and *basbosa* along with fruit juice drinks.Wikipedia:Citation needed

In the 20th century, many fast-food chains opened franchises in Mecca, catering to locals and pilgrims alike. Exotic foods, such as fruits from India and Japan, are often brought by the pilgrims.

Demographics

Population density in Mecca is very high. Most long-term residents of Mecca live in the Old City, and many work in the industry known locally as the *Hajj Industry*. Iyad Madani, Saudi Arabia's minister for Hajj, was quoted as saying, "We never stop preparing for the Hajj." Year-round, pilgrims stream into the city to perform the rites of Umrah, and during the last weeks of Dhu al-Qi'dah, on average 4 million Muslims arrive in the city to take part in the rites known as Hajj.

Pilgrims are from varying ethnicities and backgrounds, mainly Central Asia, South Asia, Southeast Asia, Europe, the Middle East, and Africa. Many of these pilgrims have remained and become residents of the city. The Burmese are an older, more established community who number roughly 250,000. Adding to the Hajj-related diversity, the oil-boom of the past 50 years has brought hundreds of thousands of working immigrants.

Non-Muslims are not permitted to enter Mecca under Saudi law, and using fraudulent documents to do so may result in arrest and prosecution. The prohibition extends to Ahmadis, as they are considered non-Muslims. Nevertheless, many non-Muslims and Ahmadis have visited the city. The first such recorded example of non-Muslims is that of Ludovico di Varthema of Bologna in 1503. Guru Nanak Sahib, the founder of Sikhism, visited Mecca in December 1518.[50] One of the most famous was Richard Francis Burton, who traveled as a Qadiriyyah Sufi from Afghanistan in 1853. The Saudi government supports their position usingWikipedia:Citation needed Sura 9:28 from the Qur'an: *O ye who believe! Truly the Pagans are unclean; so let them not, after this year of theirs, approach the Sacred Mosque.*

Education

Formal education started to be developed in the late Ottoman period continuing slowly into and Hashimite times. The first major attempt to improve the situation was made by a Jeddah merchant, Muhammad ʿAlī Zaynal Riḍā, who founded the Madrasat al-Falāḥ in Mecca in 1911–12 that cost £400,000.

The school system in Mecca has many public and private schools for both males and females. As of 2005, there were 532 public and private schools for males and another 681 public and private schools for female students.[51] The medium of instruction in both public and private schools is Arabic with emphasis on English as a second language, but some private schools founded by foreign entities such as International schools use the English language for medium of instruction. They also allow mixing between males and females while other schools do not.

For higher education, the city has only one university, Umm Al-Qura University, which was established in 1949 as a college and became a public university in 1979.

Paleontology

In 2010, the Mecca area became an important site for paleontology with respect to primate evolution, with the discovery of a *Saadanius* fossil. Saadanius is considered to be a primate closely related to the common ancestor of the Old World monkeys and apes. The fossil habitat, near what is now the Red Sea in western Saudi Arabia, was a damp forest area between 28 million and 29 million years ago.

Paleontologists involved in the research hope to find further fossils in the area.

Communications

Telecommunications in the city were emphasized early under the Saudi reign. King Abdul Aziz Al-Saud (Ibn Saud) pressed them forward as he saw them as a means of convenience and better governance. While in King Husayn's time there were about 20 telephones in the entire city; in 1936 the number jumped to 450, totalling about half the telephones in the country. During that time, telephone lines were extended to Jeddah and Ta'if, but not to the capital Riyadh. By 1985, Mecca, like other Saudi cities, possessed modern telephone, telex, radio and television communications.[52]

Limited radio communication was established within the Kingdom under the Hashimites. In 1929, wireless stations were set up in various towns of the region, creating a network that would become fully functional by 1932. Soon after World War II, the existing network was greatly expanded and improved. Since then, radio communication has been used extensively in directing the pilgrimage and addressing the pilgrims. This practice started in 1950, with the initiation of broadcasts the Day of Arafa, and increased until 1957, at which time Radio Makka became the most powerful station in the Middle East at 50 kW. Later, power was increased to 450 kW. Music was not immediately broadcast, but gradually introduced.

Transportation

Air

Mecca has only the small Mecca East Airport with no airline service, so Mecca is served by King Abdulaziz International Airport (IATA: **JED**, ICAO: **OEJN**) located at Jeddah, about 100 kilometres from the city centre. To cater the large number of Hajj pilgrims, this airport has a specifically built Hajj terminal which can accommodate 47 planes simultaneously and it can receive 3,800 pilgrims per hour during the Hajj season.

Figure 17: *Hajj terminal*

Rail

Al Mashaaer Al Mugaddassah Metro

Al Mashaaer Al Mugaddassah Metro is a metro line in mecca opened in 13 November 2010. This 18.1 kilometer elevated metro transports pilgrims to holy sites Mount Arafat, Muzdalifah and Mina in the city during hajj reducing the congestion on the roads.

Mecca Metro

Mecca Metro, officially known as **Makkah Mass Rail Transit**, is a planned four-line metro system for the city. This will be in addition to the Al Mashaaer Al Mugaddassah Metro which carries pilgrims during Hajj.

Intercity

A high speed inter-city rail line (Haramain High Speed Rail Project also known as the "Western Railway"), is under construction in Saudi Arabia. It will link along 444 kilometres (276 mi), the Muslim holy cities of Medina and Mecca via King Abdullah Economic City, Rabigh, Jeddah and King Abdulaziz International Airport. This rail line is planned to provide a safe and comfortable transport in 320 kilometres per hour (200 mph) electric trains in-turn reducing the travel time to less than two hours between Mecca and Medina. It will be built by a business consortium from Spain.[53]

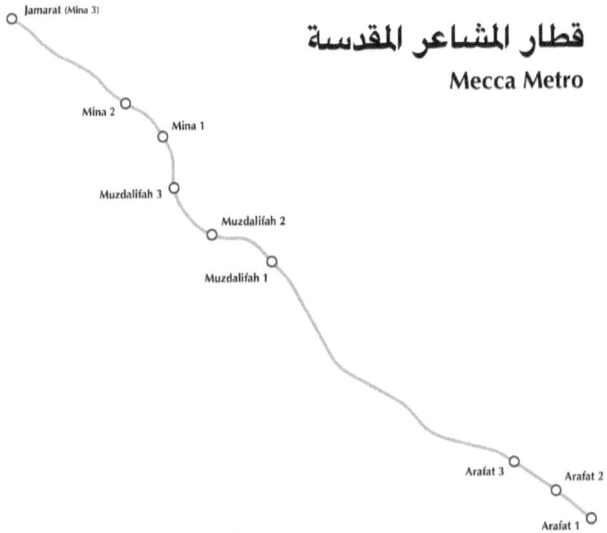

Figure 18: *Mecca Metro Route Map*

Roads

Some of the intercity highways which connects the city of Mecca are:[54,55]

- Highway 40 (Saudi Arabia) – connects Jeddah to Mecca and Mecca to Dammam.
- Highway 15 (Saudi Arabia) – connects Taif to Mecca and Mecca to Medina.

Sister cities

- Medina, Saudi Arabia
- Merv, Turkmenistan
- Istanbul, Turkey
- Taif, Saudi Arabia

References

Notes

Bibliography

Figure 19: *Entry Gate of Mecca on Jaddah Makkah Highway*

- the editors of Time-Life Books. (1999). *What life was like in the lands of the prophet: Islamic world, AD 570 – 1405.* Time-Life Books. ISBN 0-7835-5465-6.
- Lapidus, Ira M. (1988). *A History of Islamic Societies.* Cambridge University Press. ISBN 0-521-22552-3.

Further reading

See also: Bibliography of the history of Mecca

- Bianca, Stefano (2000), "Case Study 1: The Holy Cities of Islam – The Impact of Mass Transportation and Rapid Urban Change"[56], *Urban Form in the Arab World*, Zurich: ETH Zurich, ISBN 3728119725, 0500282056
- Bosworth, C. Edmund, ed. (2007). "Mecca". *Historic Cities of the Islamic World.* Leiden: Koninklijke Brill.
- Dumper, Michael R. T.; Stanley, Bruce E., eds. (2008), "Makkah", *Cities of the Middle East and North Africa*, Santa Barbara, USA: ABC-CLIO
- Rosenthal, Franz; Ibn Khaldun (1967). *The Muqaddimah: An Introduction to History.* Princeton University Press. ISBN 0-691-09797-6.
- Watt, W. Montgomery. "Makka – The pre-Islamic and early Islamic periods." *Encyclopaedia of Islam.* Edited by: P. Bearman, Th. Bianquis, C.E. Bosworth, E. van Donzel and W.P. Heinrichs. Brill, 2008. Brill Online. 6 June 2008
- Winder, R.B. "Makka – The Modern City." *Encyclopaedia of Islam.* Edited by: P. Bearman, Th. Bianquis, C.E. Bosworth, E. van Donzel and W.P. Heinrichs. Brill, 2008. Brill Online. 6 June 2008

- "Quraysh"[57]. *Encyclopædia Britannica*. Britannica Concise Encyclopedia (online). 2007. Retrieved 19 February 2007.

External links

- Holy Mecca Municipality[58]
- Saudi Information Resource – Holy Mecca[59]
- Personal Narrative of a Pilgrimage to Al Madinah and Meccah, by Richard Burton[60]

Medina

Medina
المدينة المنورة
Al-Madīnah al-Munawwarah المدينة النبي
Al Madīnat an-Nabī
Yathrib
يثرب
The Radiant City

Clockwise from top left: Al-Masjid an-Nabawi interior, Al-Masjid an-Nabawi, Medina skyline, Quba Mosque, Mount Uhud

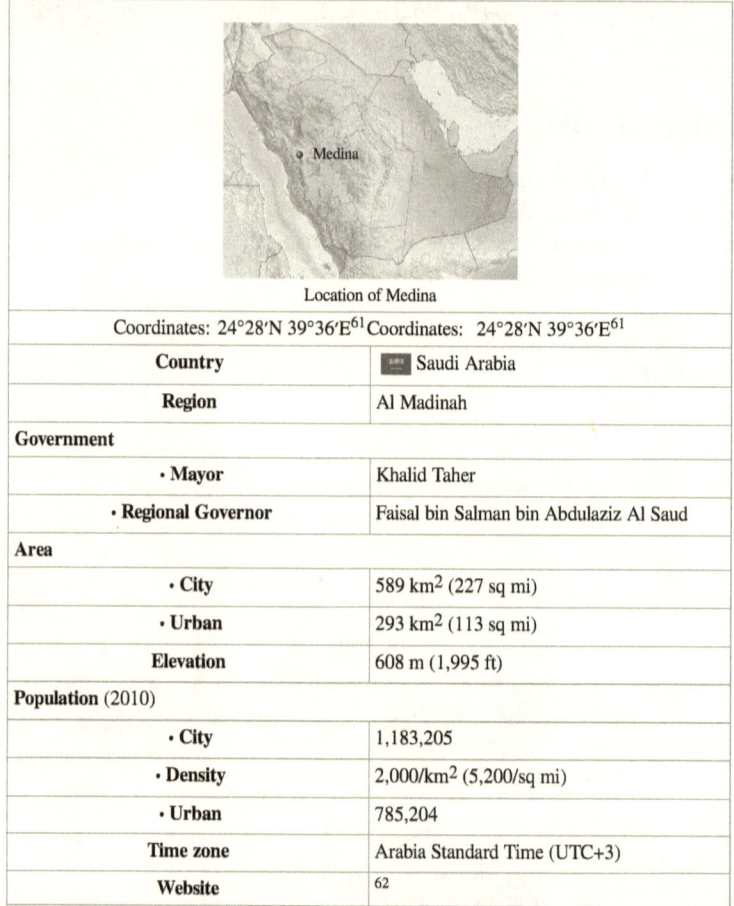

Location of Medina
Coordinates: 24°28′N 39°36′E[61] Coordinates: 24°28′N 39°36′E[61]

	Country	Saudi Arabia
	Region	Al Madinah
Government		
	• Mayor	Khalid Taher
	• Regional Governor	Faisal bin Salman bin Abdulaziz Al Saud
Area		
	• City	589 km² (227 sq mi)
	• Urban	293 km² (113 sq mi)
	Elevation	608 m (1,995 ft)
Population (2010)		
	• City	1,183,205
	• Density	2,000/km² (5,200/sq mi)
	• Urban	785,204
	Time zone	Arabia Standard Time (UTC+3)
	Website	[62]

Medina (/məˈdiːnə/; Arabic: المدينة المنورة, *al-Madīnah al-Munawwarah*, "the radiant city"; or المدينة, *al-Madīnah* (Hejazi pronunciation: [almaˈdiːna]), "the city"), also transliterated as **Madīnah**, is a city and administrative headquarters of the Al-Madinah Region of Saudi Arabia. At the city's heart is al-Masjid an-Nabawi ("the Prophet's Mosque"), which is the burial place of the Islamic prophet Muhammad, and is the second-holiest city in Islam after Mecca.

Medina was Muhammad's destination of his Hijrah (migration) from Mecca, and became the capital of a rapidly increasing Muslim Empire, under Muhammad's leadership. It served as the power base of Islam in its first century where the early Muslim community developed. Medina is home to the three oldest mosques, namely the Quba Mosque, al-Masjid an-Nabawi, and Masjid al-Qiblatayn ("the mosque of the two qiblas"). Muslims believe that the chronologically final surahs of the Quran were revealed to Muhammad in Medina, and are called Medinan surahs in contrast to the earlier Meccan surahs.[63,64]

Just like Mecca, the city is closed to anyone who is considered a non-Muslim, including members of the Ahmadiyya movement (however, not the entire city is closed) by the national government.[65]

Etymology

The Arabic word *al-Madīnah* (المدينة) simply means "the city". Before the advent of Islam, the city was known as *Yathrib* (pronounced [ˈjaθrib]; يثرب). The word *Yathrib* has been recorded in Surat al-Ahzab of the Quran.[Quran 33:13[66]]

Also called Taybah ([ˈtˤajba]; طيبة). An alternative name is *al-Madīnah an-Nabawiyyah* (المدينة النبوية) or *Madīnat an-Nabī* (مدينة النبي, "the city of the prophet").

Overview

As of 2010[67], the city of Medina has a population of 1,183,205. In addition to its Arab inhabitants, during the pre-Islamic era Yathrib was inhabited by Jewish tribes. Later the city's name was changed to *al-Madīna-tu n-Nabī* or *al-Madīnatu 'l-Munawwarah* (المدينة المنورة "the enlightened city" or "the radiant city"). Medina is celebrated for containing al-Masjid an-Nabawi and also as the city which gave refuge to him and his followers, and so ranks as the second holiest city of Islam, after Mecca.[68] Muhammad was buried in Medina, under the Green Dome, as were the first two Rashidun caliphs, Abu Bakr and Umar, who were buried next to him in what used to be Muhammad's house.

Medina is 210 miles (340 km) north of Mecca and about 120 miles (190 km) from the Red Sea coast. It is situated in the most fertile part of all the Hejaz territory, the streams of the vicinity tending to converge in this locality. An immense plain extends to the south; in every direction the view is bounded by hills and mountains.

The historic city formed an oval, surrounded by a strong wall, 30 to 40 feet (9.1 to 12.2 m) high, dating from the 12th century CE, and was flanked with towers, while on a rock, stood a castle. Of its four gates, the *Bab-al-Salam*, or Egyptian gate, was remarkable for its beauty. Beyond the walls of the city, west and south were suburbs consisting of low houses, yards, gardens and plantations. These suburbs also had walls and gates. Almost all of the historic

Figure 20: *The Green Dome of the Prophet's Mosque*

city has been demolished in the Saudi era. The rebuilt city is centred on the vastly expanded al-Masjid an-Nabawi.

The graves of Fatimah (Muhammad's daughter) and Hasan (Muhammad's grandson), across from the mosque at Jannat al-Baqi, and Abu Bakr (first caliph and the father of Muhammad's wife, Aisha), and of Umar (Umar ibn Al-Khattab), the second caliph, are also here. The mosque dates back to the time of Muhammad, but has been twice reconstructed.[69]

Because of the Saudi government's religious policy and concern that historic sites could become the focus for idolatry, much of Medina's Islamic physical heritage has been altered.

Religious significance in Islam

Medina's importance as a religious site derives from the presence of al-Masjid an-Nabawi. The mosque was expanded by the Umayyad Caliph Al-Walid I. Mount Uhud is a mountain north of Medina which was the site of the second battle between Muslim and Meccan forces.

The first mosque built during Muhammad's time is also located in Medina and is known as the Quba Mosque. It was destroyed by lightning, probably about 850 CE, and the graves were almost forgotten. In 892, the place was cleared up, the graves located and a fine mosque built, which was destroyed by fire in 1257 CE and almost immediately rebuilt. It was restored by Qaitbay, the Egyptian ruler, in 1487.

Masjid al-Qiblatain is another mosque also historically important to Muslims. It is where the command was sent to Muhammad to change the direction of prayer (qibla) from Jerusalem to Mecca according to a Hadith.

Like Mecca, the city of Medina only permits Muslims to enter, although the haram (area closed to non-Muslims) of Medina is much smaller than that of Mecca, with the result that many facilities on the outskirts of Medina are open to non-Muslims, whereas in Mecca the area closed to non-Muslims extends well beyond the limits of the built-up area. Both cities' numerous mosques are the destination for large numbers of Muslims on their Umrah (second pilgrimage after Hajj). Hundreds of thousands of Muslims come to Medina annually while performing pilgrimage Hajj. Al-Baqi' is a significant cemetery in Medina where several family members of Muhammad, caliphs and scholars are buried.

Islamic scriptures emphasise the sacredness of Medina. Medina is mentioned several times as being sacred in the Quran, for example ayah; 9:101, 9:129, 59:9, and ayah 63:7. Medinan suras are typically longer than their Mecca counterparts. There is also a book within the hadith of Bukhari titled 'virtues of Medina'.[70]

Sahih Bukhari says:

> *Narrated Anas: The Prophet said, "Medina is a sanctuary from that place to that. Its trees should not be cut and no heresy should be innovated nor any sin should be committed in it, and whoever innovates in it an heresy or commits sins (bad deeds), then he will incur the curse of God, the angels, and all the people."*

History

Jewish roots

By the fourth century, Arab tribes began to encroach from Yemen, and there were three prominent Jewish tribes that inhabited the city into the 7th century AD: the Banu Qaynuqa, the Banu Qurayza, and Banu Nadir.[71] Ibn Khordadbeh later reported that during the Persian Empire's domination in Hejaz, the Banu Qurayza served as tax collectors for the shah.[72]

The situation changed after the arrival from Yemen of two new Arab tribes named Banu Aus (or Banu 'Aws) and Banu Khazraj. At first, these tribes were allied with Jewish rulers, but later they revolted and became independent.[73]

Figure 21: *Historic Medina*

Toward the end of the 5th century,[74] the Jewish rulers lost control of the city to Banu Aus and Banu Khazraj. The Jewish Encyclopedia states that "by calling in outside assistance and treacherously massacring at a banquet the principal Jews", Banu Aus and Banu Khazraj finally gained the upper hand at Medina.

Most modern historians accept the claim of the Muslim sources that after the revolt, the Jewish tribes became clients of the Aus and the Khazraj.[75] However, according to scholar of Islam William Montgomery Watt, the clientship of the Jewish tribes is not borne out by the historical accounts of the period prior to 627, and he maintained that the Jewish populace retained a measure of political independence.

Early Muslim chronicler Ibn Ishaq tells of a pre-Islamic conflict between the last Yemenite king of the Himyarite Kingdom[76] and the residents of Yathrib. When the king was passing by the oasis, the residents killed his son, and the Yemenite ruler threatened to exterminate the people and cut down the palms. According to Ibn Ishaq, he was stopped from doing so by two rabbis from the Banu Qurayza tribe, who implored the king to spare the oasis because it was the place "to which a prophet of the Quraysh would migrate in time to come, and it would be his home and resting-place." The Yemenite king thus did not destroy the town and converted to Judaism. He took the rabbis with him, and in Mecca, they reportedly recognised the Ka'ba as a temple built by Abraham and advised the king "to do what the people of Mecca did: to circumambulate the temple, to venerate and honour it, to shave his head and to behave with all humility until he had left its precincts." On approaching Yemen, tells ibn Ishaq, the rabbis demonstrated to the local people a miracle by coming out of a fire unscathed and the Yemenites accepted Judaism.[77]

Eventually the Banu Aus and the Banu Khazraj became hostile to each other and by the time of Muhammad's Hijra (emigration) to Medina in 622 AD/1 AH, they had been fighting for 120 years and were the sworn enemies of each other.[78] The Banu Nadir and the Banu Qurayza were allied with the Aus, while the Banu Qaynuqa sided with the Khazraj.[79] They fought a total of four wars.

Their last and bloodiest battle was the Battle of Bu'ath that was fought a few years before the arrival of Muhammad. The outcome of the battle was inconclusive, and the feud continued. Abd-Allah ibn Ubayy, one Khazraj chief, had refused to take part in the battle, which earned him a reputation for equity and peacefulness. Until the arrival of Muhammad, he was the most respected inhabitant of Yathrib. To solve the ongoing feud, concerned residents of the city met secretly with Muhammad in Al-Aqaba, a place between Makkah and Mina, inviting him and his small band of believers to come to Yathrib, where Muhammad could serve as disinterested mediator between the factions and his community could practice its faith freely.

Muhammad's arrival

In 622 AD/1 AH, Muhammad and around 70 Meccan Muhajirun believers left Mecca for sanctuary in Yathrib, an event that transformed the religious and political landscape of the city completely; the longstanding enmity between the Aus and Khazraj tribes was dampened as many of the two Arab tribes and some local Jews embraced Islam. Muhammad, linked to the Khazraj through his great-grandmother, was agreed on as civic leader. The Muslim converts native to Yathrib of whatever background—pagan Arab or Jewish—were called *Ansar* ("the Patrons" or "the Helpers").

According to Ibn Ishaq, the local pagan Arab tribes, the Muslim Muhajirun from Mecca, the local Muslims (Ansar), and the Jewish population of the area signed an agreement, the Constitution of Medina, which committed all parties to mutual co-operation under the leadership of Muhammad. The nature of this document as recorded by Ibn Ishaq and transmitted by Ibn Hisham is the subject of dispute among modern Western historians, many of whom maintain that this "treaty" is possibly a collage of different agreements, oral rather than written, of different dates, and that it is not clear exactly when they were made. Other scholars, however, both Western and Muslim, argue that the text of the agreement—whether a single document originally or several—is possibly one of the oldest Islamic texts we possess.[80] In Yemenite Jewish sources, another

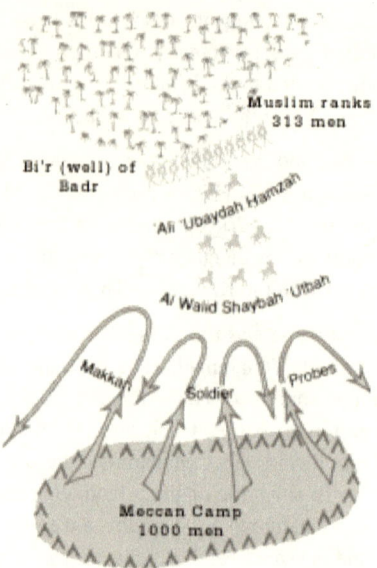

Figure 22: *Battle positions at Badr*

treaty was drafted between Muhammad and his Jewish subjects, known as *kitāb ḏimmat al-nabi*, written in the 17th year of the Hijra (638 CE), and which gave express liberty unto Jews living in Arabia to observe the Sabbath and to grow-out their side-locks, but were required to pay the jizya (poll-tax) annually for their protection by their patrons.[81]

Battle of Badr

The Battle of Badr was a key battle in the early days of Islam and a turning point in Muhammad's struggle with his opponents among the Quraysh in Mecca.

In the spring of 624, Muhammad received word from his intelligence sources that a trade caravan, commanded by Abu Sufyan ibn Harb and guarded by thirty to forty men, was travelling from Syria back to Mecca. Muhammad gathered an army of 313 men, the largest army the Muslims had put in the field yet. However, many early Muslim sources, including the Quran, indicate that no serious fighting was expected,[82] and the future Caliph Uthman ibn Affan stayed behind to care for his sick wife.

As the caravan approached Medina, Abu Sufyan began hearing from travellers and riders about Muhammad's planned ambush. He sent a messenger named Damdam to Mecca to warn the Quraysh and get reinforcements. Alarmed, the Quraysh assembled an army of 900–1,000 men to rescue the caravan. Many of the Qurayshi nobles, including Amr ibn Hishām, Walid ibn Utba, Shaiba, and Umayyah ibn Khalaf, joined the army. However, some of the army was to later return to Mecca before the battle.

The battle started with champions from both armies emerging to engage in combat. The Muslims sent out Ali, Ubaydah ibn al-Harith (Obeida), and Hamza ibn 'Abd al-Muttalib. The Muslims dispatched the Meccan champions in a three-on-three mêlée, Hamzah killed his opponent with the very first strike, although Ubaydah was mortally wounded.[83]

Now both armies began firing arrows at each other. Two Muslims and an unknown number of Quraysh were killed. Before the battle started, Muhammad had given orders for the Muslims to attack with their ranged weapons, and only engage the Quraysh with melee weapons when they advanced.[84] Now he gave the order to charge, throwing a handful of pebbles at the Meccans in what was probably a traditional Arabian gesture while yelling "Defaced be those faces!"[85,86] The Muslim army yelled *"Yā manṣūr amit!"*[87] and rushed the Qurayshi lines. The Meccans, although substantially outnumbering the Muslims, promptly broke and ran. The battle itself only lasted a few hours and was over by the early afternoon. The Quran describes the force of the Muslim attack in many verses, which refer to thousands of angels descending from Heaven at Badr to slaughter the Quraysh.[88] Early Muslim sources take this account literally, and there are several hadith where Muhammad discusses the Angel Jibreel and the role he played in the battle.

Ubaydah ibn al-Harith (Obeida) was given the honour of "he who shot the first arrow for Islam" as Abu Sufyan ibn Harb altered course to flee the attack. In retaliation for this attack Abu Sufyan ibn Harb requested an armed force from Mecca.[89]

Throughout the winter and spring of 623 other raiding parties were sent by Muhammad from Medina.

Battle of Uhud

In 625, Abu Sufyan ibn Harb, Chieftain of the Quraish of Mecca, who paid tax to the Byzantine empire regularly, once again led a Meccan force against Medina. Muhammad marched out to meet the force but before reaching the battle, about one third of the troops under Abd-Allah ibn Ubayy withdrew. With a smaller force, the Muslim army had to find a strategy to gain the upper hand. A group of archers were ordered to stay on a hill to keep an eye on the Meccan's cavalry forces and to provide protection at the rear of the Muslim's army. As the battle heated up, the Meccans were forced to somewhat retreat. The battle front was pushed further and further away from the archers, whom, from the start of the battle, had really nothing to do but watch. In their growing impatience to be part of the battle, and seeing that they were somewhat

Figure 23: *Mount Uhud*

gaining advantage over the Kafirun (Infidels) these archers decided to leave their posts to pursue the retreating Meccans. A small party, however, stayed behind; pleading all along to the rest to not disobey their commanders' orders. But their words were lost among the enthusiastic yodels of their comrades.

However, the Meccans' retreat was actually a manufactured manoeuvre that paid off. The hillside position had been a great advantage to the Muslim forces, and they had to be lured off their posts for the Meccans to turn the table over. Seeing that their strategy had actually worked, the Meccans cavalry forces went around the hill and re-appeared behind the pursuing archers. Thus, ambushed in the plain between the hill and the front line, the archers were systematically slaughtered, watched upon by their desperate comrades who stayed behind up in the hill, shooting arrows to thwart the raiders, but to little effect.

However, the Meccans did not capitalise on their advantage by invading Medina and returned to Mecca. The Medinans suffered heavy losses, and Muhammad was injured.

Battle of the Trench

In 627, Abu Sufyan ibn Harb once more led Meccan forces against Medina. Because the people of Medina had dug a trench to further protect the city, this event became known as the Battle of the Trench. After a protracted siege and various skirmishes, the Meccans withdrew again. During the siege, Abu Sufyan ibn Harb had contacted the remaining Jewish tribe of Banu Qurayza and formed an agreement with them, to attack the defenders from behind the lines. It was however discovered by the Muslims and thwarted. This was in breach of the Constitution of Medina and after the Meccan withdrawal, Muhammad immediately marched against the Qurayza and laid siege to their strongholds. The Jewish forces eventually surrendered. Some members of the Banu Aus now interceded on behalf of their old allies and Muhammad agreed to the appointment of one of their chiefs, Sa'd ibn Mua'dh, as judge. Sa'ad judged by Jewish Law that all male members of the tribe should be killed and the women and children enslaved as was the law stated in the Old Testament for treason (Deutoronomy).[90] This action was conceived of as a defensive measure to ensure that the Muslim community could be confident of its continued survival in Medina. The historian Robert Mantran argues that from this point of view it was successful — from this point on, the Muslims were no longer primarily concerned with survival but with expansion and conquest.

Capital city of early Islam and the caliphate

In the ten years following the hijra, Medina formed the base from which Muhammad and the Muslim army attacked and were attacked, and it was from here that he marched on Mecca, entering it without battle in 629 AD/8 AH, all parties acquiescing to his leadership. Afterwards, however, despite Muhammad's tribal connection to Mecca and the ongoing importance of the Meccan kaaba for Islamic pilgrimage (hajj), Muhammad returned to Medina, which remained for some years the most important city of Islam and the capital of the early caliphate.

Yathrib was renamed Medina from *Madinat al-Nabi* ("city of the Prophet" in Arabic) in honour of Muhammad's prophethood and death there. (Alternatively, Lucien Gubbay suggests the name Medina could also have been a derivative from the Aramaic word *Medinta*, which the Jewish inhabitants could have used for the city.)

Under the first three caliphs Abu Bakr, Umar, and Uthman, Medina was the capital of a rapidly increasing Muslim Empire. During the period of Uthman, the third caliph, a party of Arabs from Egypt, disgruntled at his political decisions, attacked Medina in 656 AD/35 AH and murdered him in his own home. Ali, the fourth caliph, changed the capital of the caliphate from Medina to Kufa

Figure 24: *Old depiction of Medina during Ottoman times*

in Iraq. After that, Medina's importance dwindled, becoming more a place of religious importance than of political power.

In 1256 AD Medina was threatened by a lava flow from the Harrat Rahat volcanic area.[91]

After the fragmentation of the caliphate, the city became subject to various rulers, including the Mamluks of Cairo in the 13th century and finally, in 1517, the Ottoman Empire.

World War I to Saudi control

In the beginning of the 20th century, during World War I, Medina witnessed one of the longest sieges in history. Medina was a city of the Turkish Ottoman Empire. Local rule was in the hands of the Hashemite clan as Sharifs or Emirs of Mecca. Fakhri Pasha was the Ottoman governor of Medina. Ali bin Hussein, the Sharif of Mecca and leader of the Hashemite clan, revolted against the Caliph in Constantinople (Istanbul) and sided with Great Britain. The city of Medina was besieged by the Sharif's forces, and Fakhri Pasha tenaciously held on during the Siege of Medina from 1916 till 10 January 1919. He refused to surrender and held on another 72 days after the Armistice of Moudros, until he was arrested by his own men.[92] In anticipation of the plunder and destruction to follow, Fakhri Pasha secretly sent the Sacred Relics of Medina to Istanbul.[93]

Figure 25: *Modern city of Medina*

As of 1920, the British described Medina as "much more self-supporting than Mecca." After the First World War, the Hashemite Sayyid Hussein bin Ali was proclaimed King of an independent Hejaz. Soon after, in 1924, he was defeated by Ibn Saud, who integrated Medina and the whole of the Hejaz into the modern kingdom of Saudi Arabia.

Medina today

Today, Medina ("Madinah" officially in Saudi documents), in addition to being the second most important Islamic pilgrimage destination after Mecca, is an important regional capital of the western Saudi Arabian province of Al Madinah. In addition to the sacred core of the old city, which is off limits to non-Muslims, Medina is a modern, multi-ethnic city inhabited by Saudi Arabs and an increasing number of Muslim and non-Muslim expatriate workers: other Arab nationalities (Egyptians, Jordanians, Lebanese, etc.), South Asians (Bangladeshis, Indians, Pakistanis, etc.), and Filipinos.

Geography

The soil surrounding Medina consists of mostly basalt, while the hills, especially noticeable to the south of the city, are volcanic ash which dates to the first geological period of the Paleozoic Era.

Al Madinah Al Munawarah is located at Eastern Part of Al Hijaz Region in the Kingdom of Saudi Arabia on longitude 39° 36' E and latitude 24° 28' N.

Madinah is located in the north-western part of the Kingdom, to the east of the Red Sea, which lies only 250 kilometres (160 miles) away from it. It is surrounded by a number of mountains: Al-Hujaj, or Pilgrims' Mountain to the west, Salaa to the north-west, Al-E'er or Caravan Mountain to the south and Uhad to the north. Madinah is situated on a flat mountain plateau at the junction of the three valleys of Al-Aql, Al-Aqiq, and Al-Himdh. For this reason, there are large green areas amidst a dry mountainous region. The city is 620 metres (2,030 feet) above sea level. Its western and southwestern parts have many volcanic rocks. Madinah lies at the meeting-point of longitude 39°36' east and latitude 24°28' north. It covers an area of about 50 square kilometres (19 square miles).

Al Madinah Al Munawwarah is a desert oasis surrounded with mountains and stony areas from all sides. It was mentioned in several references and sources. It was known as Yathrib in Writings of ancient Maeniand, this is obvious evidence that the population structure of this desert oasis is a combination of north Arabs and South Arabs, who settled there and built their civilisation during the thousand years before Christ.

Climate

Medina has a hot desert climate (Köppen climate classification *BWh*). Summers are extremely hot with daytime temperatures averaging about 43 °C (109 °F) with nights about 29 °C (84 °F). Temperatures above 45 °C (113 °F) are not unusual between June and September. Winters are milder, with temperatures from 12 °C (54 °F) at night to 25 °C (77 °F) in the day. There is very little rainfall, which falls almost entirely between November and May.

Medina

Climate data for Medina (1985–2010)

Month	Jan	Feb	Mar	Apr	May	Jun	Jul	Aug	Sep	Oct	Nov	Dec	Year
Record high °C (°F)	33.2 (91.8)	36.6 (97.9)	40.0 (104)	43.0 (109.4)	46.0 (114.8)	47.0 (116.6)	49.0 (120.2)	48.4 (119.1)	46.4 (115.5)	42.8 (109)	36.8 (98.2)	32.2 (90)	49.0 (120.2)
Average high °C (°F)	24.2 (75.6)	26.6 (79.9)	30.6 (87.1)	35.3 (95.5)	39.6 (103.3)	42.9 (109.2)	42.9 (109.2)	43.7 (110.7)	42.3 (108.1)	37.3 (99.1)	30.6 (87.1)	26.0 (78.8)	35.2 (95.4)
Daily mean °C (°F)	17.9 (64.2)	20.2 (68.4)	23.9 (75)	28.5 (83.3)	33.0 (91.4)	36.3 (97.3)	36.5 (97.7)	37.1 (98.8)	35.6 (96.1)	30.4 (86.7)	24.2 (75.6)	19.8 (67.6)	28.6 (83.5)
Average low °C (°F)	11.6 (52.9)	13.4 (56.1)	16.8 (62.2)	21.2 (70.2)	25.5 (77.9)	28.4 (83.1)	29.1 (84.4)	29.9 (85.8)	27.9 (82.2)	22.9 (73.2)	17.7 (63.9)	13.6 (56.5)	21.5 (70.7)
Record low °C (°F)	1.0 (33.8)	3.0 (37.4)	7.0 (44.6)	11.5 (52.7)	14.0 (57.2)	21.7 (71.1)	22.0 (71.6)	23.0 (73.4)	18.2 (64.8)	11.6 (52.9)	9.0 (48.2)	3.0 (37.4)	1.0 (33.8)
Average precipitation mm (inches)	6.3 (0.248)	3.1 (0.122)	9.8 (0.386)	9.6 (0.378)	5.1 (0.201)	0.1 (0.004)	1.1 (0.043)	4.0 (0.157)	0.4 (0.016)	2.5 (0.098)	10.4 (0.409)	7.8 (0.307)	60.2 (2.37)
Average rainy days	2.6	1.4	3.2	4.1	2.9	0.1	0.4	1.5	0.6	2.0	3.3	2.5	24.6
Average relative humidity (%)	38	31	25	22	17	12	14	16	14	19	32	38	23

Source: Jeddah Regional Climate Center

Religion

As with most cities in Saudi Arabia, Islam is the religion adhered by the majority of the population of Medina. Sunnis of different schools (Hanafi, Maliki, Shafi'i and Hanbali) constitute the majority while there is a significant Shia minority in and around Medina, such as the Nakhawila. Outside the city centre (reserved for Muslims only), there are significant numbers of non-Muslim migrant workers and expats.

Economy

Historically, Medina is known for growing dates. As of 1920, 139 varieties of dates were being grown in the area. Medina also was known for growing many types of vegetables.

The Medina Knowledge Economic City project, a city focused on knowledge-based industries, has been planned and is expected to boost development and increase the number of jobs in Medina.[94]

The city is served by the Prince Mohammad Bin Abdulaziz Airport which opened in 1974. It handles on average 20–25 flights a day, although this number triples during the Hajj season and school holidays.

With the increasing number of pilgrim visiting each year, many hotels are being constructed.

Education

Universities include:

- Islamic University of Madinah
- Taibah University

Transport

Air

Medina is served by Prince Mohammad bin Abdulaziz Airport (IATA: **MED**, ICAO: **OEMA**) located about 15 kilometres (9.3 miles) from the city centre. This airport handles mostly domestic destinations and it has limited international services to regional destinations such as Cairo, Bahrain, Doha, Dubai, Istanbul and Kuwait.

Figure 26: *Masjid Nabawi at sunset*

Figure 27: *Panel representing the Mosque of Medina. Found in İznik, Turkey, 18th century. Composite body, silicate coat, transparent glaze, underglaze painted.*

Rail

A high speed inter-city rail line (Haramain High Speed Rail Project also known as the "Western Railway"), is under construction in Saudi Arabia. It will link along 444 kilometres (276 miles), the Muslim holy city of Medina and Mecca via King Abdullah Economic City, Rabigh, Jeddah and King Abdulaziz International Airport. A three-line metro is also planned.

Road

Major roads that connect city of medina to other parts of the country are,
- Highway 15 (Saudi Arabia) – connects Medina to Mecca, Abha, Khamis Mushait and Tabuk.
- Highway 60 (Saudi Arabia) – connects Medina to Buraidah

Figure 28: *Prince Mohammad bin Abdulaziz Airport*

Bus

Medina Bus Transport finds the route to nearest Bus station/stop and al-Masjid an-Nabawi ("the Prophet's Mosque").

Destruction of heritage

Saudi Arabia is hostile to any reverence given to historical or religious places of significance for fear that it may give rise to *shirk* (idolatry). As a consequence, under Saudi rule, Medina has suffered from considerable destruction of its physical heritage including the loss of many buildings over a thousand years old. Critics have described this as "Saudi vandalism" and claim that in Medina and Mecca over the last 50 years, 300 historic sites linked to Muhammad, his family or companions have been lost.[95] In Medina, examples of historic sites which have been destroyed include the Salman al-Farsi Mosque, the Raj'at ash-Shams Mosque, the Jannat al-Baqi cemetery, and the house of Muhammed.[96]

External links

- Media related to Medina at Wikimedia Commons
- Media related to Category:Medina at Wikimedia Commons
- Medina travel guide from Wikivoyage
- "Medina". *New International Encyclopedia*. 1905.

St. Peters Basilica

St. Peter's Basilica

St. Peter's Basilica	
Papal Basilica of St. Peter in the Vatican	
<ul><li>*Basilica Papale di San Pietro in Vaticano* (Italian)</li><li>*Basilica Sancti Petri* (Latin)</li></ul>	
 Main façade and dome of St. Peter's Basilica	
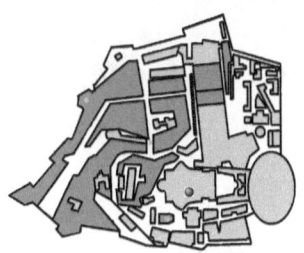 Location on a map of Vatican City	
41°54′08″N 12°27′12″E[97] Coordinates: 41°54′08″N 12°27′12″E[97]	
Location	Vatican City
Country	Holy See
Denomination	Roman Catholic

Tradition	Latin Rite
Website	St. Peter's Basilica[98]
History	
Dedication	Saint Peter
Consecrated	18 November 1626
Architecture	
Status	Papal major basilica
Architect(s)	• Donato Bramante • Antonio da Sangallo the Younger • Michelangelo • Giacomo Barozzi da Vignola • Giacomo della Porta • Carlo Maderno • Gian Lorenzo Bernini • Carlo Fontana
Style	Renaissance and Baroque
Groundbreaking	18 April 1506
Completed	18 November 1626
Specifications	
Length	730 feet (220 m)
Width	500 feet (150 m)
Height	448.1 feet (136.6 m)
Nave height	151.5 feet (46.2 m)
Dome diameter (outer)	137.7 feet (42.0 m)
Dome diameter (inner)	136.1 feet (41.5 m)
Administration	
Diocese	Rome
Clergy	
Archpriest	Angelo Comastri
UNESCO World Heritage Site	
Official name	Vatican City
Type	Cultural
Criteria	i, ii, iv, vi
Designated	1984 (8th session)

St. Peter's Basilica

Reference no.	286[99]
State Party	Holy See
Region	Europe and North America

The **Papal Basilica of St. Peter in the Vatican** (Italian: *Basilica Papale di San Pietro in Vaticano*), or simply **St. Peter's Basilica** (Latin: *Basilica Sancti Petri*), is an Italian Renaissance church in Vatican City, the papal enclave within the city of Rome.

Designed principally by Donato Bramante, Michelangelo, Carlo Maderno and Gian Lorenzo Bernini, St. Peter's is the most renowned work of Renaissance architecture and the largest church in the world. While it is neither the mother church of the Catholic Church nor the cathedral of the Diocese of Rome, St. Peter's is regarded as one of the holiest Catholic shrines. It has been described as "holding a unique position in the Christian world"[100] and as "the greatest of all churches of Christendom".[101]

Catholic tradition holds that the Basilica is the burial site of Saint Peter, one of Jesus's Apostles and also the first Pope. Saint Peter's tomb is supposedly directly below the high altar of the Basilica. For this reason, many Popes have been interred at St. Peter's since the Early Christian period, and there has been a church on this site since the time of the Roman emperor Constantine the Great. Construction of the present basilica, which would replace Old St. Peter's Basilica from the 4th century CE, began on 18 April 1506 and was completed on 18 November 1626.

St. Peter's is famous as a place of pilgrimage and for its liturgical functions. The Pope presides at a number of liturgies throughout the year, drawing audiences of 15,000 to over 80,000 people, either within the Basilica or the adjoining St. Peter's Square.[102] St. Peter's has many historical associations, with the Early Christian Church, the Papacy, the Protestant Reformation and Catholic Counter-reformation and numerous artists, especially Michelangelo. As a work of architecture, it is regarded as the greatest building of its age. St. Peter's is one of the four churches in the world that hold the rank of Major Basilica, all four of which are in Rome. Contrary to popular misconception, it is not a cathedral because it is not the seat of a bishop; the *Cathedra* of the Pope as Bishop of Rome is in the Archbasilica of St. John Lateran.

Figure 29: *Facade of Saint Peter's Basilica at night*

Overview

St. Peter's is a church built in the Renaissance style located in the Vatican City west of the River Tiber and near the Janiculum Hill and Hadrian's Mausoleum. Its central dome dominates the skyline of Rome. The basilica is approached via St. Peter's Square, a forecourt in two sections, both surrounded by tall colonnades. The first space is oval and the second trapezoid. The façade of the basilica, with a giant order of columns, stretches across the end of the square and is approached by steps on which stand two 5.55 metres (18.2 ft) statues of the 1st-century apostles to Rome, Saints Peter and Paul.

The basilica is cruciform in shape, with an elongated nave in the Latin cross form but the early designs were for a centrally planned structure and this is still in evidence in the architecture. The central space is dominated both externally and internally by one of the largest domes in the world. The entrance is through a narthex, or entrance hall, which stretches across the building. One of the decorated bronze doors leading from the narthex is the Holy Door, only opened during jubilees.

The interior is of vast dimensions when compared with other churches. One author wrote: "Only gradually does it dawn upon us – as we watch people draw near to this or that monument, strangely they appear to shrink; they are,

Figure 30: *View from the Tiber on Ponte Sant'Angelo and the Basilica. The iconic dome dominates the skyline of Rome.*

Figure 31: *St. Peter's Basilica at night from Via della Conciliazione in Rome.*

Figure 32: *St Peter's, Bernini's colonnade and Maderno's fountain*

of course, dwarfed by the scale of everything in the building. This in its turn overwhelms us."[103]

The nave which leads to the central dome is in three bays, with piers supporting a barrel-vault, the highest of any church. The nave is framed by wide aisles which have a number of chapels off them. There are also chapels surrounding the dome. Moving around the basilica in a clockwise direction they are: The Baptistery, the Chapel of the Presentation of the Virgin, the larger Choir Chapel, the Clementine Chapel with the altar of Saint Gregory, the Sacristy Entrance, the left transept with altars to the Crucifixion of Saint Peter, Saint Joseph and Saint Thomas, the altar of the Sacred Heart, the Chapel of the Madonna of Colonna, the altar of Saint Peter and the Paralytic, the apse with the Chair of Saint Peter, the altar of Saint Peter raising Tabitha, the altar of the Archangel Michael, the altar of the Navicella, the right transept with altars of Saint Erasmus, Saints Processo and Martiniano, and Saint Wenceslas, the altar of Saint Basil, the Gregorian Chapel with the altar of the Madonna of Succour, the larger Chapel of the Holy Sacrament, the Chapel of Saint Sebastian and the Chapel of the Pietà.[104] At the heart of the basilica, beneath the high altar, is the *Confessio* or *Chapel of the Confession*, in reference to the confession of faith by St. Peter, which led to his martyrdom. Two curving marble staircases lead to this underground chapel at the level of the Constantinian church and immediately above the purported burial place of Saint Peter.

The entire interior of St. Peter's is lavishly decorated with marble, reliefs, architectural sculpture and gilding. The basilica contains a large number of tombs of popes and other notable people, many of which are considered outstanding artworks. There are also a number of sculptures in niches and chapels, including Michelangelo's *Pietà*. The central feature is a baldachin, or canopy over the Papal Altar, designed by Gian Lorenzo Bernini. The sanctuary culminates in a sculptural ensemble, also by Bernini, and containing the symbolic *Chair of Saint Peter*.

One observer wrote: "St Peter's Basilica is the reason why Rome is still the center of the civilized world. For religious, historical, and architectural reasons it by itself justifies a journey to Rome, and its interior offers a palimpsest of artistic styles at their best ..."[105]

The American philosopher Ralph Waldo Emerson described St. Peter's as "an ornament of the earth ... the sublime of the beautiful."[106]

File:Vatican StPeter Square.jpg

Panorama of St. Peter's Square

Status

St. Peter's Basilica is one of the Papal Basilicas (previously styled "patriarchal basilicas")[107] and one of the four Major Basilicas of Rome, the other Major Basilicas (all of which are also Papal Basilicas) being the Basilicas of St. John Lateran, St. Mary Major, and St. Paul outside the Walls. The rank of major basilica confers on St. Peter's Basilica precedence before all minor basilicas worldwide. However, unlike all the other Papal Major Basilicas, it is wholly within the territory, and thus the sovereign jurisdiction, of the Vatican City State, and not that of Italy.[108]

It is the most prominent building in the Vatican City. Its dome is a dominant feature of the skyline of Rome. Probably the largest church in Christendom,[109] it covers an area of 2.3 hectares (5.7 acres). One of the holiest sites of Christianity and Catholic Tradition, it is traditionally the burial site of its titular, St. Peter, who was the head of the twelve Apostles of Jesus and, according to tradition, the first Bishop of Antioch and later the first Bishop of Rome, rendering him the first Pope. Although the New Testament does not mention

Figure 33: *Bishops at the Second Vatican Council in 1962.*

St. Peter's martyrdom in Rome, tradition, based on the writings of the Fathers of the Church,Wikipedia:Please clarify holds that his tomb is below the baldachin and altar of the Basilica in the "Confession". For this reason, many Popes have, from the early years of the Church, been buried near Pope St. Peter in the necropolis beneath the Basilica. Construction of the current basilica, over the old Constantinian basilica, began on 18 April 1506 and finished in 1615. At length, on 18 November 1626 Pope Urban VIII solemnly dedicated the Basilica.

St. Peter's Basilica is neither the Pope's official seat nor first in rank among the Major Basilicas of Rome. This honour is held by the Pope's cathedral, the Archbasilica of St. John Lateran which is the mother church of all churches in communion with the Catholic Church. However, St. Peter's is certainly the Pope's principal church in terms of use because most Papal liturgies and ceremonies take place there due to its size, proximity to the Papal residence, and location within the Vatican City proper. The "Chair of Saint Peter", or cathedra, an ancient chair sometimes presumed to have been used by St. Peter himself, but which was a gift from Charles the Bald and used by many popes, symbolises the continuing line of apostolic succession from St. Peter to the reigning Pope. It occupies an elevated position in the apse of the Basilica, supported symbolically by the Doctors of the Church and enlightened symbolically by the Holy Spirit.

St. Peter's Basilica   59

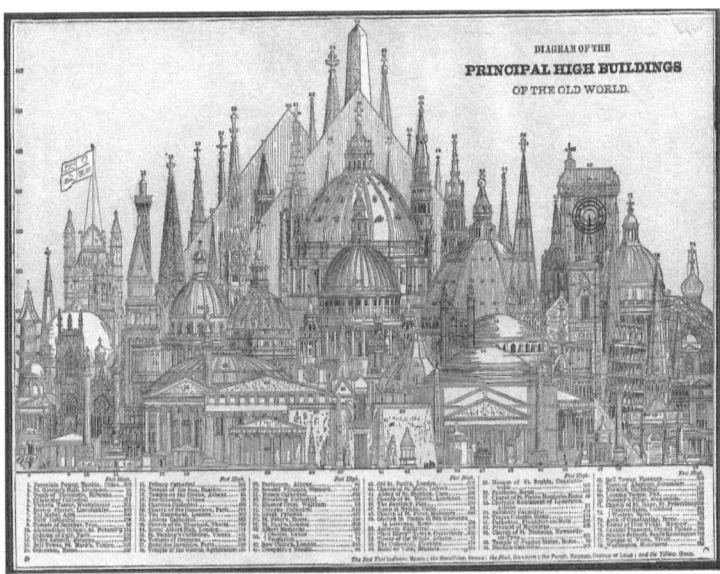

Figure 34: *The relative and absolute heights of the tallest buildings and structures of the Old World, with St. Peter's Basilica at the center*

As one of the constituent structures of the historically and architecturally significant Vatican City, St. Peter's Basilica was inscribed as a UNESCO World Heritage Site in 1984 under criteria (i), (ii), (iv), and (vi). With an exterior area of 21,095 square metres (227,060 sq ft), an interior area of 15,160 square metres (163,200 sq ft), and a volume of 5,000,000 cubic metres (180,000,000 cu ft), St. Peter's Basilica is the largest Christian church building in the world by the two latter metrics and the second largest by the first as of 2016[110]. The top of its dome, at 448.1 feet (136.6 m), also places it as the second tallest building in Rome as of 2016[110]. The dome's soaring height placed it among the tallest buildings of the Old World, and it continues to hold the title of tallest dome in the world. Though the largest dome in the world by diameter at the time of its completion, it no longer holds this distinction.

Figure 35: *Crepuscular rays are seen in St. Peter's Basilica at certain times each day.*

History

Saint Peter's burial site

After the crucifixion of Jesus, it is recorded in the Biblical book of the Acts of the Apostles that one of his twelve disciples, Simon known as Saint Peter, a fisherman from Galilee, took a leadership position among Jesus' followers and was of great importance in the founding of the Christian Church. The name Peter is "Petrus" in Latin and "Petros" in Greek, deriving from "*petra*" which means "stone" or "rock" in Greek, and is the literal translation of the Aramaic "Kepa", the name given to Simon by Jesus. (John 1:42, and see Matthew 16:18)

Catholic tradition holds that Peter, after a ministry of thirty-four years, traveled to Rome and met his martyrdom there along with Paul on 13 October, 64 CE during the reign of the Roman Emperor Nero. His execution was one of the many martyrdoms of Christians following the Great Fire of Rome. According to Origen, Peter was crucified head downwards, by his own request because he considered himself unworthy to die in the same manner as Jesus. The crucifixion took place near an ancient Egyptian obelisk in the Circus of Nero. The obelisk now stands in St. Peter's Square and is revered as a "witness" to Peter's death. It is one of several ancient Obelisks of Rome.[111]

According to tradition, Peter's remains were buried just outside the Circus, on the Mons Vaticanus across the Via Cornelia from the Circus, less than 150 metres (490 ft) from his place of death. The Via Cornelia was a road which ran east-to-west along the north wall of the Circus on land now covered by the southern portions of the Basilica and St. Peter's Square. A shrine was built on this site some years later. Almost three hundred years later, Old St. Peter's Basilica was constructed over this site.

The area now covered by the Vatican City had been a cemetery for some years before the Circus of Nero was built. It was a burial ground for the numerous executions in the Circus and contained many Christian burials, because for many years after the burial of Saint Peter many Christians chose to be buried near Peter.

In 1939, in the reign of Pope Pius XII, 10 years of archaeological research began, under the crypt of the basilica, an area inaccessible since the 9th century. The excavations revealed the remains of shrines of different periods at different levels, from Clement VIII (1594) to Callixtus II (1123) and Gregory I (590–604), built over an aedicula containing fragments of bones that were folded in a tissue with gold decorations, tinted with the precious murex purple. Although it could not be determined with certainty that the bones were those of Peter, the rare vestments suggested a burial of great importance. On 23 December 1950, in his pre-Christmas radio broadcast to the world, Pope Pius XII announced the discovery of Saint Peter's tomb.

Old St. Peter's Basilica

Old St. Peter's Basilica was the 4th-century church begun by the Emperor Constantine the Great between 319 and 333 CE. It was of typical basilical form, a wide nave and two aisles on each side and an apsidal end, with the addition of a transept or bema, giving the building the shape of a tau cross. It was over 103.6 metres (340 ft) long, and the entrance was preceded by a large colonnaded atrium. This church had been built over the small shrine believed to mark the burial place of St. Peter. It contained a very large number of burials and memorials, including those of most of the popes from St. Peter to the 15th century. Like all of the earliest churches in Rome, both this church and its successor had the entrance to the east and the apse at the west end of the building. Since the construction of the current basilica, the name *Old St. Peter's Basilica* has been used for its predecessor to distinguish the two buildings.

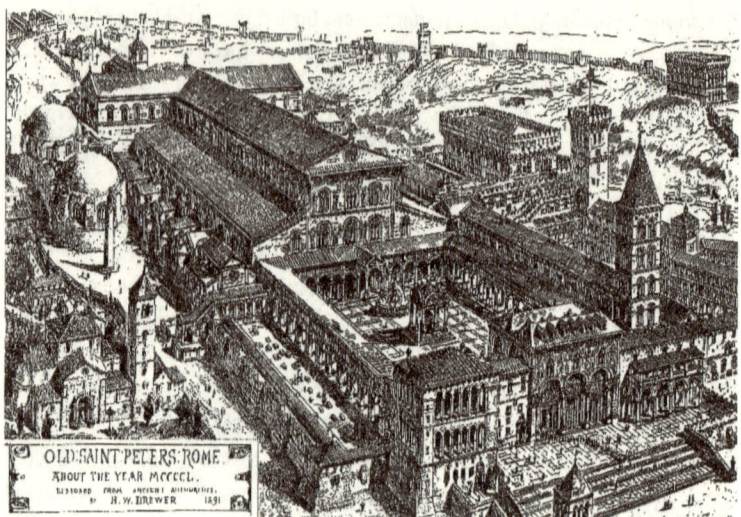

Figure 36: *A conjectural view of the Old St. Peter's Basilica by H. W. Brewer, 1891*

The plan to rebuild

By the end of the 15th century, having been neglected during the period of the Avignon Papacy, the old basilica had fallen into disrepair. It appears that the first pope to consider rebuilding, or at least making radical changes was Pope Nicholas V (1447–55). He commissioned work on the old building from Leone Battista Alberti and Bernardo Rossellino and also had Rossellino design a plan for an entirely new basilica, or an extreme modification of the old. His reign was frustrated by political problems and when he died, little had been achieved. He had, however, ordered the demolition of the Colosseum and by the time of his death, 2,522 cartloads of stone had been transported for use in the new building.[112] The foundations were completed for a new transept and choir to form a domed Latin cross with the preserved nave and side aisles of the old basilica. Some walls for the choir had also been built.

Pope Julius II planned far more for St Peter's than Nicholas V's program of repair or modification. Julius was at that time planning his own tomb, which was to be designed and adorned with sculpture by Michelangelo and placed within St Peter's.[113] In 1505 Julius made a decision to demolish the ancient basilica and replace it with a monumental structure to house his enormous tomb and "aggrandize himself in the popular imagination". A competition was held, and a number of the designs have survived at the Uffizi Gallery. A succession of popes and architects followed in the next 120 years, their combined efforts resulting in the present building. The scheme begun by Julius II continued through the reigns of Leo X (1513–1521), Hadrian VI (1522–1523). Clement VII (1523–1534), Paul III (1534–1549), Julius III (1550–1555), Marcellus II (1555), Paul IV (1555–1559), Pius IV (1559–1565), Pius V (saint) (1565–1572), Gregory XIII (1572–1585), Sixtus V (1585–1590), Urban VII (1590), Gregory XIV (1590–1591), Innocent IX (1591), Clement VIII (1592–1605), Leo XI (1605), Paul V (1605–1621), Gregory XV (1621–1623), Urban VIII (1623–1644) and Innocent X (1644–1655).

Financing with indulgences

One method employed to finance the building of St. Peter's Basilica was the granting of indulgences in return for contributions. A major promoter of this method of fund-raising was Albrecht, Archbishop of Mainz and Magdeburg, who had to clear debts owed to the Roman Curia by contributing to the rebuilding program. To facilitate this, he appointed the German Dominican preacher Johann Tetzel, whose salesmanship provoked a scandal.[114]

A German Augustinian priest, Martin Luther, wrote to Archbishop Albrecht arguing against this "selling of indulgences". He also included his "Disputation of Martin Luther on the Power and Efficacy of Indulgences", which came to be known as *The 95 Theses*.[115] This became a factor in starting the Reformation, the birth of Protestantism.

Architecture

Successive plans

Pope Julius' scheme for the grandest building in Christendom was the subject of a competition for which a number of entries remain intact in the Uffizi Gallery, Florence. It was the design of Donato Bramante that was selected, and for which the foundation stone was laid in 1506. This plan was in the form of an enormous Greek Cross with a dome inspired by that of the huge circular Roman temple, the Pantheon. The main difference between Bramante's design and that of the Pantheon is that where the dome of the Pantheon is supported by a continuous wall, that of the new basilica was to be supported only on four large piers. This feature was maintained in the ultimate design. Bramante's dome was to be surmounted by a lantern with its own small dome but otherwise very similar in form to the Early Renaissance lantern of Florence Cathedral designed for Brunelleschi's dome by Michelozzo.

Bramante had envisioned that the central dome would be surrounded by four lower domes at the diagonal axes. The equal chancel, nave and transept arms were each to be of two bays ending in an apse. At each corner of the building

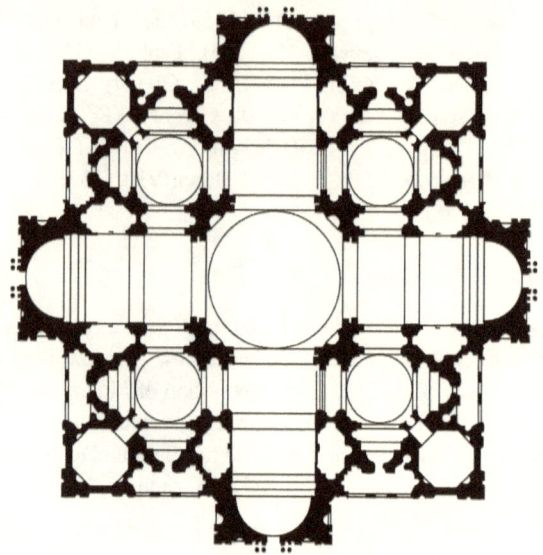

Figure 37: *Bramante's plan*

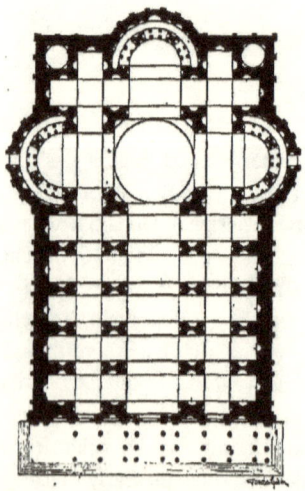

Figure 38: *Raphael's plan*

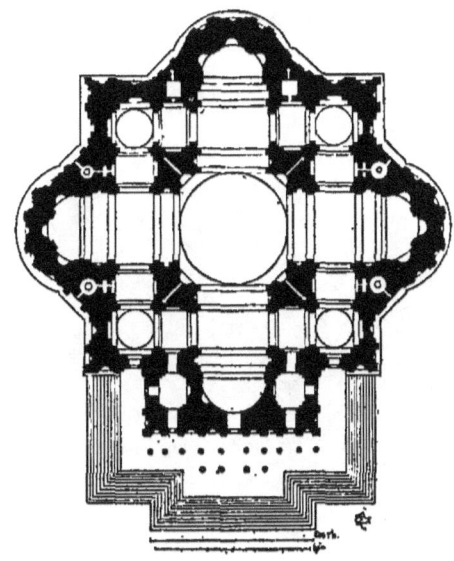

Figure 39: *Michelangelo's plan*

was to stand a tower, so that the overall plan was square, with the apses projecting at the cardinal points. Each apse had two large radial buttresses, which squared off its semi-circular shape.[116]

When Pope Julius died in 1513, Bramante was replaced with Giuliano da Sangallo, Fra Giocondo and Raphael. Sangallo and Fra Giocondo both died in 1515, Bramante himself having died the previous year. The main change in Raphael's plan is the nave of five bays, with a row of complex apsidal chapels off the aisles on either side. Raphael's plan for the chancel and transepts made the squareness of the exterior walls more definite by reducing the size of the towers, and the semi-circular apses more clearly defined by encircling each with an ambulatory.[117]

In 1520 Raphael also died, aged 37, and his successor Baldassare Peruzzi maintained changes that Raphael had proposed to the internal arrangement of the three main apses, but otherwise reverted to the Greek Cross plan and other features of Bramante.[118] This plan did not go ahead because of various difficulties of both Church and state. In 1527 Rome was sacked and plundered by Emperor Charles V. Peruzzi died in 1536 without his plan being realized.

At this point Antonio da Sangallo the Younger submitted a plan which combines features of Peruzzi, Raphael and Bramante in its design and extends the

Figure 40: *View of the interior shows the transept arms to right and left, and the chancel beyond the baldacchino.*

building into a short nave with a wide façade and portico of dynamic projection. His proposal for the dome was much more elaborate of both structure and decoration than that of Bramante and included ribs on the exterior. Like Bramante, Sangallo proposed that the dome be surmounted by a lantern which he redesigned to a larger and much more elaborate form.[119] Sangallo's main practical contribution was to strengthen Bramante's piers which had begun to crack.

On 1 January 1547 in the reign of Pope Paul III, Michelangelo, then in his seventies, succeeded Sangallo the Younger as "Capomaestro", the superintendent of the building program at St Peter's. He is to be regarded as the principal designer of a large part of the building as it stands today, and as bringing the construction to a point where it could be carried through. He did not take on the job with pleasure; it was forced upon him by Pope Paul, frustrated at the death of his chosen candidate, Giulio Romano and the refusal of Jacopo Sansovino to leave Venice. Michelangelo wrote "I undertake this only for the love of God and in honour of the Apostle." He insisted that he should be given a free hand to achieve the ultimate aim by whatever means he saw fit.

Michelangelo's contribution

Michelangelo took over a building site at which four piers, enormous beyond any constructed since ancient Roman times, were rising behind the remaining nave of the old basilica. He also inherited the numerous schemes designed and redesigned by some of the greatest architectural and engineering minds of the 16th century. There were certain common elements in these schemes. They all called for a dome to equal that engineered by Brunelleschi a century earlier and which has since dominated the skyline of Renaissance Florence, and they all called for a strongly symmetrical plan of either Greek Cross form, like the iconic St. Mark's Basilica in Venice, or of a Latin Cross with the transepts of identical form to the chancel, as at Florence Cathedral.

Even though the work had progressed only a little in 40 years, Michelangelo did not simply dismiss the ideas of the previous architects. He drew on them in developing a grand vision. Above all, Michelangelo recognized the essential quality of Bramante's original design. He reverted to the Greek Cross and, as Helen Gardner expresses it: "Without destroying the centralising features of Bramante's plan, Michelangelo, with a few strokes of the pen converted its snowflake complexity into massive, cohesive unity."

As it stands today, St. Peter's has been extended with a nave by Carlo Maderno. It is the chancel end (the ecclesiastical "Eastern end") with its huge centrally placed dome that is the work of Michelangelo. Because of its location within the Vatican State and because the projection of the nave screens the dome from sight when the building is approached from the square in front of it, the work of Michelangelo is best appreciated from a distance. What becomes apparent is that the architect has greatly reduced the clearly defined geometric forms of Bramante's plan of a square with square projections, and also of Raphael's plan of a square with semi-circular projections.[120] Michelangelo has blurred the definition of the geometry by making the external masonry of massive proportions and filling in every corner with a small vestry or stairwell. The effect created is of a continuous wall-surface that is folded or fractured at different angles, but lacks the right-angles which usually define change of direction at the corners of a building. This exterior is surrounded by a giant order of Corinthian pilasters all set at slightly different angles to each other, in keeping with the ever-changing angles of the wall's surface. Above them the huge cornice ripples in a continuous band, giving the appearance of keeping the whole building in a state of compression.[121]

Dome: successive and final designs

The dome of St. Peter's rises to a total height of 136.57 metres (448.1 ft) from the floor of the basilica to the top of the external cross. It is the tallest dome in the world.[122] Its internal diameter is 41.47 metres (136.1 ft), slightly smaller than two of the three other huge domes that preceded it, those of the Pantheon of Ancient Rome, 43.3 metres (142 ft), and Florence Cathedral of the Early Renaissance, 44 metres (144 ft). It has a greater diameter by approximately 30 feet (9.1 m) than Constantinople's Hagia Sophia church, completed in 537. It was to the domes of the Pantheon and Florence duomo that the architects of St. Peter's looked for solutions as to how to go about building what was conceived, from the outset, as the greatest dome of Christendom.

Figure 41: *Bramante's dome*

Bramante and Sangallo, 1506 and 1513

The dome of the Pantheon stands on a circular wall with no entrances or windows except a single door. The whole building is as high as it is wide. Its dome is constructed in a single shell of concrete, made light by the inclusion of a large amount of the volcanic stones tuff and pumice. The inner surface of the dome is deeply coffered which has the effect of creating both vertical and horizontal ribs, while lightening the overall load. At the summit is an ocular opening 8 metres (26 ft) across which provides light to the interior.

Bramante's plan for the dome of St. Peter's (1506) follows that of the Pantheon very closely, and like that of the Pantheon, was designed to be constructed in Tufa Concrete for which he had rediscovered a formula. With the exception of the lantern that surmounts it, the profile is very similar, except that in this case the supporting wall becomes a drum raised high above ground level on four massive piers. The solid wall, as used at the Pantheon, is lightened at St. Peter's by Bramante piercing it with windows and encircling it with a peristyle.

In the case of Florence Cathedral, the desired visual appearance of the pointed dome existed for many years before Brunelleschi made its construction feasible.[123] Its double-shell construction of bricks locked together in herringbone pattern (re-introduced from Byzantine architecture), and the gentle upward slope of its eight stone ribs made it possible for the construction to take place

Figure 42: *Sangallo's design*

without the massive wooden formwork necessary to construct hemispherical arches. While its appearance, with the exception of the details of the lantern, is entirely Gothic, its engineering was highly innovative, and the product of a mind that had studied the huge vaults and remaining dome of Ancient Rome.

Sangallo's plan (1513), of which a large wooden model still exists, looks to both these predecessors. He realised the value of both the coffering at the Pantheon and the outer stone ribs at Florence Cathedral. He strengthened and extended the peristyle of Bramante into a series of arched and ordered openings around the base, with a second such arcade set back in a tier above the first. In his hands, the rather delicate form of the lantern, based closely on that in Florence, became a massive structure, surrounded by a projecting base, a peristyle and surmounted by a spire of conic form. According to James Lees-Milne the design was "too eclectic, too pernickety and too tasteless to have been a success".

Michelangelo and Giacomo della Porta, 1547 and 1585

Michelangelo redesigned the dome in 1547, taking into account all that had gone before. His dome, like that of Florence, is constructed of two shells of brick, the outer one having 16 stone ribs, twice the number at Florence but far fewer than in Sangallo's design. As with the designs of Bramante and Sangallo, the dome is raised from the piers on a drum. The encircling peristyle

Figure 43: *St. Peter's Basilica from Castel Sant'Angelo showing the dome rising behind Maderno's façade.*

of Bramante and the arcade of Sangallo are reduced to 16 pairs of Corinthian columns, each of 15 metres (49 ft) high which stand proud of the building, connected by an arch. Visually they appear to buttress each of the ribs, but structurally they are probably quite redundant. The reason for this is that the dome is ovoid in shape, rising steeply as does the dome of Florence Cathedral, and therefore exerting less outward thrust than does a hemispherical dome, such as that of the Pantheon, which, although it is not buttressed, is countered by the downward thrust of heavy masonry which extends above the circling wall.

The ovoid profile of the dome has been the subject of much speculation and scholarship over the past century. Michelangelo died in 1564, leaving the drum of the dome complete, and Bramante's piers much bulkier than originally designed, each 18 metres (59 ft) across. Following his death, the work continued under his assistant Jacopo Barozzi da Vignola with Giorgio Vasari appointed by Pope Pius V as a watchdog to make sure that Michelangelo's plans were carried out exactly. Despite Vignola's knowledge of Michelangelo's intentions, little happened in this period. In 1585 the energetic Pope Sixtus appointed Giacomo della Porta who was to be assisted by Domenico Fontana. The five-year reign of Sixtus was to see the building advance at a great rate.

Figure 44: *The engraving by Stefan du Pérac was published in 1569, five years after the death of Michelangelo*

Michelangelo left a few drawings, including an early drawing of the dome, and some drawings of details. There were also detailed engravings published in 1569 by Stefan du Pérac who claimed that they were the master's final solution. Michelangelo, like Sangallo before him, also left a large wooden model. Giacomo della Porta subsequently altered this model in several ways, in keeping with changes that he made to the design. Most of these changes were of a cosmetic nature, such as the adding of lion's masks over the swags on the drum in honour of Pope Sixtus and adding a circlet of finials around the spire at the top of the lantern, as proposed by Sangallo. The major change that was made to the model, either by della Porta, or Michelangelo himself before his death, was to raise the outer dome higher above the inner one.

A drawing by Michelangelo indicates that his early intentions were towards an ovoid dome, rather than a hemispherical one. In an engraving in Galasso Alghisi' treatise (1563), the dome may be represented as ovoid, but the perspective is ambiguous.[124] Stefan du Pérac's engraving (1569) shows a hemispherical dome, but this was perhaps an inaccuracy of the engraver. The profile of the wooden model is more ovoid than that of the engravings, but less so than the finished product. It has been suggested that Michelangelo on his death bed reverted to the more pointed shape. However Lees-Milne cites Giacomo della

Porta as taking full responsibility for the change and as indicating to Pope Sixtus that Michelangelo was lacking in the scientific understanding of which he himself was capable.

Helen Gardner suggests that Michelangelo made the change to the hemispherical dome of lower profile in order to establish a balance between the dynamic vertical elements of the encircling giant order of pilasters and a more static and reposeful dome. Gardner also comments "The sculpturing of architecture [by Michelangelo] ... here extends itself up from the ground through the attic stories and moves on into the drum and dome, the whole building being pulled together into a unity from base to summit."

It is this sense of the building being sculptured, unified and "pulled together" by the encircling band of the deep cornice that led Eneide Mignacca to conclude that the ovoid profile, seen now in the end product, was an essential part of Michelangelo's first (and last) concept. The sculptor/architect has, figuratively speaking, taken all the previous designs in hand and compressed their contours as if the building were a lump of clay. The dome *must* appear to thrust upwards because of the apparent pressure created by flattening the building's angles and restraining its projections. If this explanation is the correct one, then the profile of the dome is not merely a structural solution, as perceived by Giacomo della Porta; it is part of the integrated design solution that is about visual tension and compression. In one sense, Michelangelo's dome may appear to look backward to the Gothic profile of Florence Cathedral and ignore the Classicism of the Renaissance, but on the other hand, perhaps more than any other building of the 16th century, it prefigures the architecture of the Baroque.

Completion

Giacomo della Porta and Domenico Fontana brought the dome to completion in 1590, the last year of the reign of Sixtus V. His successor, Gregory XIV, saw Fontana complete the lantern and had an inscription to the honour of Sixtus V placed around its inner opening. The next pope, Clement VIII, had the cross raised into place, an event which took all day, and was accompanied by the ringing of the bells of all the city's churches. In the arms of the cross are set two lead caskets, one containing a fragment of the True Cross and a relic of St. Andrew and the other containing medallions of the Holy Lamb.

In the mid 18th century, cracks appeared in the dome, so four iron chains were installed between the two shells to bind it, like the rings that keep a barrel from bursting. As many as ten chains have been installed at various times, the earliest possibly planned by Michelangelo himself as a precaution, as Brunelleschi did at Florence Cathedral.

St. Peter's Basilica

Figure 45: *The dome was brought to completion by Giacomo della Porta and Fontana.*

Around the inside of the dome is written, in letters 1.4 metres (4.6 ft) high:

TV ES PETRVS ET SVPER HANC PETRAM AEDIFICABO ECCLESIAM MEAM. TIBI DABO CLAVES REGNI CAELORVM

(... *you are Peter, and on this rock I will build my church. ... I will give you the keys of the kingdom of heaven* ... Vulgate, Matthew 16:18–19[125].)

Beneath the lantern is the inscription:

S. PETRI GLORIAE SIXTVS PP. V. A. M. D. XC. PONTIF. V.
(*To the glory of St Peter; Sixtus V, pope, in the year 1590, the fifth of his pontificate.*)

Discovery of Michelangelo draft

On 7 December 2007, a fragment of a red chalk drawing of a section of the dome of the basilica, almost certainly by the hand of Michelangelo, was discovered in the Vatican archives. The drawing shows a small precisely drafted section of the plan of the entabulature above two of the radial columns of the cupola drum. Michelangelo is known to have destroyed thousands of his drawings before his death.[126] The rare survival of this example is probably due to its fragmentary state and the fact that detailed mathematical calculations had been made over the top of the drawing.

Figure 46: *Architectural details of the dome at Saint Peter's Basilica in Vatican city, Vatican*

Changes of plan

On 18 February 1606, under Pope Paul V, the dismantling of the remaining parts of the Constantinian basilica began. The marble cross that had been set at the top of the pediment by Pope Sylvester and Constantine the Great was lowered to the ground. The timbers were salvaged for the roof of the Borghese Palace and two rare black marble columns, the largest of their kind, were carefully stored and later used in the narthex. The tombs of various popes were opened, treasures removed and plans made for re-interment in the new basilica.

The Pope had appointed Carlo Maderno in 1602. He was a nephew of Domenico Fontana and had demonstrated himself as a dynamic architect. Maderno's idea was to ring Michelangelo's building with chapels, but the Pope was hesitant about deviating from the master's plan, even though he had been dead for forty years. The *Fabbrica* or building committee, a group drawn from various nationalities and generally despised by the Curia who viewed the basilica as belonging to Rome rather than Christendom, were in a quandary as to how the building should proceed. One of the matters that influenced their thinking was the Counter-Reformation which increasingly associated a Greek Cross plan with paganism and saw the Latin Cross as truly symbolic of Christianity.

St. Peter's Basilica

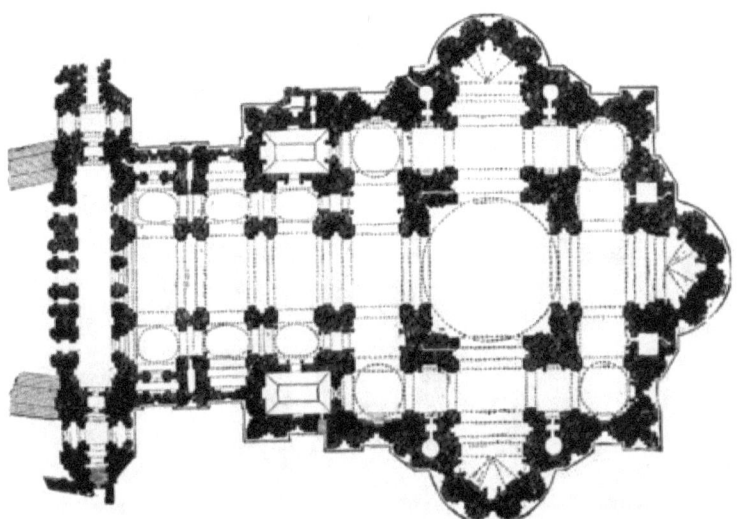

Fig. 4 und 5. Längenfchnitt und Grundriß von St. Peter in Rom.

Figure 47: *Michelangelo's plan extended with Maderno's nave and narthex*

Another influence on the thinking of both the Fabbrica and the Curia was a certain guilt at the demolition of the ancient building. The ground on which it and its various associated chapels, vestries and sacristies had stood for so long was hallowed. The only solution was to build a nave that encompassed the whole space. In 1607 a committee of ten architects was called together, and a decision was made to extend Michelangelo's building into a nave. Maderno's plans for both the nave and the facade were accepted. The building began on 7 May 1607, and proceeded at a great rate, with an army of 700 labourers being employed. The following year, the façade was begun, in December 1614 the final touches were added to the stucco decoration of the vault and early in 1615 the partition wall between the two sections was pulled down. All the rubble was carted away, and the nave was ready for use by Palm Sunday.

Maderno's facade

The facade designed by Maderno, is 114.69 metres (376.3 ft) wide and 45.55 metres (149.4 ft) high and is built of travertine stone, with a giant order of Corinthian columns and a central pediment rising in front of a tall attic surmounted by thirteen statues: Christ flanked by eleven of the Apostles (except Saint Peter, whose statue is left of the stairs) and John the Baptist.[127] The inscription below the cornice on the 1 metre (3.3 ft) tall frieze reads:

Figure 48: *Maderno's façade, with the statues of Saint Peter (left) and Saint Paul (right) flanking the entrance stairs*

IN HONOREM PRINCIPIS APOST PAVLVS V BVRGHESIVS ROMANVS PONT MAX AN MDCXII PONT VII
(*In honour of the Prince of Apostles, Paul V Borghese, a Roman, Supreme Pontiff, in the year 1612, the seventh of his pontificate*)

(Paul V (Camillo Borghese), born in Rome but of a Sienese family, liked to emphasize his "Romanness.")

The facade is often cited as the least satisfactory part of the design of St. Peter's. The reasons for this, according to James Lees-Milne, are that it was not given enough consideration by the Pope and committee because of the desire to get the building completed quickly, coupled with the fact that Maderno was hesitant to deviate from the pattern set by Michelangelo at the other end of the building. Lees-Milne describes the problems of the façade as being too broad for its height, too cramped in its details and too heavy in the attic story. The breadth is caused by modifying the plan to have towers on either side. These towers were never executed above the line of the facade because it was discovered that the ground was not sufficiently stable to bear the weight. One effect of the facade and lengthened nave is to screen the view of the dome, so that the building, from the front, has no vertical feature, except from a distance.

Figure 49: *The narthex*

Narthex and portals

Behind the façade of St. Peter's stretches a long portico or "narthex" such as was occasionally found in Italian Romanesque churches. This is the part of Maderno's design with which he was most satisfied. Its long barrel vault is decorated with ornate stucco and gilt, and successfully illuminated by small windows between pendentives, while the ornate marble floor is beamed with light reflected in from the piazza. At each end of the narthex is a theatrical space framed by ionic columns and within each is set a statue, an equestrian figure of Charlemagne by Cornacchini (18th century) in the south end and Constantine the Great by Bernini (1670) in the north end.

Five portals, of which three are framed by huge salvaged antique columns, lead into the basilica. The central portal has a bronze door created by Antonio Averulino in 1455 for the old basilica and somewhat enlarged to fit the new space.

Maderno's nave

To the single bay of Michelangelo's Greek Cross, Maderno added a further three bays. He made the dimensions slightly different from Michelangelo's bay, thus defining where the two architectural works meet. Maderno also tilted the axis of the nave slightly. This was not by accident, as suggested by his critics.

Figure 50: *Maderno's nave, looking towards the chancel*

An ancient Egyptian obelisk had been erected in the square outside, but had not been quite aligned with Michelangelo's building, so Maderno compensated, in order that it should, at least, align with the Basilica's façade.

The nave has huge paired pilasters, in keeping with Michelangelo's work. The size of the interior is so "stupendously large" that it is hard to get a sense of scale within the building.[128] The four cherubs who flutter against the first piers of the nave, carrying between them two holy water basins, appear of quite normal cherubic size, until approached. Then it becomes apparent that each one is over 2 metres high and that real children cannot reach the basins unless they scramble up the marble draperies. The aisles each have two smaller chapels and a larger rectangular chapel, the Chapel of the Sacrament and the Choir Chapel. These are lavishly decorated with marble, stucco, gilt, sculpture and mosaic. Remarkably, there are very few paintings, although some, such as Raphael's *Sistine Madonna* have been reproduced in mosaic. The most precious painting is a small icon of the Madonna, removed from the old basilica.

Maderno's last work at St. Peter's was to design a crypt-like space or "Confessio" under the dome, where the cardinals and other privileged persons could descend in order to be nearer to the burial place of the apostle. Its marble steps are remnants of the old basilica and around its balustrade are 95 bronze lamps.

Influence on church architecture

The design of St. Peter's Basilica, and in particular its dome, has greatly influenced church architecture in Western Christendom. Within Rome, the huge domed church of Sant'Andrea della Valle was designed by Giacomo della Porta before the completion of St Peter's Basilica, and subsequently worked on by Carlo Maderno. This was followed by the domes of San Carlo ai Catinari, Sant'Agnese in Agone, and many others. Christopher Wren's dome at St Paul's Cathedral (London, England), the domes of Karlskirche (Vienna, Austria), St. Nicholas Church (Prague, Czech Republic), and the Pantheon (Paris, France) all pay homage to St Peter's Basilica.

The 19th and early-20th-century architectural revivals brought about the building of a great number of churches that imitate elements of St Peter's to a greater or lesser degree, including St. Mary of the Angels in Chicago, St. Josaphat's Basilica in Milwaukee, Immaculate Heart of Mary in Pittsburgh and Mary, Queen of the World Cathedral in Montreal, which replicates many aspects of St Peter's on a smaller scale. Post-Modernism has seen free adaptations of St Peter's in the Basilica of Our Lady of Licheń, and the Basilica of Our Lady of Peace of Yamoussoukro.

Bernini's furnishings

Pope Urban VIII and Bernini

As a young boy Gian Lorenzo Bernini (1598–1680) visited St. Peter's with the painter Annibale Carracci and stated his wish to build "a mighty throne for the apostle". His wish came true. As a young man, in 1626, he received the patronage of Pope Urban VIII and worked on the embellishment of the Basilica for 50 years. Appointed as Maderno's successor in 1629, he was to become regarded as the greatest architect and sculptor of the Baroque period. Bernini's works at St. Peter's include the baldachin (baldaquin, from Italian: **baldacchino**), the Chapel of the Sacrament, the plan for the niches and loggias in the piers of the dome and the chair of St. Peter.

Baldacchino and niches

Bernini's first work at St. Peter's was to design the baldacchino, a pavilion-like structure 28.74 metres (94.3 ft) tall and claimed to be the largest piece of bronze in the world, which stands beneath the dome and above the altar. Its design is based on the *ciborium*, of which there are many in the churches of Rome, serving to create a sort of holy space above and around the table on which the Sacrament is laid for the Eucharist and emphasizing the significance of this ritual. These *ciboria* are generally of white marble, with inlaid coloured

Figure 51: *The apse with St. Peter's Cathedra supported by four Doctors of the Church*

stone. Bernini's concept was for something very different. He took his inspiration in part from the baldachin or canopy carried above the head of the pope in processions, and in part from eight ancient columns that had formed part of a screen in the old basilica. Their twisted barley-sugar shape had a special significance as they were modeled on those of the Temple of Jerusalem and donated by the Emperor Constantine. Based on these columns, Bernini created four huge columns of bronze, twisted and decorated with laurel leaves and bees, which were the emblem of Pope Urban.

The baldacchino is surmounted not with an architectural pediment, like most baldacchini, but with curved Baroque brackets supporting a draped canopy, like the brocade canopies carried in processions above precious iconic images. In this case, the draped canopy is of bronze, and all the details, including the olive leaves, bees, and the portrait heads of Urban's niece in childbirth and her newborn son, are picked out in gold leaf. The baldacchino stands as a vast free-standing sculptural object, central to and framed by the largest space within the building. It is so large that the visual effect is to create a link between the enormous dome which appears to float above it, and the congregation at floor level of the basilica. It is penetrated visually from every direction, and is visually linked to the *Cathedra Petri* in the apse behind it and to the four piers containing large statues that are at each diagonal.

Figure 52: *The altar with Bernini's baldacchino*

As part of the scheme for the central space of the church, Bernini had the huge piers, begun by Bramante and completed by Michelangelo, hollowed out into niches, and had staircases made inside them, leading to four balconies. There was much dismay from those who thought that the dome might fall, but it did not. On the balconies Bernini created showcases, framed by the eight ancient twisted columns, to display the four most precious relics of the basilica: the spear of Longinus, said to have pierced the side of Christ, the veil of Veronica, with the miraculous image of the face of Christ, a fragment of the True Cross discovered in Jerusalem by Constantine's mother, Helena, and a relic of Saint Andrew, the brother of Saint Peter. In each of the niches that surround the central space of the basilica was placed a huge statue of the saint associated with the relic above. Only *Saint Longinus* is the work of Bernini. (See below)

Bernini's Towers

Urban had long been a critic of Bernini's predecessor, Carlo Maderno. His disapproval of the architect's work stemmed largely from the Maderno's design for the longitudinal nave of St. Peters, which was widely condemned for obscuring Michelangelo's dome. When the Pope gave the commission to Bernini he therefore requested that a new design for the facade's bell towers to be submitted for consideration. Baldinucci describes Bernini's tower as consisting of "two orders of columns and pilasters, the first order being Corinthian" and "a

Figure 53: *Bernini's Cathedra Petri and Gloria*

third or attic story formed of pilasters and two columns on either side of the open archway in the center".

Urban desired the towers to be completed by a very specific date: 29 June 1641, the feast day dedicated to Saints Peter and Paul. To this end an order was issued which stated that "all work should take a second seat to that of the campanile." The south tower was completed on time even in spite of these issues, but records show that in the wake of the unveiling the Pope was not content with what he saw and he ordered the top level of Bernini's tower removed so that the structure could be made even grander. The tower continued to grow, and as the construction began to settle the first cracks started to appear followed by Urban's infamous public admonishment of his architect.

In 1642 all work on both towers came to a halt. Bernini had to pay the cost for the demolition; eventually the idea of completing the bell towers was abandoned.

Cathedra Petri and Chapel of the Blessed Sacrament

Bernini then turned his attention to another precious relic, the so-called *Cathedra Petri* or "throne of St. Peter" a chair which was often claimed to have been used by the apostle, but appears to date from the 12th century. As the chair itself was fast deteriorating and was no longer serviceable, Pope Alexander

St. Peter's Basilica

Figure 54: *St. Peter's Basilica and the piazza at night*

VII determined to enshrine it in suitable splendor as the object upon which the line of successors to Peter was based. Bernini created a large bronze throne in which it was housed, raised high on four looping supports held effortlessly by massive bronze statues of four Doctors of the Church, Saints Ambrose and Augustine representing the Latin Church and Athanasius and John Chrysostom, the Greek Church. The four figures are dynamic with sweeping robes and expressions of adoration and ecstasy. Behind and above the Cathedra, a blaze of light comes in through a window of yellow alabaster, illuminating, at its center, the Dove of the Holy Spirit. The elderly painter, Andrea Sacchi, had urged Bernini to make the figures large, so that they would be seen well from the central portal of the nave. The chair was enshrined in its new home with great celebration of 16 January 1666.

Bernini's final work for St. Peter's, undertaken in 1676, was the decoration of the Chapel of the Sacrament. To hold the sacramental Host, he designed a miniature version in gilt bronze of Bramante's Tempietto, the little chapel that marks the place of the death of St. Peter. On either side is an angel, one gazing in rapt adoration and the other looking towards the viewer in welcome. Bernini died in 1680 in his 82nd year.

St. Peter's Piazza

To the east of the basilica is the *Piazza di San Pietro*, (St. Peter's Square). The present arrangement, constructed between 1656 and 1667, is the Baroque

Figure 55: *One of the two fountains which form the axis of the piazza.*

inspiration of Bernini who inherited a location already occupied by an Egyptian obelisk which was centrally placed, (with some contrivance) to Maderno's facade.[129] The obelisk, known as "The Witness", at 25.5 metres (84 ft) and a total height, including base and the cross on top, of 40 metres (130 ft), is the second largest standing obelisk, and the only one to remain standing since its removal from Egypt and re-erection at the Circus of Nero in 37 AD, where it is thought to have stood witness to the crucifixion of Saint Peter. Its removal to its present location by order of Pope Sixtus V and engineered by Domenico Fontana on 28 September 1586, was an operation fraught with difficulties and nearly ending in disaster when the ropes holding the obelisk began to smoke from the friction. Fortunately this problem was noticed by Benedetto Bresca, a sailor of Sanremo, and for his swift intervention, his town was granted the privilege of providing the palms that are used at the basilica each Palm Sunday.

The other object in the old square with which Bernini had to contend was a large fountain designed by Maderno in 1613 and set to one side of the obelisk, making a line parallel with the facade. Bernini's plan uses this horizontal axis as a major feature of his unique, spatially dynamic and highly symbolic design. The most obvious solutions were either a rectangular piazza of vast proportions so that the obelisk stood centrally and the fountain (and a matching companion) could be included, or a trapezoid piazza which fanned out from the facade of the basilica like that in front of the Palazzo Pubblico in Siena. The problems of the square plan are that the necessary width to include the fountain would entail the demolition of numerous buildings, including some of the Vatican, and would minimize the effect of the facade. The trapezoid plan, on the other hand, would maximize the apparent width of the facade, which was already perceived as a fault of the design.

Bernini's ingenious solution was to create a piazza in two sections. That part which is nearest the basilica is trapezoid, but rather than fanning out from the facade, it narrows. This gives the effect of countering the visual perspective. It means that from the second part of the piazza, the building looks nearer than it is, the breadth of the facade is minimized and its height appears greater in proportion to its width. The second section of the piazza is a huge elliptical circus which gently slopes downwards to the obelisk at its center. The two distinct areas are framed by a colonnade formed by doubled pairs of columns supporting an entablature of the simple Tuscan Order.

The part of the colonnade that is around the ellipse does not entirely encircle it, but reaches out in two arcs, symbolic of the arms of "the Catholic Church reaching out to welcome its communicants". The obelisk and Maderno's fountain mark the widest axis of the ellipse. Bernini balanced the scheme with another fountain in 1675. The approach to the square used to be through a jumble of old buildings, which added an element of surprise to the vista that opened up upon passing through the colonnade. Nowadays a long wide street, the Via della Conciliazione, built by Mussolini after the conclusion of the Lateran Treaties, leads from the River Tiber to the piazza and gives distant views of St. Peter's as the visitor approaches, with the basilica acting as a terminating vista.

Bernini's transformation of the site is entirely Baroque in concept. Where Bramante and Michelangelo conceived a building that stood in "self-sufficient isolation", Bernini made the whole complex "expansively relate to its environment". Banister Fletcher says "No other city has afforded such a wide-swept approach to its cathedral church, no other architect could have conceived a design of greater nobility ... (it is) the greatest of all atriums before the greatest of all churches of Christendom."

Treasures

Tombs and relics

There are over 100 tombs within St. Peter's Basilica (extant to various extents), many located beneath the Basilica. These include 91 popes, Saint Ignatius of Antioch, Holy Roman Emperor Otto II, and the composer Giovanni Pierluigi da Palestrina. Exiled Catholic British royalty James Francis Edward Stuart and his two sons, Charles Edward Stuart and Henry Benedict Stuart,

Figure 56: *View of Rome from the Dome of St. Peter's Basilica*

Figure 57: *Air vents for the crypt in St. Peter's Basilica*

Cardinal Bishop of Frascati, are buried here, having been granted asylum by Pope Clement XI. Also buried here are Maria Clementina Sobieska, wife of James Francis Edward Stuart, Queen Christina of Sweden, who abdicated her throne in order to convert to Catholicism, and Countess Matilda of Tuscany, supporter of the Papacy during the Investiture Controversy. The most recent interment was Pope John Paul II, on 8 April 2005. Beneath, near the crypt, is the recently discovered vaulted 4th-century "Tomb of the Julii". (See below for some descriptions of tombs).

Artworks

The towers and narthex

- In the towers to either side of the facade are two clocks. The clock on the left has been operated electrically since 1931. Its oldest bell dates from 1288.
- One of the most important treasures of the basilica is a mosaic set above the central external door. Called the "Navicella", it is based on a design by Giotto (early 14th century) and represents a ship symbolizing the Christian Church. The mosaic is mostly a 17th-century copy of Giotto's original.
- At each end of the narthex is an equestrian figure, to the north Constantine the Great by Bernini (1670) and to the south Charlemagne by Cornacchini (18th century).
- Of the five portals from the narthex to the interior, three contain notable doors. The central portal has the Renaissance bronze door by Antonio Averulino (called Filarete) (1455), enlarged to fit the new space. The southern door, the *Door of the Dead*, was designed by 20th-century sculptor Giacomo Manzù and includes a portrait of Pope John XXIII kneeling before the crucified figure of Saint Peter.
- The northernmost door is the "Holy Door" which, by tradition, is walled-up with bricks, and opened only for holy years such as the Jubilee year by the Pope. The present door is bronze and was designed by Vico Consorti in 1950 and cast in Florence by the Ferdinando Marinelli Artistic Foundry. Above it are inscriptions commemorating the opening of the door: PAVLVS V PONT MAX ANNO XIII and GREGORIVS XIII PONT MAX.

Recently installed commemorative plaques read as follows:

PAVLVS VI PONT MAX HVIVS PATRIARCALIS VATICANAE BA-
SILICAE PORTAM SANCTAM APERVIT ET CLAVSIT ANNO IVBI-
LAEI MCMLXXV
Paul VI, Pontifex Maximus, opened and closed the holy door of this patriarchal Vatican basilica in the jubilee year of 1975.

IOANNES PAVLVS II P.M. PORTAM SANCTAM ANNO IVBILAEI MCMLXXVI A PAVLO PP VI RESERVATAM ET CLAVSAM APERVIT ET CLAVSIT ANNO IVB HVMANE REDEMP MCMLXXXIII – MCMLXXXIV

John Paul II, Pontifex Maximus, opened and closed again the holy door closed and set apart by Pope Paul VI in 1976 in the jubilee year of human redemption 1983–4.

IOANNES PAVLVS II P.M. ITERVM PORTAM SANCTAM APERVIT ET CLAVSIT ANNO MAGNI IVBILAEI AB INCARNATIONE DOMINI MM-MMI

John Paul II, Pontifex Maximus, again opened and closed the holy door in the year of the great jubilee, from the incarnation of the Lord 2000–2001.

FRANCISCVS PP PORTAM SANCTAM ANNO MAGNI IVB MM-MMI A IOANNES PAVLVS PP II RESERVATAM ET CLAVSAM APERVIT ET CLAVSIT ANNO IVB MISERICORDIAE MMXV- MMXVI

Pope Francis opened and closed again the holy door closed and set apart by Pope John Paul II in the year of the great jubilee 2000-2001, in the jubilee year of Mercy 2015-2016.

The nave

- On the first piers of the nave are two Holy Water basins held by pairs of cherubs each 2 metres high, commissioned by Pope Benedict XIII from designer Agostino Cornacchini and sculptor Francesco Moderati, (1720s).
- Along the floor of the nave are markers showing the comparative lengths of other churches, starting from the entrance.
- On the decorative pilasters of the piers of the nave are medallions with relief depicting 56 of the first popes.
- In niches between the pilasters of the nave are statues depicting 39 founders of religious orders.
- Set against the north east pier of the dome is a statue of *Saint Peter Enthroned*, sometimes attributed to late 13th-century sculptor Arnolfo di Cambio, with some scholars dating it to the 5th century. One foot of the statue is largely worn away by pilgrims kissing it for centuries.
- The sunken Confessio leading to the Vatican Grottoes (see above) contained a large kneeling statue by Canova of Pope Pius VI, who was captured and mistreated by Napoleon Bonaparte's army. This has now been moved to the back (eastern) end of the grottoes.
- In the Confessio is the *Niche of the Pallium* ("Niche of Stoles") which contains a bronze urn, donated by Pope Benedict XIV, to contain white stoles embroidered with black crosses and woven with the wool of lambs blessed on St. Agnes' day.

- The High Altar is surmounted by Bernini's baldachin. (See above)
- Set in niches within the four piers supporting the dome are the statues associated with the basilica's primary holy relics: Saint Helena holding the True Cross and the Holy Nails, by Andrea Bolgi; Saint Longinus holding the spear that pierced the side of Jesus, by Bernini (1639); Saint Andrew with the St. Andrew's Cross, by Francois Duquesnoy and Saint Veronica holding her veil with the image of Jesus' face, by Francesco Mochi.

Figure 58: *Saint Helena by Andrea Bolgi*

Figure 59: *Saint Longinus by Bernini*

Figure 60: *Saint Andrew by Francois Duquesnoy*

Figure 61: *Saint Veronica by Francesco Mochi*

Figure 62: *Pilgrim touching the foot of Saint Peter Enthroned*

North aisle

- In the first chapel of the north aisle is Michelangelo's *Pietà*.[130]
- On the first pier in the right aisle is the monument of Queen Christina of Sweden, who abdicated in 1654 in order to convert to Catholicism.
- The second chapel, dedicated to Saint Sebastian, contains the statues of popes Pius XI and Pius XII. The space below the altar used to be the resting place of Pope Innocent XI but his remains were moved to the *Altar of the Transfiguration* on 8 April 2011. This was done to make way for the body of Pope John Paul II. His remains were placed beneath the altar on 2 May 2011.
- The large chapel on the right aisle is the *Chapel of the Blessed Sacrament* which contains the tabernacle by Bernini (1664) resembling Bramante's *Tempietto* at San Pietro in Montorio supported by two kneeling angels and with behind it a painting of the Holy Trinity by Pietro da Cortona.
- Near the altar of *Our Lady of Succour* are the monuments of popes Gregory XIII by Camillo Rusconi (1723) and Gregory XIV.
- At the end of the aisle is an altar containing the relics of Saint Petronilla and with an altarpiece *The Burial of St Petronilla* by Guercino (Giovanni Francesco Barbieri), 1623.

South aisle

- The first chapel in the south aisle is the baptistry, commissioned by Pope Innocent XII and designed by Carlo Fontana, (great nephew of Domenico Fontana). The font, which was previously located in the opposite chapel, is the red porphyry sarcophagus of Probus, the 4th-century Prefect of Rome. The lid came from a different sarcophagus, which had once held the remains of the Emperor Hadrian and in removing it from the Vatican Grotto where it had been stored, the workmen broke it into ten pieces. Fontana restored it expertly and surmounted it with a gilt-bronze figure of the "Lamb of God".
- Against the first pier of the aisle is the Monument to the Royal Stuarts, James and his sons, Charles Edward, known as "Bonnie Prince Charlie" and Henry, Cardinal and Duke of York. The tomb is a Neo-Classical design by Canova unveiled in 1819. Opposite it is the memorial of James Francis Edward Stuart's wife, Maria Clementina Sobieska.
- The second chapel is that of the *Presentation of the Virgin* and contains the memorials of Pope Benedict XV and Pope John XXIII.
- Against the piers are the tombs of Pope Pius X and Pope Innocent VIII.
- The large chapel off the south aisle is the *Choir Chapel* which contains the altar of the *Immaculate Conception*.
- At the entrance to the Sacristy is the tomb of Pope Pius VIII
- The south transept contains the altars of Saint Thomas, Saint Joseph and the *Crucifixion of Saint Peter*.
- The tomb of Fabio Chigi, Pope Alexander VII, towards the end of the aisle, is the work of Bernini and called by Lees-Milne "one of the greatest tombs of the Baroque Age". It occupies an awkward position, being set in a niche above a doorway into a small vestry, but Bernini has utilized the doorway in a symbolic manner. Pope Alexander kneels upon his tomb, facing outward. The tomb is supported on a large draped shroud in patterned red marble, and is supported by four female figures, of whom only the two at the front are fully visible. They represent Charity and Truth. The foot of Truth rests upon a globe of the world, her toe being pierced symbolically by the thorn of Protestant England. Coming forth, seemingly, from the doorway as if it were the entrance to a tomb, is the skeletal winged figure of Death, its head hidden beneath the shroud, but its right hand carrying an hourglass stretched upward towards the kneeling figure of the pope.

St. Peter's Basilica

Figure 63: *The Holy Door is opened only for great celebrations.*

Figure 64: *The tomb of Alexander VII. UNIQ-ref-0-b39fd6ad4c903d20-QINU*

Figure 65: *The bronze statue of Saint Peter holding the keys of heaven, attributed to Arnolfo di Cambio.*

Figure 66: *The Pietà by Michelangelo is in the north aisle.*

Figure 67: *Cardinals at Mass in Saint Peter's Basilica two days before a papal conclave, 16 April 2005.*

Archpriests since 1053

List of archpriests of the Vatican Basilica:[131]

- Giovanni (1053)
- Deusdedit (1092)
- Azzo (1103–1104)
- Rustico de' Rustici (ca. 1128–1131?)
- Griffone (1138–1139)
- Pietro (ca.1140?–1144)
- Bernard (1145?–1176?)
- Giovanni da Sutri (1176/78–1180)
- Ugolino di Segni (ca.1191/1200–1206)
- Guido Pierleoni (1206/7–1228)
- Stefano Conti (1229–1254)
- Riccardo Annibaldi (1254–1276)
- Giovanni Gaetano Orsini (1276–1277)
- Matteo Orsini Rosso (1278–1305)
- Napoleone Orsini Frangipani (1306–1342)
- Annibaldo di Ceccano (1342–1350)
- Guillaume de La Jugie (1362–1365)

Figure 68: *The inauguration of Pope Francis in 2013*

- Rinaldo Orsini (1366–1374)
- Hugues de Saint-Martial (1374–1378)
- Philippe d'Alençon (1378–1397)
- Cristoforo Maroni (1397–1404)
- Angelo Acciaioli (1404–1408)
- Antonio Calvi (1408–1411)
- Pedro Fernandez de Frias (1412–1420)
- Antonio Correr (1420–1429)
- Lucido Conti (1429–1434)
- Giordano Orsini (1434–1438)
- Giuliano Cesarini (1439–1444)
- Pietro Barbo (1445–1464)
- Richard Olivier (1464–1470)
- Giovanni Battista Zeno (1470–1501)
- Juan López (1501)
- Ippolito d'Este (1501–1520)
- Marco Cornaro (1520)
- Franciotto Orsini (1520–1530)
- Francesco Cornaro (1530–1543)
- Alessandro Farnese (1543–1589)
- Giovanni Evangelista Palotta (1589–1620)

- Scipione Caffarelli-Borghese (1620–1633)
- Francesco Barberini (1633–1667)
- Carlo Barberini (1667–1704)
- Francesco Nerli (1704–1708)
- Annibale Albani (1712–1751)
- Henry Benedict Stuart (1751–1807)
- Romualdo Braschi-Onesti (1807–1817)
- Alessandro Mattei (1817–1820)
- Pietro Francesco Galleffi (6 May 1820 – 18 June 1837)
- Giacomo Giustiniani (1 July 1837 – 24 February 1843)
- Mario Mattei (11 March 1843 – 7 October 1870)
- Niccola Clarelli Parracciani (8 October 1870 – 7 July 1872)
- Edoardo Borromeo (10 July 1872 – 30 November 1881)
- Edward Henry Howard (12 December 1881 – 16 September 1892)
- Francesco Ricci Paracciani (6 October 1892 – 9 March 1894)
- Mariano Rampolla del Tindaro (21 March 1894 – 16 December 1913)
- Rafael Merry del Val (12 January 1914 – 26 February 1930)
- Eugenio Pacelli (25 March 1930 – 2 March 1939)
- Federico Tedeschini (14 March 1939 – 2 November 1959)
- Domenico Tardini (14 November 1959 – 30 July 1961)
- Paolo Marella (14 August 1961 – 8 February 1983)
- Aurelio Sabattani (8 February 1983 – 1 July 1991)
- Virgilio Noè (1 July 1991 – 24 April 2002)
- Francesco Marchisano (24 April 2002 – 10 October 2006)
- Angelo Comastri (10 October 2006 – present)

Specifications

- Cost of construction of the basilica: more than 46,800,052 ducats[132]
- Geographic orientation: chancel west, nave east
- Total length: 730 feet (220 m)
- Total width: 500 feet (150 m)
- Interior length including vestibule: 693.8 feet (211.5 m), more than ⅛ mile.
- Length of the transepts in interior: 451 feet (137 m)
- Width of nave: 90.2 feet (27.5 m)
- Width at the tribune: 78.7 feet (24.0 m)
- Internal width at transepts: 451 feet (137 m)
- Internal height of nave: 151.5 feet (46.2 m) high
- Total area: 227,070 square feet (21,095 m^2), more than 5 acres (20,000 m^2).
- Internal area: 163,182.2 square feet (3.75 acres; 15,160.12 m^2)

Figure 69: *Silhouette of St. Peter's Basilica at sundown (view from Castel Sant'Angelo).*

- Height from pavement to top of cross: 448.1 feet (136.6 m)
- Façade: 167 feet (51 m) high by 375 feet (114 m) wide
- Vestibule: 232.9 feet (71.0 m) wide, 44.2 feet (13.5 m) deep, and 91.8 feet (28.0 m) high
- The internal columns and pilasters: 92 feet (28 m) tall
- The circumference of the central piers: 240 feet (73 m)
- Outer diameter of dome: 137.7 feet (42.0 m)
- The drum of the dome: 630 feet (190 m) in circumference and 65.6 feet (20.0 m) high, rising to 240 feet (73 m) from the ground
- The lantern: 63 feet (19 m) high
- The ball and cross: 8 and 16 feet (2.4 and 4.9 m), respectively
- St. Peter's Square: 1,115 feet (340 m) long, 787.3 feet (240.0 m) wide
- Each arm of the colonnade: 306 feet (93 m) long, and 64 feet (20 m) high
- The colonnades have 284 columns, 88 pilasters, and 140 statues
- Obelisk: 83.6 feet (25.5 m). Total height with base and cross, 132 feet (40 m).
- Weight of obelisk: 360.2 short tons (326,800 kg; 720,400 lb)

Bibliography

Bannister, Turpin (1968). "The Constantinian Basilica of Saint Peter at Rome". *Journal of the Society of Architectural Historians.* **27** (1): 3–32. JSTOR 988425[133]. OCLC 19640446[134]. doi: 10.2307/988425[135].(subscription required)

Baumgarten, Paul Maria (1913). "Basilica of St. Peter". In Herbermann, Charles. *Catholic Encyclopedia.* New York: Robert Appleton Company.

Betts, Richard J. (1993). "Structural Innovation and Structural Design in Renaissance Architecture". *Journal of the Society of Architectural Historians.* **52** (1): 5–25. JSTOR 990755[136]. doi: 10.2307/990755[137].

Boorsch, Suzanne (1982). "The Building of the Vatican: The Papacy and Architecture". *The Metropolitan Museum of Art Bulletin.* New York. **XL** (3): 4–64. JSTOR 3258914[138]. OCLC 39642638[139]. doi: 10.2307/3258914[140].

Dzyubanskyy, Taras (2010). *The Development of the Cult of St. Peter in the Vatican: from the poor man's grave to the largest basilica in the world.* Lviv.

Finch, Margaret (1991). "The Cantharus and Pigna at Old Saint Peter's". *Gesta.* **30** (1): 16–26. JSTOR 767006[141]. doi: 10.2307/767006[142].(subscription required)

Fletcher, Banister (1975). *History of Architecture on the Comparative Method for the student, craftsman, and amateur*[143]. New York: Macmillan Pub Company. ISBN 99974-605-5-3.Wikipedia:Please clarify

——— (2001) [First published 1896]. *Sir Banister Fletcher's a History of Architecture* (20th ed.). London: Architectural Press. ISBN 0-7506-2267-9.Wikipedia:Please clarify

Frommel, Christoph (1986). "Papal Policy: The Planning of Rome during the Renaissance in The Evidence of Art: Images and Meaning in History". *Journal of Interdisciplinary History.* Cambridge: MIT Press. **17** (1): 39–65. ISSN 0022-1953[144]. JSTOR 204124[145]. doi: 10.2307/204124[146].(subscription required)

Gardner, Helen; Kleiner, Fred S.; Mamiya, Christin J. (2005). *Gardner's Art through the Ages: The Western Perspective.* **2** (12th ed.). Belmont: Wadsworth. pp. 499–500, 571–575. ISBN 0-495-00479-0.

Goldscheider, Ludwig (1996). *Michelangelo* (6th ed.). Oxford: Phaidon. ISBN 0-7148-3296-0.

Hartt, Frederick (2006). *History of Italian Renaissance Art* (6th ed.). Englewood Cliffs: Prentice Hall. ISBN 0-13-188247-3.

Hintzen-Bohlen, Brigitte; Sorges, Jürgen (2001). *Rome and the Vatican City*. Köln: Könemann. ISBN 3-8290-3109-2.

Korn, Frank J. (2002). *Hidden Rome*. New York: Paulist Press. ISBN 0-8091-4109-4.

Lanciani, Rodolfo (1892). "Chapter III: Christian Churches". *Pagan and Christian Rome*[147]. Boston and New York: Houghton, Mifflin and Company.

Lees-Milne, James (1967). "Saint Peter's – the story of Saint Peter's Basilica in Rome"[148]. London: Hamish Hamilton. OCLC 1393052[149].

McClendon, Charles (1989). "The History of the Site of St. Peter's Basilica, Rome". *Perspecta: the Yale Architectural Journal*. MIT Press. **25**: 32–65. ISSN 0079-0958[150]. JSTOR 1567138[151]. doi: 10.2307/1567138[152].

Pevsner, Nikolaus (1963). *An Outline of European Architecture* (7th ed.). Baltimore: Penguin Books. ISBN 978-0-14-020109-3. OCLC 2208913[153].

Pinto, Pio (1975). *The Pilgrim's Guide to Rome*. San Francisco: Harper & Row. ISBN 0-06-013388-0.

Scotti, R. A. (2007). *Basilica: the Splendor and the Scandal – Building of St. Peter's*. New York: Plume. ISBN 0-452-28860-6.

"Inside the Vatican"[154]. *National Geographic News*. National Geographic Society. 28 October 2010 [2004]. Retrieved 30 December 2008.

"Saint Peter's – Truth Unveiled: Bernini's Bell Towers and the Allegory of Truth: Urban VIII's Bell Towers"[155]. Archived from the original[156] on 10 June 2014.

External links

- Vaticanstate.va[157] – official website with images and information about the Basilica
- "Virtual Reality Tour of the Basilica of Saint Peter"[158]
- St Peter's Basilica.info[159] – unofficial website on the basilica, with images and text from different books.
- 360 Degree Photographs Inside Saint Peter's Basilica[160]
- Google Maps[161]: Vatican – Satellite image of the Basilica

Records		
Preceded by **Unknown**	**Tallest building in Rome** 1626–2012 136.6 metres (448 ft)	Succeeded by **Torre Eurosky**
Preceded by **Unknown**	**Tallest dome in the world** 1626–present 136.6 metres (448 ft)	**Current holder**

Mahabodhi Temple

Mahabodhi Temple

Mahabodhi Temple

Mahabodhi Temple

UNESCO World Heritage Site	
Location	Bodh Gaya, India
Coordinates	24°41'46"N 84°59'29"E[162]
Criteria	Cultural: (i), (ii), (iii), (iv), (vi)
Reference	1056[163]
Inscription	2002 (26th Session)

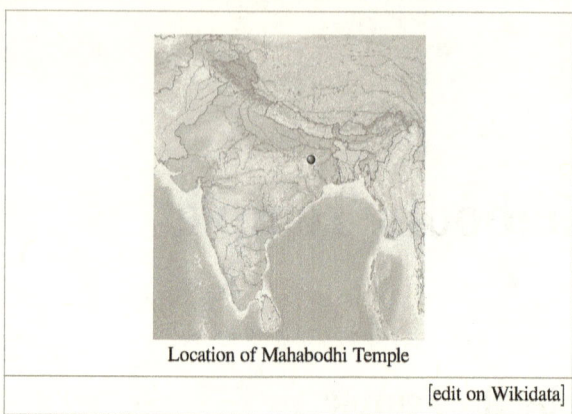

Location of Mahabodhi Temple

[edit on Wikidata]

The **Mahabodhi Temple** (literally: "Great Awakening Temple"), a UNESCO World Heritage Site, is an ancient, but much rebuilt and restored, Buddhist temple in Bodh Gaya, marking the location where the Buddha is said to have attained enlightenment. Bodh Gaya (in Gaya district) is about 96 km (60 mi) from Patna, Bihar state, India.

The site contains a descendant of the Bodhi Tree under which Buddha gained enlightenment, and has been a major pilgrimage destination for Buddhists for well over two thousand years, and some elements probably date to the period of Asoka (died c.232 BCE). What is now visible on the ground essentially dates from the 7th century CE, or perhaps somewhat earlier, as well as several major restorations since the 19th century. But the structure now may well incorporate large parts of earlier work, possibly from the 2nd or 3rd century CE.[164]

Many of the oldest sculptural elements have been moved to the museum beside the temple, and some, such as the carved stone railing wall around the main structure, have been replaced by replicas. The main temple's survival is especially impressive, as it was mostly made of brick covered with stucco, materials that are much less durable than stone. But this means that very little of the original scultural decoration has survived.[165]

The temple complex includes two large straight-sided shikhara towers, the largest over 55 metres (180 feet) high. This is a stylistic feature that has continued in Jain and Hindu temples to the present day, and influenced Buddhist architecture in other countries, in forms like the pagoda.[166]

Figure 70: *A Buddhist devotee offering prayers to the Buddha at the temple*

The Buddha

Traditional accounts say that, around 589 BCE,Wikipedia:Citation needed Siddhartha Gautama, a young prince who saw the suffering of the world and wanted to end it, reached the forested banks of the Phalgu river, near the city of Gaya, India. There he sat in meditation under a peepul tree (*Ficus religiosa* or Sacred Fig) which later became known as the Bodhi tree. According to Buddhist scriptures, after three days and three nights, Siddharta attained enlightenment and the answers that he had sought. In that location, Mahabodhi Temple was built by Emperor Ashoka in around 260 BCE.

The Buddha then spent the succeeding seven weeks at seven different spots in the vicinity meditating and considering his experience. Several specific places at the current Mahabodhi Temple relate to the traditions surrounding these seven weeks:

- The first week was spent under the Bodhi tree.
- During the second week, the Buddha remained standing and stared, uninterrupted, at the Bodhi tree. This spot is marked by the Animeshlocha Stupa, that is, the unblinking stupa or shrine, to the north-east of the Mahabodhi Temple complex. There stands a statue of Buddha with his eyes fixed towards the Bodhi tree.

Figure 71: *The Mahabodhi Tree*

- The Buddha is said to have walked back and forth between the location of the Animeshlocha Stupa and the Bodhi tree. According to legend, lotus flowers sprung up along this route; it is now called Ratnachakrama or the jewel walk.
- He spent the fourth week near Ratnagar Chaitya, to the north-east side.
- During the fifth week, Buddha answered in details to the queries of Brahmins under the Ajapala Nigodh tree, now marked by a pillar.
- He spent the sixth week next to the Lotus pond.
- He spent the seventh week under the Rajyatna tree.

Bodhi Tree

The Bodhi tree at Bodhgaya is directly connected to the life of the historical Buddha, Siddhartha Gautama, who attained enlightenment or perfect insight when he was meditating under it. The temple was built directly to the east of the Bodhi tree, supposedly a direct descendant of the original Bodhi Tree.

According to Buddhist mythology, if no Bodhi tree grows at the site, the ground around the Bodhi tree is devoid of all plants for a distance of one royal karīsa. Through the ground around the Bodhi tree no being, not even an elephant, can travel.

Figure 72: *Illustration of the temple built by Asoka at Bodh-Gaya around the Bodhi tree. Sculpture of the Satavahana period at Sanchi, 1st century CE.*

According to the Jatakas, the navel of the earth lies at this spot,[167] and no other place can support the weight of the Buddha's attainment.[168] Another Buddhist tradition claims that when the world is destroyed at the end of a kalpa, the Bodhimanda is the last spot to disappear, and will be the first to appear when the world emerges into existence again. Tradition also claims that a lotus will bloom there, and if a Buddha is born during that the new kalpa, the lotus flowers in accordance with the number of Buddhas expected to arise.[169] According to legend, in the case of Gautama Buddha, a Bodhi tree sprang up on the day he was born.[170]

Temple construction

Mauryan establishment

In approximately 250 BCE, about 200 years after the Buddha attained Enlightenment, Buddhist Emperor Asoka visited Bodh Gaya in order to establish a monastery and shrine on the holy site, which have today disappeared.

There remains however the Diamond throne, which he had established at the foot of the Bodhi tree.[171] The Diamond throne, or *Vajrasana*, is thought to have been built by Emperor Ashoka of the Maurya Empire between 250-233

Figure 73: *Discovery of the Diamond throne, built by Ashoka c.250 BCE.*

BCE,.[172] at the location where the Buddha reached enlightenment.[173] It is worshiped today, and is the center of many festivities at the Mahabodhi Temple.

Representations of the early temple structure meant to protect the Bodhi tree are found at Sanchi, on the toraṇas of Stūpa I, dating from around 25 BCE, and on a relief carving from the stupa railing at Bhārhut, from the early Shunga period (c. 185–c. 73 BCE).[174]

Sunga structures

Columns with pot-shaped bases

Additional structures were brought in by the Sungas. In particular, columns with pot-shaped bases were found around the Diamond throne. These columns are thought to date to the 1st century BCE, towards the end of the Sungas. These columns, which were found through archaeological research at the Buddha's Walk in the Mahabodhi Temple, quite precisely match the columns described on the reliefs found on the gateway pillars.[176]

Figure 74: *Reconstitution of the Sunga period pillars at Bodh Gaya, from archaeology (left) and from artistic relief (right). They are dated to the 1st century BCE. Reconstitution done by Alexander Cunningham.*[175]

Railings

The railing also around the Mahabodhi Temple at Bodh Gaya is quite ancient. These are old sandstone posts dating about 150 BCE, during the Sunga period. There are carved panels as well as medallions, with many scene similar to those of the contemporary Sunga railings at Bharhut (150 BCE) and Sanchi (115 BCE), although the reliefs at Sanchi Stupa No.2 are often considered as the oldest of all.[177,178] The railing was extended during the following century, down to the end of Gupta period (7th century), with coarse granite decorated with elaborate foliate ornaments and small figures as well as stupas.[179] Many parts of the initial railing have been dismantled and are now in museums, such as the Indian Museum in Kolkota, and have been replaced by plaster copies.

Sunga railings at Bodh Gaya	
Original railings	
Early photographs of the railings (Henry Baily Wade Garrick, 1880).	
Remains of the railings in the Indian Museum, Kolkata.	
Devotion scenes	

Animals
Stories
Individual elements
The railings today at Bodh Gaya (mainly plaster duplicates)

Figure 75: *Plaster copy and reconstruction of original Sunga railing.*

Figure 76: *Post relief (plaster copy).*

Figure 77: *Adoration of the wheel of the Law (plaster copy).*

Figure 78: *Bodh Gaya original railings, Indian Museum, Calcutta.*

Figure 79: *Bodh Gaya original railings, Indian Museum, Calcutta.*

Figure 80: *Railing post.*

Figure 81: *Another railing post.*

Figure 82: *Bodh Gaya Sunga pillar.*

Figure 83: *Bodh Gaya Sunga railing.*

Figure 84: *Bodh Gaya Sunga railing.*

Figure 85: *Bodh Gaya Sunga railing.*

Figure 86: *Bodh Gaya Sunga railing.*

Figure 87: *1903 photograph.*

Current temple by the Guptas

While Asoka is considered the Mahabodhi temple's founder, the current structure dates from the Gupta Empire, in the 5th–6th century CE. The pyramidal temple probably replaced an open pavilion that had been constructed around the tree and the Asokan platform. The new Mahabodhi temple included a diamond throne (called the *Vajrasana*) to mark the exact spot of the Buddha's enlightenment. The Temple was restored by the British and India post independence.

Decline

Buddhism declined when the dynasties patronizing it declined, following Huna invasions and the early Arab Islamic invasions such as that of Muhammad bin Qasim. A strong revival occurred under the Pala Empire in the northeast of the subcontinent (where the temple is situated). Mahayana Buddhism flourished under the Palas between the 8th and the 12th century. However, after the defeat of the Palas by the Hindu Sena dynasty, Buddhism's position again began to erode and became nearly extinct in India. During the 12th century CE, Bodh Gaya and the nearby regions were invaded by Muslim Turk armies. During this period, the Mahabodhi Temple fell into disrepair and was largely abandoned. Over the following centuries, the monastery's abbot or mahant position became occupied by the area's primary landholder, who claimed ownership of the Mahabodhi Temple grounds.

Figure 88: *Temple before restoration*

In the 13th century, Burmese Buddhists built a temple with the same name and modelled on the original Mahabodhi Temple.[180] Wikipedia:Citing sources

Mucalinda Lake

It is said that four weeks after the Buddha began meditating under the Bodhi Tree, the heavens darkened for seven days, and a prodigious rain descended. However, the mighty king of serpents, Mucalinda, came from beneath the earth and protected with his hood the one who is the source of all protection. When the great storm had cleared, the serpent king assumed his human form, bowed before the Buddha, and returned in joy to his palace.

The subject of Buddha meditating under the protection of Mucalinda is very common in Lao Buddhist art. One modern rendition is present in Bunleua Sulilat's sculpture park Sala Keoku.

Restoration

During the 11th century and the 19th century, Burmese rulers undertook restoration of the temple complex and surrounding wall. In the 1880s, the then-British colonial government of India began to restore Mahabodhi Temple under the direction of Sir Alexander Cunningham and Joseph David Beglar.

Figure 89: *A statue of Mucalinda protecting the Buddha in Mucalinda Lake, Mahabodhi Temple*

Figure 90: *The temple as it appeared immediately after its restoration in 1880s*

Figure 91: *A Bodh Gaya railing post.*

In 1885, Sir Edwin Arnold visited the site and under guidance from Ven. Weligama Sri Sumangala published several articles drawing the attention of the Buddhists to the deplorable conditions of Buddhagaya.[181,182]

Architectural style

Mahabodhi Temple is constructed of brick and is one of the oldest brick structures to have survived in eastern India. It is considered to be a fine example of Indian brickwork, and was highly influential in the development of later architectural traditions. According to UNESCO, "the present temple is one of the earliest and most imposing structures built entirely in brick from Gupta period" (300–600 CE). Mahabodhi Temple's central tower rises 55 metres (180 ft), and were heavily renovated in the 19th century. The central tower is surrounded by four smaller towers, constructed in the same style.

The Mahabodhi Temple is surrounded on all four sides by stone railings, about two metres high. The railings reveal two distinct types, both in style as well as the materials used. The older ones, made of sandstone, date to about 150 BCE, and the others, constructed from unpolished coarse granite, are believed to be of the Gupta period. The older railings have scenes such as Lakshmi, the Hindu/Buddhist goddess of wealth, being bathed by elephants; and Surya, the Hindu sun god, riding a chariot drawn by four horses. The newer railings

Figure 92: *Bodh Gaya quadriga relief of the sun god Surya riding between Buddhist pillars (detail of a railing post), 2nd-1st century BCE.*

have figures of stupas (reliquary shrines) and garudas (eagles). Images of lotus flowers also appear commonly.

Images of the site include Avalokiteśvara (Padmapani, Khasarpana), Vajrapani, Tara, Marichi, Yamantaka, Jambhala and Vajravārāhī. Images of Vishnu, Shiva, Surya and other Vedic deities are also associated with the site. Images of Vishnu, Shiva, Surya and other Vedic deities are also associated with the site.

Control of the site

In 1891, a campaign to return control of the temple to Buddhists, over the objections of the Hindu mahant.

The campaign was partially successful in 1949, when control passed from the Hindu mahant to the state government of Bihar, which established a Bodh Gaya Temple Management Committee (BTMC) under the Bodh Gaya Temple Act of 1949.[183] The committee has nine members, a majority of whom, including the chairman, must by law be Hindus. Mahabodhi's first head monk under the management committee was Anagarika Munindra, a Bengali man who had been an active member of the Maha Bodhi Society. In 2013, the

Figure 93: *The temple undergoing repairs (from January, 2006).*

Bihar government amended the Bodh Gaya Temple Act of 1949, allowing for a non-Hindu to head the temple committee.

Current status and management

The Bihar state government assumed responsibility for the protection, management, and monitoring of temple and its properties when India gained its independence. Pursuant to the Bodh Gaya Temple Act of 1949, such responsibilities are shared with the Bodhgaya Temple Management Committee, and an advisory board. By law, the Committee must consist of four Buddhist and four Hindu representatives, including the head of Sankaracharya Math monastery as an ex-officio Hindu member.[184] The Committee serves for a three-year term. A 2013 Amendment to Bodhgaya Temple Management Act allows the Gaya District Magistrate to be the Chairman of committee, even if he is not Hindu. The Advisory Board consists of the governor of Bihar and twenty to twenty-five other members, half of them from foreign Buddhist countries.

In June 2002, the Mahabodhi Temple became a UNESCO World Heritage Site. All finds of religious artifacts in the area are legally protected under the Treasure Trove Act of 1878.

The temple's head monk, Bhikkhu Bodhipala, resigned in 2007 after he was charged with cutting the branches of Holy Bodhi Tree on a regular basis and selling them to foreigners for significant amounts of money. A newspaper alleged that wealthy Thai buyers bought a branch with the cooperation of senior members of the temple's management committee.[185] While the temple's spokesman stated that botanists had pruned the tree, the Bihar home secretary ordered the tree examined.[186] A criminal charge was filed against Bodhipala.Wikipedia:Citation needed If convicted, Bodhipala would be subject to at least 10 years' imprisonment.

Following the expiration of the Committee's term in September 2007, Bihar's government delayed appointing a new Committee and the district magistrate administered the temple pending such appointment. Eventually, on May 16, 2008 the government announced the appointment of a new Temple Management Committee.

As of June 2017, the temples head monk was Bhikkhu Chalinda.[187]

Recent events

In 2013, the upper portion of the temple was covered with gold. The gold was a gift from the King of Thailand and devotees from Thailand, and installed with the approval of the Archaeological Survey of India.

2013 attack

On 7 July 2013, ten low-intensity bombs exploded in the temple complex, injuring 5 people. One bomb was near the statue of Buddha and another was near the Mahabodhi tree. Three unexploded bombs were also found and defused. The blasts took place between 5.30 a.m. and 6.00 a.m. The main temple was undamaged. The Intelligence Bureau of India may have alerted state officials of possible threats around 15 days prior to the bombing. On 4 November 2013, the National Investigation Agency announced that the Islamic terrorist group Indian Mujahideen was responsible for the bombings.

References

- Harle, J.C., *The Art and Architecture of the Indian Subcontinent*, 2nd edn. 1994, Yale University Press Pelican History of Art, ISBN 0300062176
- Michell, George, *The Penguin Guide to the Monuments of India, Volume 1: Buddhist, Jain, Hindu*, 1989, Penguin Books, ISBN 0140081445

Further reading

- Horner, I.B. (trans.) (1975; reprinted 2000). *The Minor Anthologies of the Pali Canon (Part III): 'Chronicle of Buddhas' (Buddhavamsa) and 'Basket of Conduct' (Cariyapitaka)*. Oxford: Pali Text Society. ISBN 0-86013-072-X.
- Doyle, Tara N. (2003-09-11). *Liberate the Mahabodhi Temple! Socially Engaged Buddhism, Dalit-Style.* In: Steven Heine, Charles Prebish (eds), *Buddhism in the Modern World*[188]. Oxford University Press. pp. 249–280. ISBN 0-19-514698-0.
- Kinnard, Jacob N. (1998). When Is The Buddha Not the Buddha? The Hindu/Buddhist Battle over Bodhgayā and Its Buddha Image[189], Journal of the American Academy of Religion 66 (4), 817-839
- Knopf, Rainer (2000). Bodh-Gaya: Ein internationales Zentrum des Buddhismus in nicht-buddhistischer Umgebung[190], Internationales Asienforum 31 (3-4), 289-314
- NCERT (2012). *An Introduction to Indian Art*[191] (PDF). NCERT. ISBN 978-93-5007-187-8.

External links

 Wikimedia Commonshas media related to: *Mahabodhi Temple*(category)

- Land Enlightenment of the Buddha[192]
- Mahabodhi Temple and attraction around it[193]
- Bodhgaya News[194]
- UNESCO World Heritage[195]
- Mahabodhi Temple in Bihar[196]

Golden Temple

Golden Temple

**Harmandir Sahib
Golden Temple**
ਸ੍ਰੀ ਹਰਿਮੰਦਰ ਸਾਹਿਬ

The Harmandir Sahib (Golden Temple)

Location within Punjab

Alternative names	Darbar Sahib Golden Temple of Amritsar
General information	
Town or city	Amritsar
Coordinates	31°37'12"N 74°52'37"E[197] Coordinates: 31°37'12"N 74°52'37"E[197]
Construction started	December 1581[198]
Completed	1589 (Temple), 1604 (with Adi Granth)[198]
Website	
Sri Harmandir Sahib (Gurmukhi)[199]	

Sri Harmandir Sahib (lit. "the abode of God"), also known as **Golden Temple** and the **Darbar Sahib**, is the holiest Gurdwara and the most important pilgrimage site of Sikhism.[200] It is located in the city of Amritsar, Punjab, India.[200]

The temple is built around a man-made pool (*sarovar*) that was completed by Guru Ram Das in 1577.[201,202] Guru Arjan – the fifth Guru of Sikhism, requested Sai Mian Mir – a Muslim Pir of Lahore to lay its foundation stone in 1589.[198] In 1604, Guru Arjan placed a copy of the Adi Granth in Harmandir Sahib, calling the site *Ath Sath Tirath* (lit. "shrine of 68 pilgrimages"). The temple was repeatedly rebuilt by the Sikhs after it became a target of persecution and was destroyed several times by the Muslim armies from Afghanistan and the Mughal Empire.[200] The army led by Ahmad Shah Abdali, for example, demolished it in 1757 and again in 1762, then filled the pool with garbage.[203] Maharaja Ranjit Singh after founding the Sikh Empire, rebuilt it in marble and copper in 1809, overlaid the sanctum with gold foil in 1830. This has led to the name the Golden Temple.[204]

The temple is spiritually the most significant shrine in Sikhism. It became a center of the Singh Sabha Movement between 1883 and 1920s. In the early 1980s, the temple became a center of conflict between the Indian government led by Indira Gandhi, some Sikh groups and a militant movement led by Jarnail Singh Bhindranwale seeking to carve out a new nation named Khalistan from parts of India and Pakistan. In 1984, Gandhi sent in the army, leading to numerous deaths of militants, soldiers and civilians, as well as causing much damage to the temple and the destruction of Akal Takht. The temple complex was rebuilt again after the 1984 damage.[200,205]

The Harmandir Sahib is an open house of worship for all men and women, from all walks of life and faith. It has a square plan with four entrances, has a circumambulation path around the pool. The temple is a collection of buildings around the sanctum and the pool. One of these is Akal Takht, the chief center of religious authority of Sikhism.[200] Additional buildings include a clock

Figure 94: *The Harimandir Sahib was repeatedly destroyed and rebuilt, the last time in 1830 with marble, copper and gold by Ranjit Singh.*

tower, the offices of Gurdwara Committee, a Museum and a langar – a free Sikh community run kitchen that serves a simple vegetarian meal to all visitors without discrimination.[200] Over 100,000 people visit the holy shrine daily for worship.

Nomenclature

The Harmandir Sahib is also spelled as Harimandar, Harimandir or Harmandar Sahib. It is also called the *Darbar Sahib* (Punjabi pronunciation: [dərbɑr sɑhɪb]) which means "sacred audience", as well as the Golden Temple for its gold foil covered sanctum center.[200] The word "Harmandir" is composed of two words, "Hari" which scholars variously translate either as "God" or "Vishnu", and "mandir" which means temple or house.[206] The Sikh tradition has several Gurdwaras named "Harmandir Sahib" such as those in Kiratpur and Patna. Of these, the one in Amritsar is most revered.[207]

History

According to the Sikh historical records, the land that became Amritsar and houses the Harimandar Sahib was chosen by Guru Amar Das – the third Guru of the Sikh tradition. It was then called Guru Da Chakk, after he had asked his disciple Ram Das to find land to start a new town with a man made pool as its central point.[202,201] After Ram Das succeeded Guru Amar Das in 1574, and given the hostile opposition he faced from the sons of Guru Amar Das,[208]

Figure 95: *Maharaja Ranjit Singh listening to Guru Granth Sahib near Harmandir Sahib*

Guru Ram Das founded the town that came to be known as "Ramdaspur". He started by completing the pool with the help of Baba Buddha (not to be confused with the Buddha of Buddhism). Guru Ram Das built his new official centre and home next to it. He invited merchants and artisans from other parts of India to settle into the new town with him.

Ramdaspur town expanded during the time of Guru Arjan financed by donations and constructed by voluntary work. The town grew to become the city of Amritsar, and the pool area grew into the Golden Temple complex.[209] The construction activity between 1574 and 1604 is described in *Mahima Prakash Vartak*, a semi-historical Sikh hagiography text likely composed in 1741, and the earliest known document dealing with the lives of all the ten Gurus. Guru Arjan installed the scripture of Sikhism inside the new temple in 1604.[209] Continuing the efforts of Guru Ram Das, Guru Arjan established Amritsar as a primary Sikh pilgrimage destination. He wrote a voluminous amount of Sikh scripture including the popular Sukhmani Sahib.[210]

Construction

Guru Ram Das acquired the land for the site. Two versions of stories exist on how he acquired this land. In one based on a Gazetteer record, the land was purchased with Sikh donations of 700 rupees from the owners of the village of Tung. In another version, Emperor Akbar is stated to have donated the land to the wife of Guru Ram Das.[211]

In 1581, Guru Arjan initiated the construction of the Gurdwara.[198] During the construction the pool was kept empty and dry. It took 8 years to complete the first version of the Harmandir Sahib. Guru Arjan planned a temple at a level lower than the city to emphasize humility and the need to efface one's ego before entering the premises to meet the Guru.[198] He also demanded that the temple compound be open on all sides to emphasize that it was open to all. The sanctum inside the pool where his Guru seat was had only one bridge to emphasize that the end goal was one, states Arvind-Pal Singh Mandair.[198] In 1589, the temple made with bricks was complete. Guru Arjan invited Sufi saint Mian Mir of Lahore to lay its foundation stone, signaling pluralism and that the Sikh tradition welcomed all.[198] After the inauguration, the pool was filled with water. On August 16, 1604, Guru Arjan completed expanding and compiling the first version of the Sikh scripture and placed a copy of the Adi Granth in the temple. He appointed Baba Buddha as the first Granthi.[212]

Guru Arjan called the site *Ath Sath Tirath* which means "shrine of 68 pilgrimages".[213] The temple complex marks the place of this announcement with a raised canopy on the *parkarma* (circumambulation marble path around the pool). The name, state W. Owen Cole and other scholars, reflects the belief that visiting this temple is equivalent to 68 Hindu pilgrimage sites in the Indian subcontinent, or that a Tirath to the Golden Temple has the efficacy of all 68 Tiraths combined.[214] The completion of the first version of the Golden Temple was a major milestone for Sikhism, states Arvind-Pal Singh Mandair, because it provided a central pilgrimage place and a rallying point for the Sikh community, set within a hub of trade and activity.[198]

Mughal Empire era destruction and rebuilding

The growing influence and success of Guru Arjan drew the attention of the Mughal Empire. Guru Arjan was arrested under the orders of the Mughal Emperor Jahangir and asked to convert to Islam. He refused, was tortured and executed in 1606 CE.[215,216] Guru Arjan's son and successor Guru Hargobind left Amritsar and moved into the Shivalik Hills to avoid persecution and to save the Sikh panth.[217] For about a century after Guru Arjan martyrdom, state Louis E. Fenech and W. H. McLeod, the Golden Temple was not occupied by the actual Sikh Gurus and it remained in hostile sectarian hands.[217] In 18th century, Guru Gobind Singh and his newly founded Khalsa Sikhs came back and fought to liberate it.[217] The Golden Temple was viewed by the Mughal rulers and Afghan Sultans as the center of Sikh faith and it remained the main target of persecution.

The Golden Temple was the center of historic events in Sikh history:[218,204]

- In 1709, the governor of Lahore sent in his army to suppress and prevent the Sikhs from gathering for their festivals of Baisakhi and Divali. But the Sikhs defied by gathering in the Golden Temple. In 1716, Banda Singh and numerous Sikhs were arrested and executed.
- In 1737, the Mughal governor ordered the capture of the custodian of the Golden Temple named Mani Singh and executed him. He appointed Masse Khan as the police commissioner who then occupied the Temple and converted it into his entertainment center with dancing girls. He befouled the pool. Sikhs avenged the sacrilege of the Golden Temple by assassinating Masse Khan inside the Temple in August 1740.
- In 1746, another Lahore official Diwan Lakhpat Rai working for Yahiya Khan, and seeking revenge for the death of his brother, filled the pool with sand. In 1749, Sikhs restored the pool when Muin ul-Mulk slackened Mughal operations against Sikhs and sought their help during his operations in Multan.
- In 1757, the Afghani ruler Ahmad Shah Durrani, also known as Ahmad Shah Abdali, attacked Amritsar and desecrated the Golden Temple. He had waste poured into the pool along with entrails of slaughtered cows, before departing for Afghanistan. The Sikhs restored it again.
- In 1762, Ahmad Shah Durrani returned and had the Golden Temple blown up with gunpowder. Sikhs returned and celebrated Divali in its premises. In 1764, Jassa Singh Ahluvalia collected donations to rebuild the Golden Temple. A new main gateway (Darshani Deorhi), causeway and sanctum were completed in 1776, while the floor around the pool was completed in 1784. The Sikhs also completed a canal to bring in fresh water from Ravi River for the pool.

Ranjit Singh era reconstruction

Ranjit Singh founded the nucleus of the Sikh Empire at the age of 21 with help of Sukkarchakkia *misl* forces he inherited and those of his mother-in-law Rani Sada Kaur. In 1802, at age 22, he took Amritsar from the Bhangi Sikh *misl*, paid homage at the Golden Temple and announced that he would renovate and rebuild it with marble and gold. The Temple was renovated in marble and copper in 1809, and in 1830 Ranjit Singh donated gold to overlay the sanctum with gold foil.[204]

The management and operation of Darbar Sahib – a term that refers to the entire Golden Temple complex of buildings, was taken over by Ranjit Singh. He appointed Desa Singh Majithia to manage it, and made land grants whose collected revenue was assigned to pay for the Temple's maintenance and operation. Ranjit Singh also made the position of Temple officials hereditary.

Figure 96: *A 1880 photograph of the Golden Temple, sacred pool and the nearby buildings. The walled courtyard and entrances were added later.*

Description

The Golden Temple's architecture reflects different architectural practices prevalent in the Indian subcontinent, as various iterations of temple were rebuilt and restored. The Temple is described by Ian Kerr, and other scholars, as a mixture of the Indo-Islamic Mughal and the Hindu Rajput architecture.[219]

The sanctum is a 12.25 x 12.25 metre square with two storeys and a gold foil dome. This sanctum has a marble platform that is a 19.7 x 19.7 metre square. It sits inside an almost square (154.5 x 148.5 m2) pool called *amritsar* or *amritsarovar* (*amrit* means nectar, *sar* is short form of *sarovar* and means pool). The pool is 5.1 metre deep and is surrounded by a 3.7 metre wide circumambulatory marble passage that is circled clockwise. The sanctum is connected to the platform by a causeway and the gateway into the causeway is called the Darshani Deorhi (from *Darshana Dvara*). For those who wish to take a dip in the pool, the Temple provides a half hexagonal shelter and holy steps to Har ki Pauri.[220] Bathing in the pool is believed by many Sikhs to have restorative powers, purifying one's *karma*. Some carry bottles of the pool water home particularly for sick friends and relatives. The pool is maintained by volunteers who perform *kar seva* (community service) by draining and desilting it periodically.

The Golden Temple map

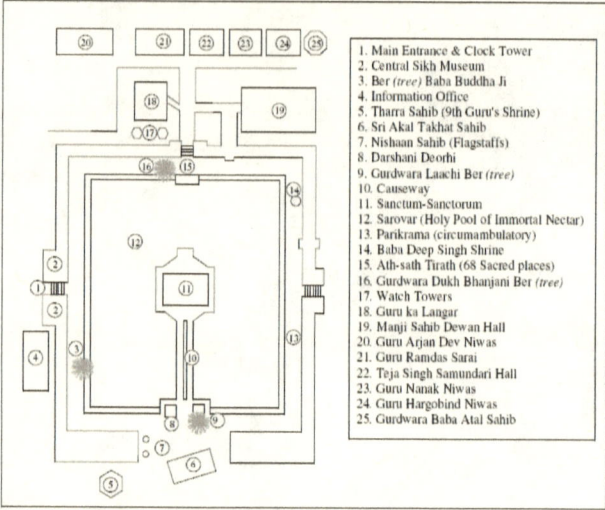

Figure 97: *The Golden temple complex map*

Left: Causeway to the sanctum with people, behind the pool is Ath Sath Tirath; Right: Entrance view

The sanctum has two floors. The Sikh Scripture *Guru Granth Sahib* is seated on the lower square floor for about 20 hours everyday, and for 4 hours it is taken to its bedroom inside Akal Takht with elaborate ceremonies in a palki, for *sukhasana* and *prakash*. The floor with the seated scripture is raised a few steps above the entrance causeway level. The upper floor in the sanctum is a gallery and connected by stairs. The ground floor is lined with white marble, as is the path surrounding the sanctum. The sanctum's exterior has gilded copper plates. The doors are gold foil covered copper sheets with nature motifs such as birds and flowers. The ceiling of the upper floor is gilded, embossed and decorated with jewels. The sanctum dome is semi-spherical with a pinnacle ornament. The sides are embellished with arched copings and small solid domes, the corners adorning cupolas, all of which are covered with gold foil covered gilded copper.

The floral designs on the marble panels of the walls around the sanctum are Arabesque. The arches include verses from the Sikh scripture in gold letters. The frescoes follow the Indian tradition and include animal, bird and nature motifs rather than being purely geometrical. The stair walls have murals of Sikh Gurus such as the falcon carrying Guru Gobind Singh riding a horse.[221]

The Darshani Deorhi is a two storey structure that houses the temple management offices and treasury. At the exit of path leading away from the sanctum is the *prasada* facility, where volunteers serve a flour-based sweet offering called *karah prasad*. Typically, the pilgrims to the Golden Temple enter and make a clockwise circumambulation around the pool before entering the sanctum. There are four entrances to the gurdwara complex signifying the openness to all sides, but a single entrance to the sanctum of the temple through a causeway.

Left: Akal Takht illuminated; Right: One of the entrance gates

Akal Takht and Teja Singh Samundri Hall

In front of the sanctum and the causeway is the Akal Takht building. It is the chief *Takht*, a center of authority in Sikhism. It is also the headquarters of the main political party of the Indian state of Punjab, Shiromani Akali Dal (Supreme Akali Party).[200] The Akal Takht issues edicts or writs (*hukam*) on matters related to Sikhism and the solidarity of the Sikh community. Its name *Akal Takht* means "throne of the Timeless (God)". The institution was established by Guru Hargobind after the martyrdom of his father Guru Arjan, as a place to conduct ceremonial, spiritual and secular affairs, issuing binding writs on Sikh Gurdwaras far from his own location. A building was later

Figure 98: *A 1860s photo of the Golden Temple with the Gothic clock tower under construction during the colonial British era. This clock tower was demolished later.*

constructed over the Takht founded by Guru Hargobind, and this came to be known as Akal Bunga. The Akal Takht is also known as Takht Sri Akal Bunga. The Sikh tradition has five Takhts, all of which are major pilgrimage sites in Sikhism. These are in Anandpur, Patna, Nanded, Talwandi Sabo and Amritsar. The Akal Takht in the Golden Temple complex is the primary seat and chief.[222]

The Teja Singh Samundri Hall is the office of the Shiromani Gurdwara Parbandhak Committee (Supreme Committee of Temple Management). It is located in a building near the Langar-kitchen and Assembly Hall. This office coordinates and oversees the operations of major Sikh temples.[200,223]

Clock Tower

The Clock Tower did not exist in the original version of the temple. In its location was a building, now called the "lost palace". The officials of the British India wanted to demolish the building after the Second Anglo-Sikh war and once they had annexed the Sikh Empire. The Sikhs opposed the demolition, but this opposition was ignored. In its place, the clock tower was added. The clock tower was designed by John Gordon in a Gothic cathedral style with red bricks. The clock tower construction started in 1862 and was completed in 1874. The tower was demolished by the Sikh community about 70 years later. In its place, a new entrance was constructed with a design more harmonious with the Temple. This entrance on the north side has a clock, houses a museum on its upper floor, and it continues to be called *ghanta ghar deori*.

Figure 99: *The historic Dukh Bhanjani Ber tree inside the courtyard, next to Ath Sath Tirath.*

Ber trees

The Golden Temple complex originally was open and had numerous trees around the pool. It is now a walled, two storey courtyard with four entrances, that preserve three Ber trees (jujube). One of them is to the right of the main *ghanta ghar deori* entrance with the clock, and it is called the *Ber Baba Buddha*. It is believed in the Sikh tradition to be the tree where Baba Buddha sat to supervise the construction of the pool and first temple.[214]

A second tree is called *Laachi Ber*, believed to the one under which Guru Arjan rested while the temple was being built.[214] The third one is called *Dukh Bhanjani Ber*, located on the other side of the sanctum, across the pool. It is believed in the Sikh tradition that this tree was the location where a Sikh was cured of his leprosy after taking a dip in the pool, giving the tree the epithet of "suffering remover".[206] There is a small Gurdwara underneath the tree.[214] The *Ath Sath Tirath*, or the spot equivalent to 68 pilgrimages, is in the shade underneath the *Dukh Bhanjani Ber* tree. Sikh devotees, states Charles Townsend, believe that bathing in the pool near this spot delivers the same fruits as a visit to 68 pilgrimage places in India.[214]

Figure 100: *The ceiling of Harmandir Sahib is covered with gold foil and studded with precious stones.*

Sikh history museums

The main *ghanta ghar deori* north entrance has a Sikh history museum on the first floor, according to the Sikh tradition. The display shows various paintings, of gurus and martyrs, many narrating the persecution of Sikhs over their history, as well as historical items such as swords, kartar, comb, chakkars. A new underground museum near the clock tower, but outside the temple courtyard also shows Sikh history.[224,225] According to Louis E. Fenech, the display does not present the parallel traditions of Sikhism and is partly ahistorical such as a headless body continuing to fight, but a significant artwork and reflects the general trend in Sikhism of presenting their history to be one of persecution, martyrdoms and bravery in wars.

The main entrance to the Gurdwara has many memorial plaques that commemorate past Sikh historical events, saints and martyrs, contributions of Ranjit Singh, as well as commemorative inscriptions of all the Sikh soldiers who died fighting in the two World Wars and the various Indo-Pakistan wars.

Guru Ram Das Langar

Harmandir Sahib complex has a Langar, a community run free kitchen and dining hall. It is attached to the east side of the courtyard near the *Dukh Bhanjani Ber*, outside of the entrance. Food is served here to all visitors who want it, regardless of faith, gender or economic background. Vegetarian food is served and all people eat together as equals. Everyone sits on the floor in rows, which is called *pangat*. The meal is served by volunteers as part of their *kar seva* ethos.[214] A simple meal is served round the clock.

Daily ceremonies

Left: A palanquin being prepared for the daily *sukhasan* ritual to carry the scripture to a bedroom; Right: A Sikh pilgrim. Some Sikh take a dip in the pool.

There are several rituals performed everyday in the Golden Temple as per the historic Sikh tradition. These rituals treat the scripture as a living person, a Guru out of respect. The rituals include:[226]

- Closing ritual called *sukhasan* (*sukh* means "comfort or rest", *asan* means "position"). At night, after a series of devotional kirtans and three part ardās, the *Guru Granth Sahib* is closed, carried on the head, placed into and then carried in a flower decorated, pillow-bed palki (palanquin), with chanting. Its bedroom is in the Akal Takht, on the first floor. Once it arrives there, the scripture is tucked into a bed.[226]
- Opening ritual called *prakash* which means "light". About dawn everyday, the *Guru Granth Sahib* is taken out its bedroom, carried on the head, placed and carried in a flower decorated palki with chanting and bugle sounding across the causeway. It is brought to the sanctum. Then after ritual singing of a series of Var Asa kirtans and ardas, a random page is opened. This is the *mukhwak* of the day, it is read out loud, and then written out for the pilgrims to read over that day.[226]

Influence on contemporary era Sikhism

Singh Sabha movement

The Singh Sabha movement was a late-19th century movement within the Sikh community to rejuvenate and reform Sikhism at a time when Christian, Hindu and Muslim proselytizers were actively campaigning to convert Sikhs to their religion.[227] The movement was triggered by the conversion of Ranjit Singh's son Duleep Singh and other well known people to Christianity. Started in 1870s, the Singh Sabha movement's aims were to propagate the true Sikh religion, restore and reform Sikhism to bring back into the Sikh fold the apostates who had left Sikhism.[228,229] There were three main groups with different viewpoints and approaches, of which the Tat Khalsa group prevailed by early 1900s.[230] Before 1905, the Golden Temple had idols and images for at least a century.[231] In 1905, with the campaign of the Tat Khalsa, these idols and images were removed from the Golden Temple.

Jallianwala Bagh massacre

As per tradition, the Sikhs gathered in the Golden Temple to celebrate the festival of Baisakhi in 1919. After their visit, many walked over to the Jallianwala Bagh next to it to listen to speakers protesting Rowlatt Act and other policies of the colonial British government. A large crowd had gathered, when the British general Reginald Dyer ordered his soldiers to surround the Jallianwala Bagh, then open fire into the civilian crowd. Hundreds died and thousands were wounded. The massacre strengthened the opposition to the colonial rule throughout India, and particularly Sikhs. It triggered massive non-violent protests. The protests pressured the British government to transfer the control over the management and treasury of the Golden Temple to an elected organization called Shiromani Gurudwara Prabandhak Committee (SGPC). The SGPC continues to manage the Golden Temple.[232]

Operation Blue Star

The Golden Temple and Akal Takht were occupied by various militant groups in early 1980s. These included the Dharam Yudh Morcha led by Jarnail Singh Bhindranwale, the Babbar Khalsa, the AISSF and the National Council of Khalistan. By late 1983, the Bhindranwale led group had begun to build bunkers and observations posts in and around the Golden Temple. The Golden Temple became a place for weapons training for the militants. In June 1984, the then Prime Minister of India Indira Gandhi ordered Indian Army to begin Operation Blue Star against the militants. The operation caused severe damaged and destroyed Akal Takht. Numerous soldiers, civilians and militants died in the cross fire. Within days of the Operation Bluestar, some 2,000

Sikh soldiers in India mutinied and attempted to reach Amritsar to liberate the Golden Temple. Within six months, on 31 October 1984, Indira Gandhi's Sikh bodyguards assassinated her.

In 1986, Indira Gandhi's son and the next Prime Minister of India Rajiv Gandhi ordered repairs of the Akal Takht Sahib. These repairs were removed and Sikhs rebuilt the Akal Takht Sahib in 1999.Wikipedia:Citation needed

Celebrations

One of the most important festivals is Vaisakhi, which is celebrated in the second week of April (usually the 13th). Sikhs celebrate the founding of the Khalsa on this day and it is celebrated with fervour in the Harmandir Sahib. Other important Sikh religious days such as the birth of Guru Ram Das, martyrdom day of Guru Teg Bahadur, the birthday of the Sikh founder Guru Nanak, etc., are also celebrated with religious piety. Similarly Diwali is one of the festivals which sees the Harmandir Sahib beautifully illuminated with Diyas (lamps); lights and fireworks are discharged. Most Sikhs visit Amritsar and the Harmandir Sahib at least once during their lifetime, particularly and mostly during special occasions in their life such as birthdays, marriages, childbirth, etc.

References

Bibliography

- The Editors of Encyclopaedia Britannica (2014). *Encyclopedia Britannica*[233].
- Kerr, Ian J. (2015). "Harimandar". *Encyclopaedia of Sikhism*[234]. Punjabi University Patiala.
- Pardeep Singh Arshi (1989). *The Golden Temple: history, art, and architecture*[235]. Harman. ISBN 978-81-85151-25-0.
- W. Owen Cole (2004). *Understanding Sikhism*[236]. Dunedin Academic Press. ISBN 978-1-906716-91-2.
- Louis E. Fenech; W. H. McLeod (2014). *Historical Dictionary of Sikhism*[237]. Rowman & Littlefield Publishers. ISBN 978-1-4422-3601-1.
- W.H. McLeod (1990). *Textual Sources for the Study of Sikhism*[238]. University of Chicago Press. ISBN 978-0-226-56085-4.
- Trudy Ring; Noelle Watson; Paul Schellinger (2012). *Asia and Oceania: International Dictionary of Historic Places*[239]. Routledge. ISBN 978-1-136-63979-1.

- Christopher Shackle; Arvind Mandair (2013). *Teachings of the Sikh Gurus: Selections from the Sikh Scriptures*[240]. Routledge. ISBN 978-1-136-45101-0.
- Pashaura Singh; Louis E. Fenech (2014). *The Oxford Handbook of Sikh Studies*[241]. Oxford University Press. ISBN 978-0-19-100411-7.
- Arvind-Pal Singh Mandair (2013). *Sikhism: A Guide for the Perplexed*[242]. Bloomsbury Academic. ISBN 978-1-4411-0231-7.
- Singh, Nikky-Guninder Kaur (2011). *Sikhism: An Introduction*[243]. I.B.Tauris. ISBN 978-0-85771-962-1.
- Henry Walker (2002). Kerry Brown, ed. *Sikh Art and Literature*[244]. Routledge. ISBN 978-1-134-63136-0.

External links

 Wikimedia Commons has media related to *Harmandir Sahib*.

- Website of Shiromani Gurdwara Parbandhak Committee[245]
- Golden Temple[246] at DMOZ
- photos from the 1880s[247]

Pashupatinath Temple

Pashupatinath Temple

Pashupatinath Temple पशुपतिनाथ मन्दिर	
 Night view of Pashupatinath Temple	
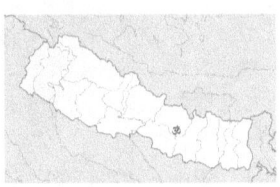 Location in Nepal	
Geography	
Coordinates	27°42′35″N 85°20′55″E[248] Coordinates: 27°42′35″N 85°20′55″E[248]
Country	Nepal
State	Bagmati Zone
District	Kathmandu
Locale	Kathmandu
Culture	

Sanctum	Shiva
Important festivals	Shivaratri, Teej, Bala Chaturdashi
Architecture	
Architectural styles	Pagoda
Number of temples	492
History and governance	
Website	pashupati.org.np[249]

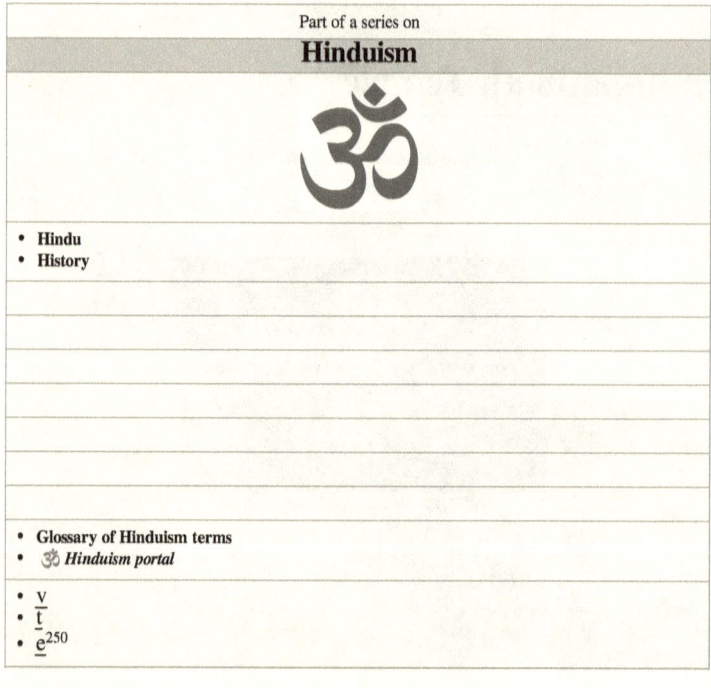

The **Pashupatinath Temple** (Nepali: पशुपतिनाथ मन्दिर) is a famous, sacred Hindu temple dedicated to Pashupatinath and is located on the banks of the Bagmati River 5 kilometres north-east of Kathmandu Valley in the eastern part of Kathmandu, the capital of Nepal. This temple is considered one of the sacred temples of Hindu faith. The temple serves as the seat of the national deity, Lord Pashupatinath.This temple complex is on UNESCO World Heritage Sites's list Since 1979. This "extensive Hindu temple precinct" is a "sprawling collection of temples, ashrams, images and inscriptions raised over the centuries along the banks of the sacred Bagmati river" and is included as one of the seven monument groups in UNESCO's designation of Kathmandu

Figure 101: *World Heritage Site, Pashupatinath Temple*

Valley as a cultural heritage site. One of the major Festivals of the temple is Maha Shivaratri on which day over 800,000 devotees visit here.

The twelve Jyotirlinga (in India) are the body and the Jyotirlinga at Pashupatinath in Kathmandu (Nepal) is the head over this body.

The temple is one of the 275 Tamil Paadal Petra Sthalams (*Holy Abodes of Shiva*) on the continent. Kotirudra Samhita, Chapter 11 on the Shivalingas of the North, in Shiva Purana mentions this Shivalinga as the bestower of all wishes.

History

The temple was erected anew in the 15th century by Lichhavi King Shupuspa after the previous building was consumed by termites.[251] Over time, countless further temples have been erected around this two-storied temple. These include the Vaishnava temple complex with a Ram temple from the 14th century and the Guhyeshwari Temple mentioned in an 11th-century manuscript.

Legend surrounding the origin of the temple

Pashupatinath Temple is the oldest Hindu temple in Kathmandu. It is not known for certain when Pashupatinath Temple was built. But according to Nepal Mahatmaya and Himvatkhanda, the deity here gained great fame there as Pashupati, the Lord of all Pashus, which are living as well as non-living beings. Pashupatinath Temple's existence dates back to 400 B.C. The richly-ornamented pagoda houses the sacred linga or holy symbol of Lord Shiva. There are many legends describing as to how the temple of Lord Aalok Pashupatinath came to existence here. Some of them are narrated below:-

The Cow Legend

Legend says that Lord Shiva once took the form of an antelope and sported unknown in the forest on Bagmati river's east bank. The gods later caught up with him and grabbing him by the horn, forced him to resume his divine form. The broken horn was worshipped as a linga but over time it was buried and lost. Centuries later astonished herdsmen found one of his cows showering the earth with milk. Digging deep at the site, he discovered the divine linga of Pashupatinath.

The Lichchhavi Legend

According to Gopalraj Aalok Vamsavali, the oldest ever chronicle in Nepal, this temple was built by Supuspa Deva, a Lichchhavi King, who according to the stone inscription erected by Jayadeva 11 in the courtyard of Pashupatinath in 753 AD, happened to be the ruler 39 generations before Manadeva (464-505 AD).

The Devalaya Legend

Another chronicle states that Pashupatinath Temple was in the form of Linga shaped Devalaya before Supuspa Deva constructed a five-storey temple of Pashupatinath in this place. As the time passed, the need for repairing and renovating this temple arose. It is learnt that this temple was reconstructed by a medieval King named Shivadeva (1099-1126 AD). It was renovated by Ananta Malla adding a roof to it. Thousands of pilgrims from all over the world come to pay homage to this temple, that is also known as 'The Temple of Living Beings'.

Other beliefs

There are several complex stories involving the origins of Pashupatinath. One story goes, in brief, that Shiva and Parvati came to the Kathmandu Valley and rested by the Bagmati while on a journey. Shiva was so impressed by its beauty and the surrounding forest that he and Parvati changed themselves into deer and walked into the forest. Many spots in the Kathmandu Valley have been identified as places where Shiva went during his time as a deer. After a while, the people and gods began to search for Shiva. Finally, after various complications, they found him in the forest, but he refused to leave. More complications ensued, but ultimately Lord Shiva announced that, since he had lived by the Bagmati river in a deer's form, he would now be known as Pashupatinath, Lord of all animals. It is said that whoever came here and beheld the lingam that appeared there would not be reborn as an animal.

Finding of Shiva Linga at Pashupatinath Temple

It is said that the wish-fulfilling cow Kamadhenu took shelter in a cave on the Chandravan mountain. Everyday Kamadhenu went down to the place the lingam was sunken into the soil and poured her milk on top of the soil. After a few thousand years some people saw Kamadhenu pouring milk on that same spot every day, and started to wonder what that would be. So they removed the soil and found the beautiful shining lingam and started worshiping it.

File:Pashupati dec 20 2009.jpg

Pashupatinath Temple Panorama of the Pashupatinath Temple from the other bank of Bagmati river, Kathmandu, Nepal.

Temple complex

The area of Pashupatinath encompasses 264 hectares of land including 518 temples and monuments. Main pagoda style temple is located in the fortified courtyard within the complex guarded by Semi-Military Nepal Police and Military Force Nepal Army and has a police outpost along with living quarter within. In front of the western door, there is a huge statue Nandi bull, in bronze. Along with many temples and shrines of both Vaishnav and saiva tradition.

Temples and Shrines in the inner courtyard

- Vasuki Nath Temple
- Unmatta Bhairav Temple
- Surya narayan Temple
- Kirti mukh bhairav shrine
- Budanil kantha shrine
- Hanuman shrine
- 184 shivaling shrine

Figure 102: *Pashupati temple surroundings*

Temples and Shrines in the outer complex

- Ram mandir
- Virat swaroop temple
- 12 jyotirlingha and Pandra Shivalaya
- Guhyeshwari Temple

Main temple architecture

This main temple is built in the Nepalese pagoda style of architecture. All the features of pagoda style are founded here like cubic constructions, beautifully carved wooden rafters on which they rest (tundal). The two level roofs are of copper with gold covering. The temple resides on a square base platform with a height of 23m 7 cm from base to pinnacle. It has four main doors, all covered with silver sheets. This temple has a gold pinnacle (Gajur).Inside are two Garbhagrihas, outer and inner.The inner garbhagriha or sanctum sanctorum is where the idol is placed and outer sanctum is an open corridor-like space.

Figure 103: *Raghavendra Bhat (right) and Girish Bhatt in traditional 4-5 kg heavy Priestly garb of Pashupatinath Temple*

The Deity

The sacro sanctum, or the main idol is a stone Mukhalinga with a silver yoni base bound with the silver serpent. The lingam is one metre high and has faced in four directions. These faces represent various aspects of Shiva; Sadyojata (also known as Barun), Vamdeva (also known as Ardha Nareshwor), Tatpurusha, Aghor & Ishana (imaginative). Facing West, North, East, South and Zenith respectively representing five primary elements namely earth, water, air, light and ether.[252] Each face has tiny protruding hands holding rudraksha mala on right hand and a kamandalu on the other. Unlike other Shiva lingams in India and Nepal this Pashupati Shiva lingam is always Dressed in its golden vastra except during abhishakam, so pouring milk and Ganga Jal is only possible during abhishakam through the main priests.

Priest

The unique feature of this temple is that only 4 priests can touch the idol. Daily rituals of Pashupatinath are carried out by two sets of priests ; one being the Bhatt priests and other Bhandari. Bhatta or Bhatt are the one who performs the daily ritual and can touch the lingam, whereas Bhandaris are the helper and temple caretaker priests who are not qualified to perform pooja rituals or to touch the deity.

Bhatta

Bhatta also spelt as *Bhat*are highly educated Vedic Dravida Brahmin Scholars from Karnataka. Unlike other Hindu temples, priesthood of Pashupatinath is not hereditary. Priests are selected from a group of scholars educated by Shri Shankaracharya Dakshinamnaya Peeth Sringeri on Rig Vedic Recitation, initiated in Pashupata Yoga by Kashi Math,Shiva Āgama and learned Recitation of Samaveda from Haridwar.After qualifying and fulfilling all those criteria they will be selected for Priesthood by Raj Guru of Pashupatinath Temple undergoing strict examination on Vedas and Shiva Agamas and then the qualifies are sent to Kathmandu for performing Puja and Daily Worship of Lord Shri Pashupatinath .

The unique feature of this temple is that only 4 Bhatta priests can touch the deity. Current Bhatt priests of the temple are;

- Ganesh Bhat (15th head priest of the Pashupatinath Temple aka Mool Bhat) from Udupi.
- Ram Karanth Bhat from Mangaluru.
- Girish Bhat from Sirsi.
- Narayan Bhat(Recently appointed) from Bhatkal
- Raghavendra Bhat (Priest for Vasuki Nath temple only)

Bhandaris

Also called Rajbhandari are the treasurers, temple caretakers, and assistant priest of the temple. These Bhandaris are the descendants of helper priests brought up by early Bhatts, but were allowed to settle in Kathmandu valley and later assimilated in existing Newar caste of Rajbhandari - a high-caste Chathariya/Kshatriya clan of Kashyapa gotra. Their main function is to help the Bhatta priest and perform maintenance of the inner Garbhagriha. They can have little or no Vedic knowledge but still qualify as assistant priests if they belong from the same family lineage and undergo some basic criteria like caste, gotra, lineage purity, educational qualification, etc. They work in a set of three and change in every full moon day. There are a total of 108 Bhandaris.

Figure 104: *Pandra Shivalaya and ghat (viewpoint for tourist from adjacent side of river Bagmati, East of the main temple)*

Entry and Darshan

Temple courtyard has 4 entrances in all directions. The western entrance is the main entrance to the temple courtyard and rests three entrances are only opened during regular time. Temple security (Armed Police Force Nepal) and Pashupatinath area development trust are selective regarding who is allowed entry into the inner courtyard. Practising Hindus and Buddhist of Nepali diaspora are only allowed into Temple courtyard. Practising Hindus of western descent are not allowed into the temple complex along with other non-Hindu Visitors with an exception to Sikh and Jain groups if they are of Indian ancestry. Others can look at the main temple from adjacent side of the river and has to pay a nominal fee of $10 (1000 Nepali rupee) for visiting hundreds of small temples in the external premises of the temple complex. The inner temple courtyard remains open from 4 am to 7 pm for the devotee but the Inner Pashupatinath Temple where the Lingam of Lord Pashupatinath is established is open from 5 am to 12 pm for the morning ritual and viewing and from 5 pm to 7 pm for evening ritual. Unlike many other Saiva temples, devotees are not allowed to enter in the inner-most Garbhagriha but are allowed to view from the exterior premises of the outer Garbhagriha.

Abhisheka

The inner sanctum where the Shiva Linga is placed, has four entrance, East, west, north, south. Normally devotees will have the Shiva Lingadarshan through western door entrance only. From 9:30 to 1:30 devotees can worship from all the 4 doors.

All the four doors are also opened during the Abhisheka time i.e. 9-11am. All the four sides of the Shiva Lingadarshan are possible during this period. One can take the abhisheka ticket at the SBI counter, available at the entrance of the temple. The basic abhisheka ticket costs around NPR.1100/-, which includes the Rudraabhisheka and various other poojas. Abhisheka will be done based on the direction the mukh is viewed. If your receipt says as eastern direction then one needs to stand in the queue at the eastern entrance, wherein the priests will do the abhisheka for the eastern mukh of the Shiva Linga.

Festivals

There are many festivals throughout the year and thousands of people attend these festivals. The most important festivals are the Maha Shiva Ratri Bala Chaturthi festival, and Teej festival. During these festivals, people from all over the world come to worship. Wikipedia:Citation needed

Controversy of 2009

In January 2009, after the forced resignation by the chief priest of Pashupatinath temple, the Maoist-led government of Nepal "hand picked" Nepalese priests to lead the temple, thus bypassing the temple's long-standing requirements. This appointment was contested by the Bhandaris of the temple, stating that they were not against the appointment of Nepalese priests but against the appointment without proper procedure. After the appointment was challenged in a civil court, the appointment was overruled by Supreme Court of Nepal. However, the government did not heed the ruling and stood by its decision. This led to public outrage and protests over a lack of transparency. The paramilitary group of the CPN (Maoist), called YCL, attacked the protesters, leading to over a dozen injuries. Lawmakers and activists from opposition parties joined protests, declaring their support for the Bhatta and other pro-Bhatta protesters. After long dissatisfaction and protest by Hindus both in and outside Nepal, the government was forced to reverse its decision that had been declared illegal by the Supreme Court of Nepal and reinstate Bhatta priests.

Figure 105: *One of the outer shrine damaged in 2015 Nepal earthquake*

2015 earthquake

The main temple complex of Pashupatinath and the sanctum sanctorum was left untouched but some of the outer buildings in the World Heritage Site were damaged by the April 2015 Nepal earthquake.

In popular culture

The buildings and street layout of the temple was used in the video game Commandos 2: Men of Courage in one stage of the game, "Target: Burma". Although the game was set in Burma, there were references to Gurkhas, soldiers of Nepali nationality.

Gallery

Pashupatinath Temple scenes

Pashupatinath Temple

Temple from the river side

Front entrance from the street side

Temple cremations on the Bagmati River

Cremations up close

Temple sadhus

A glimpse at the temple

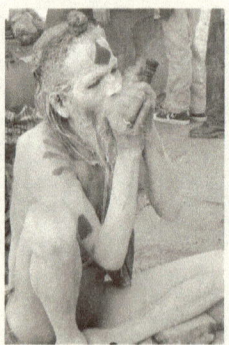

An Aghora in Pashupatinath Temple during Shivaratri

Entrance From Western side

Bridge at Bagmati river of Pashupati temple

Manson Bagmati river and temple

Evening Aarati Pray

External links

 Wikimedia Commons has media related to *Pashupatinath temple*.

- Shri Pashupatinath Mandir, Nepal[253]
- Pashupatinath Temple[254]
- Pashupatinath Darshan[255]
- Video guide to Pashupatinath Nepal[256]
- Virtual Tour of Pashupatnath Temple[257]

Mount Kailash

Mount Kailash

Mount Kailash	
Gang Rinpoche	
 The north face of Mount Kailash	
Highest point	
Elevation	6,638 m (21,778 ft)
Prominence	1,319 m (4,327 ft)
Coordinates	31°4′0″N 81°18′45″E[258] Coordinates: 31°4′0″N 81°18′45″E[258]
Geography	
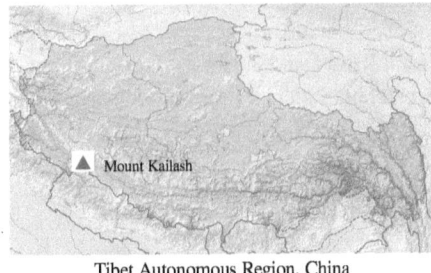 Tibet Autonomous Region, China	

Parent range	Transhimalaya

Mount Kailash (Sanskrit: कैलास, IAST: Kailāsa), **Mount Kailasa** or **Gang Rinpoche**, is a peak in the Kailash Range (Gangdisê Mountains), which forms part of Transhimalaya in the Tibet Autonomous Region of China.

The mountain lies near the source of some of the longest Asian rivers: the Indus, Sutlej, Brahmaputra, and Ghaghara (a tributary of the Ganges). Mount Kailash which is located near Lake Manasarovar and Lake Rakshastal, is considered to be sacred in four religions: Bön, Buddhism, Jainism and Hinduism.

Etymology

The mountain is known as "*Kailāsa*" (कैलास) in Sanskrit.[259,260] The name also could have been derived from the word "*kelāsa*" (केलास), which means "crystal".

In his Tibetan-English dictionary, Chandra (1902: p. 32) identifies the entry for 'kai la sha' (Wylie: *kai la sha*) which is a loan word from Sanskrit 'kailāsa' (Devanagari: कैलास).[261]

The Tibetan name for the mountain is **Gangs Rin-po-che** (Tibetan: གངས་རིན་པོ་ཆེ ; Chinese: 冈仁波齐峰). *Gangs* or *Kang* is the Tibetan word for *snow peak* analogous to *alp* or *hima*; *rinpoche* is an honorific meaning "precious one" so the combined term can be translated "precious jewel of snows".

> "Tibetan Buddhists call it Kangri Rinpoche; 'Precious Snow Mountain'. Bon texts have many names: Water's Flower, Mountain of Sea Water, Nine Stacked Swastika Mountain. For Hindus, it is the home of the mountain god Shiva and a symbol of his power symbol "Om"; for Jains it is where their first Tirthankara was enlightened; for Buddhists, the navel of the universe; and for adherents of Bon, the abode of the sky goddess Sipaimen.'[262]

Another local name for the mountain is **Tisé** mountain, which derives from *ti tse* in the Zhang-Zhung language, meaning "water peak" or "river peak", connoting the mountain's status as the source of the mythical Lion, Horse, Peacock and Elephant Rivers, and in fact the Indus, Yarlung Tsangpo/Dihang/Brahmaputra, Karnali and Sutlej all begin in the Kailash-Lake Manasarovara region.

Religious significance

In Hinduism

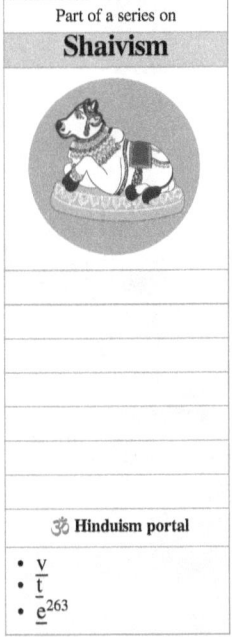

According to Hinduism, Shiva, the god of gods, resides at the summit of a legendary mountain named **Kailāsa**, where he sits in a state of perpetual meditation along with his wife Pārvatī. He is at once the Lord of Yoga and therefore the ultimate renunciate ascetic, yet he is also the divine master of Tantra.

According to Charles Allen, one description in the Vishnu Purana of the mountain states that its four faces are made of crystal, ruby, gold, and lapis lazuli. It is a pillar of the world and is located at the heart of six mountain ranges symbolizing a lotus.[264]

In Jainism

In Jainism, Kailash is also known as Mount Meru. Ashtapada, the mountain next to Mt. Kailash, is the site where the first Jain Tirthankara, Rishabhanatha, attained moksha (liberation).

Figure 106: *An illustration of the Hindu significance of Mount Kailash, depicting the holy family of Shiva, consisting of Shiva, Parvati, Ganesha and Kartikeya (Muruga)*

In Buddhism

Vajrayana Buddhists believe that Mount Kailash is the home of the buddha Cakrasaṃvara (also known as Demchok), who represents supreme bliss.

There are numerous sites in the region associated with Padmasambhava, whose tantric practices in holy sites around Tibet are credited with finally establishing Buddhism as the main religion of the country in the 7th–8th century AD.[265]

It is said that Milarepa (c. 1052 – c. 1135), champion of Vajrayana, arrived in Tibet to challenge Naro Bön-chung, champion of the Bön religion of Tibet. The two magicians engaged in a terrifying sorcerers' battle, but neither was able to gain a decisive advantage. Finally, it was agreed that whoever could reach the summit of Kailash most rapidly would be the victor. While Naro Bön-chung sat on a magic drum and soared up the slope, Milarepa's followers were dumbfounded to see him sitting still and meditating. Yet when Naro Bön-chung was nearly at the top, Milarepa suddenly moved into action and overtook him by riding on sunlight, thus winning the contest. He did, however, fling a handful of snow on to the top of a nearby mountain, since known as Bönri, bequeathing it to the Bönpo and thereby ensuring continued Bönpo connections with the region.[266,267,268]

Figure 107: *Tibetan and Nepalese Thangka depicting Mount Kailash*

In Bön

Bön, a religion native to Tibet, maintain that the entire mystical region and Kailash, which they call the "nine-story Swastika Mountain", is the axis mundi, Tagzig Olmo Lung Ring.

Pilgrimage

Every year, thousands make a pilgrimage to Kailash, following a tradition going back thousands of years. Pilgrims of several religions believe that circumambulating Mount Kailash on foot is a holy ritual that will bring good fortune. The peregrination is made in a clockwise direction by Hindus and Buddhists while Jains and Bönpos circumambulate the mountain in a counterclockwise direction.

The path around Mount Kailash is 52 km (32 mi) long. Some pilgrims believe that the entire walk around Kailash should be made in a single day, which is not considered an easy task. A person in good shape walking fast would take perhaps 15 hours to complete the entire trek. Some of the devout do accomplish this feat, little daunted by the uneven terrain, altitude sickness and harsh conditions faced in the process. Indeed, other pilgrims venture a much more demanding regimen, performing body-length prostrations over the entire length of the circumambulation: The pilgrim bends down, kneels, prostrates full-length, makes a mark with his fingers, rises to his knees, prays, and then crawls forward on hands and knees to the mark made by his/her fingers before repeating the process. It requires at least four weeks of physical endurance

Figure 108: *Stupas, with the north face of Mount Kailash (background)*

to perform the circumambulation while following this regimen. The mountain is located in a particularly remote and inhospitable area of the Tibetan Himalayas. A few modern amenities, such as benches, resting places and refreshment kiosks, exist to aid the pilgrims in their devotions. According to all religions that revere the mountain, setting foot on its slopes is a dire sin. It is a popular belief that the stairways on Mount Kailash lead to heaven.

Because of the Sino-Indian border dispute, pilgrimage to the legendary abode of Shiva was stopped from 1954 to 1978. Thereafter, a limited number of Indian pilgrims have been allowed to visit the place, under the supervision of the Chinese and Indian governments either by a lengthy and hazardous trek over the Himalayan terrain, travel by land from Kathmandu or from Lhasa where flights from Kathmandu are available to Lhasa and thereafter travel over the great Tibetan plateau by car. The journey takes four night stops, finally arriving at Darchen at elevation of 4,600 m (15,100 ft), small outpost that swells with pilgrims at certain times of year. Despite its minimal infrastructure, modest guest houses are available for foreign pilgrims, whereas Tibetan pilgrims generally sleep in their own tents. A small regional medical center serving far-western Tibet and funded by the Swiss Ngari Korsum Foundation was built here in 1997.

Walking around the mountain—a part of its official park—has to be done on foot, pony or domestic yak, taking some three days of trekking starting from a height of around 15,000 ft (4,600 m) past the Tarboche (flagpole) to cross

Figure 109: *Satellite view of Mount Kailash with lakes Rakshastal (left) and Manasarovar (right)*

the Drölma pass 18,200 ft (5,500 m), and encamping for two nights en route. First, near the meadow of Dirapuk gompa, some 2 to 3 km (1.2 to 1.9 mi) before the pass and second, after crossing the pass and going downhill as far as possible (viewing Gauri Kund in the distance).

Geology

The region around Mount Kailash and the Indus headwaters area is typified by wide scale faulting of metamorphosed late Cretaceous to mid Cenozoic sedimentary rocks which have been intruded by igneous Cenozoic granitic rocks. Mt. Kailash appears to be a metasedimentary roof pendant supported by a massive granite base. The Cenozoic rocks represent offshore marine limestones deposited before subduction of the Tethys oceanic crust. These sediments were deposited on the southern margin of the Asia block during subduction of the Tethys oceanic crust prior to the collision between the Indian and Asian continents.[269,270]

Figure 110: *North View of Mount Kailash*

Mountaineering

In 1926, Hugh Ruttledge studied the north face, which he estimated was 6,000 ft (1,800 m) high and "utterly unclimbable"[271] and thought about an ascent of the northeast ridge, but he ran out of time. Ruttledge had been exploring the area with Colonel R. C. Wilson, who was on the other side of the mountain with his Sherpa named Tseten. According to Wilson, Tseten told Wilson, "'Sahib, we can climb that!' ... as he too saw that this [the SE ridge] represented a feasible route to the summit."[272] Further excerpts from Wilson's article in the *Alpine Journal* (vol. 40, 1928) show that he was serious about climbing Kailash, but he also ran out of time. Herbert Tichy was in the area in 1936, attempting to climb Gurla Mandhata. When he asked one of the Garpons of Ngari whether Kailash was climbable, the Garpon replied, "Only a man entirely free of sin could climb Kailash. And he wouldn't have to actually scale the sheer walls of ice to do it – he'd just turn himself into a bird and fly to the summit."[273] Reinhold Messner was given the opportunity by the Chinese government to climb in the mid-1980s but he declined.

In 2001 the Chinese gave permission for a Spanish team to climb the peak, but in the face of international disapproval the Chinese decided to ban all attempts to climb the mountain. Reinhold Messner, who condemned the Spanish plans, said

If we conquer this mountain, then we conquer something in people's souls. I would suggest they go and climb something a little harder. Kailas is not so high and not so hard.

Further reading

- Albinia, Alice. (2008) *Empires of the Indus: The Story of a River.* First American Edition (2010) W. W. Norton & Company, New York. ISBN 978-0-393-33860-7.
- Nomachi, Kazuyoshi. *Tibet.* Boston: Shambhala, 1997.
- Thurman, Robert and Tad Wise, *Circling the Sacred Mountain: A Spiritual Adventure Through the Himalayas.* New York: Bantam, 1999. ISBN 0-553-37850-3 — Tells the story of a Western Buddhist making the trek around Mount Kailash.
- Snelling, John. (1990). *The Sacred Mountain: The Complete Guide to Tibet's Mount Kailas.* 1st edition 1983. Revised and enlarged edition, including: Kailas-Manasarovar Travellers' Guide. Forwards by H.H. the Dalai Lama of Tibet and Christmas Humphreys. East-West Publications, London and The Hague. ISBN 0-85692-173-4.
- (Elevation) Chinese Snow Map "Kangrinboqe", published by the Lanzhou Institute of Glaciology, Chinese Academy of Sciences.
- Allen, Charles (1982) *A Mountain in Tibet: The Search for Mount Kailas and the Sources of the Great Rivers of Asia.* (London, André Deutsch).
- Allen, Charles. (1999). *The Search for Shangri-La: A Journey into Tibetan History.* Little, Brown and Company. Reprint: Abacus, London. 2000. ISBN 0-349-11142-1.
- "A Tibetan Guide for Pilgrimage to Ti-se (Mount Kailas) and mTsho Mapham (Lake Manasarovar)." Toni Huber and Tsepak Rigzin. In: *Sacred Spaces and Powerful Places In Tibetan Culture: A Collection of Essays.* (1999) Edited by Toni Huber, pp. 125–153. The Library of Tibetan Works and Archives, Dharamsala, H.P., India. ISBN 81-86470-22-0.
- Stein, R. A. (1961). *Les tribus anciennes des marches Sino-Tibétaines: légends, classifications et histoire.* Presses Universitaires de France, Paris. (In French)
- Johnson, Russell, and Moran, Kerry. (1989). *The Sacred Mountain of Tibet: On Pilgrimage to Kailas.* Park Street Press, Rochester, Vermont. ISBN 0-89281-325-3.
- Govinda, Lama Anagarika. (1966). *The Way of the White Clouds: A Buddhist Pilgrim in Tibet.* Shambhala Publications, Inc. Boulder, Colorado. Reprint with foreword by Peter Matthiessen: Shambhala Publications, Inc. Boston, Massachusetts. 1988. ISBN 0-87773-007-5

- Thubron, Colin. (2011). "To a Mountain in Tibet." Chatto & Windus, London. ISBN 978-0-7011-8380-6

External links

 Wikimedia Commons has media related to *Mount Kailash*.

- Walk around Kailash[274] Video and still images illustrating the pilgrimage route around Mt. Kailash and parts of Lake Manasarovar, including the Saga Dawa full moon festival celebrating the life of the Buddha.

Mount Olympus

Mount Olympus

Mount Olympus	
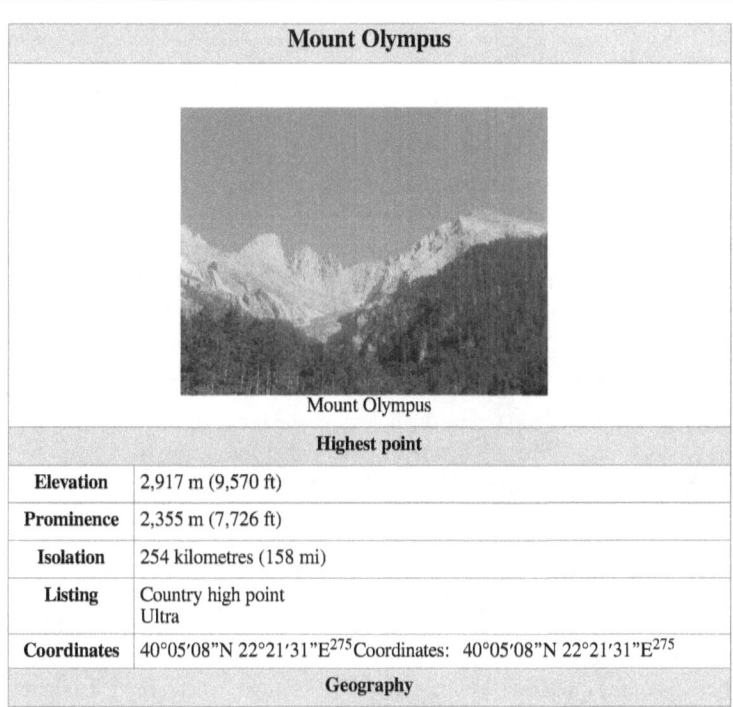 Mount Olympus	
Highest point	
Elevation	2,917 m (9,570 ft)
Prominence	2,355 m (7,726 ft)
Isolation	254 kilometres (158 mi)
Listing	Country high point Ultra
Coordinates	40°05′08″N 22°21′31″E[275]Coordinates: 40°05′08″N 22°21′31″E[275]
Geography	

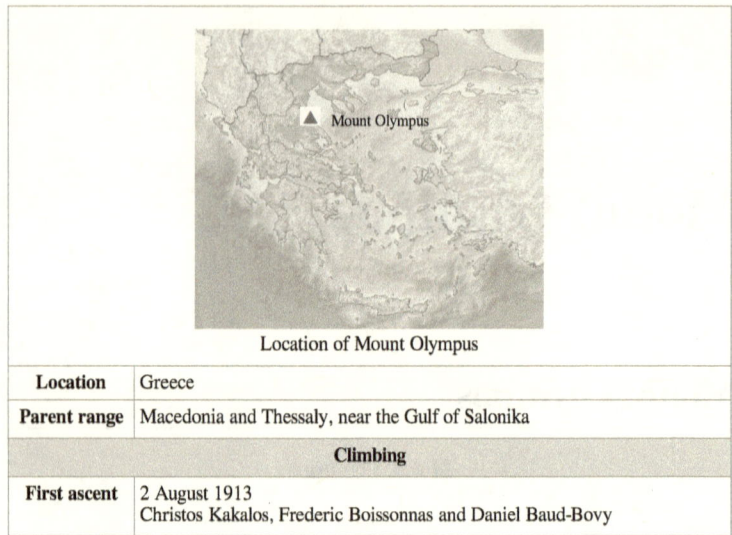
Location of Mount Olympus

Location	Greece
Parent range	Macedonia and Thessaly, near the Gulf of Salonika
Climbing	
First ascent	2 August 1913 Christos Kakalos, Frederic Boissonnas and Daniel Baud-Bovy

Mount Olympus (/oʊˈlɪmpəs, ə-/;[276] Greek: Όλυμπος [ˈolimbos] or [ˈolibos]; also transliterated as **Olympos**, and on Greek maps, **Oros Olympos**) is the highest mountain in Greece. It is located in the Olympus Range on the border between Thessaly and Macedonia, between the regional units of Pieria and Larissa, about 80 km (50 mi) southwest from Thessaloniki. Mount Olympus has 52 peaks, deep gorges, and exceptional biodiversity. The highest peak, *Mytikas*, meaning "nose", rises to 2,917 metres (9,570 ft). It is one of the highest peaks in Europe in terms of topographic prominence.

Olympus was notable in Greek mythology as the home of the Greek gods, on the Mytikas peak. Mount Olympus is also noted for its very rich flora, with several species. It has been a National Park, the first in Greece, since 1938. It is also a World's Biosphere Reserve.

Every year, thousands of people visit Olympus to admire its fauna and flora, tour its slopes, and reach its peaks. Organized mountain refuges and various mountaineering and climbing routes are available to visitors who want to explore it. The usual starting point is the town of Litochoro, on the eastern foothills of the mountain, 100 km from Thessaloniki, where, in the beginning of every summer, the Olympus Marathon terminates.

Figure 111: *Olympus' highest peak, Mytikas*

Geography

The shape of Olympus was formed by rain and wind, which produced an isolated tower almost 3,000 metres (9,800 ft) above the sea, which is only 18 kilometres (11 mi) away at Litochoro. Olympus has many peaks and an almost circular shape. The mountain has a circumference of 150 kilometres (93 mi), an average diameter of 26 kilometres (16 mi), and 600 square kilometres (230 sq mi) of area. To the northwest lies the Vlach village of Kokkinoplou. The Makryrema stream separates Olympus from the massif of Voulgara. The villages Petra, Vrontou and Dion lie to the northwest, while on the eastern side there is the town of Litochoro, where Enipeas bisects the massif of Olympus. On its southeastern side, the Ziliana gorge divides Mount Olympus from Kato Olympos (Lower Olympus), while on its southwestern foothills, there are the villages Sykaminea and Karya. The Agia Triada Sparmou Monastery and the village Pythion lie to the west. Olympus' dry foothills are known as the Xirokampi, containing chaparral and small animals. Further east, the plain of Dion is fertile and watered by the streams which originate on Olympus.

Geology

Mount Olympus is formed of sedimentary rock laid down 200 million years ago in a shallow sea. Various geological events that followed caused the emer-

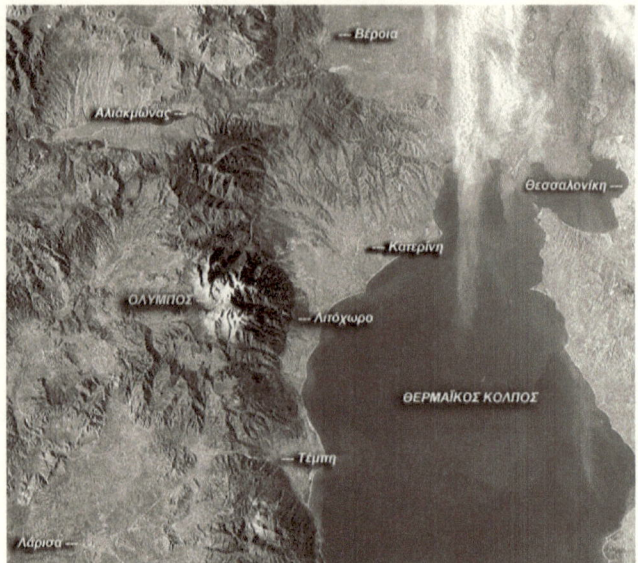

Figure 112: *Satellite photo of Olympus' region*

gence of the whole region and the sea. Around one million years ago glaciers covered Olympus and created its plateaus and depressions. With the temperature rise that followed, the ice melted and the streams that were created swept away large quantities of crushed rock in the lowest places, forming the alluvial fans, that spread out all over the region from the foothills of the mountain to the sea.

Morphology

The complicated geological past of the region is obvious from the morphology of Olympus and its National Park. Features include deep gorges and dozens of smooth peaks, many of them in altitude of more than 2,000 metres (6,600 ft), including Aghios Antonios (2,815 metres (9,236 ft)), Kalogeros (2,700 metres (8,900 ft)), Toumpa (2,801 metres (9,190 ft)) and Profitis Ilias (2,803 metres (9,196 ft)). However, it is the central, almost vertical, rocky peaks, that impress the visitor. Over the town of Litochoro, on the horizon, the relief of the mountain displays an apparent V, between two peaks of almost equal height. The left limb is the peak named Mytikas (or Pantheon - 2,918 metres (9,573 ft)). It is Greece's highest peak. Then, on the right is Stefani (or Thronos Dios [Throne of Zeus - 2,902 metres (9,521 ft)]), which presents the most impressive and steep peak of Olympus, with its last sharply rising 200

Figure 113: *The throne of Zeus (Stefani)*

Figure 114: *Mount Olympus as seen from north at Petra, Pieria*

Figure 115: *Muses' Plateau, with Stefani (or Thronos Dios) in the background*

meters presenting the greatest challenge for climbers. Further south, Skolio (second highest peak - 2,912 metres (9,554 ft)) completes an arc of about 200 degrees, with its steep slopes forming on the west side, like a wall, an impressive precipitous amphitheatrical cavity, 700 metres (2,300 ft) in depth and 1,000 metres (3,300 ft) in circumference, the 'Megala Kazania'. On the east side of the high peaks the steep slopes form zone like parallel folds, the 'Zonaria'. Even narrower and steeper scorings, the 'Loukia', lead to the peak.Wikipedia:Citation needed

On the north side, between Stefani and Profitis Ilias, extends the Muses' Plateau, at 2,550 metres (8,370 ft), while further south, almost in the center of the massif, extends the alpine tundra region of Bara, at an altitude of 2,350 metres (7,710 ft). Olympus has numerous ravines and gullies. Most distinguishable of the ravines are those of Mavrologos-Enipeas (14 km) and Mavratzas-Sparmos (13 km) near Bara and 'cut' the massif in two oval portions. On the southern foothills the great gorge of Ziliana, 13 km long, consists of a natural limit that separates the mountain from Lower Olympus. There are also many precipices and a number of caves, even nowadays unexplored. The form and layout of the rocks favor the emergence of numerous springs, mainly lower than 2,000 m, of small seasonal lakes and streams and of a small river, Enipeas, with its springs in the site Prionia and its estuary in the Aegean Sea.Wikipedia:Citation needed

Religion and mythology

In Ancient Greek religion and mythology, Olympus was the home of the Twelve Olympian gods of the ancient Greek world. It is the setting of many stories in Greek religions and myth. The Twelve Olympian gods lived in the gorges, where there were also their palaces. Pantheon (today Mytikas) was their meeting place and theater of their stormy discussions. The Throne of Zeus (today Stefani) hosted solely him, the leader of the gods. From there he unleashed his thunderbolts, expressing his divine wrath. In Pieria, at Olympus's northern foot, the mythological tradition had placed the nine Muses, patrons of the Fine Arts, daughters of Zeus and the Titanide Mnemosyne.Wikipedia:Citation needed

History

According to several sources, including here[277], Mt Olympus was originally named Mount Belus. The history of Olympus has been turbulent, as its surrounding area was not only a sacred shrine but also a battlefield for the control of the access from Thessaly to Macedonia in ancient times. In the period of the Ottoman Empire the mountain was a hiding place and base of operations for klephts and armatoloi.

In Olympus, the second armatoliki was founded, led by Kara Michalis in 1489. The action of the klephts in Olympus led the Turks to visit their outrage on the klephts' ally-village of Milia (in the late 17th century), which they destroyed. In that period Livadi in Olympus became the seat of the armatoliki of Olympus and Western Macedonia, with their first renowned commander Panos Zidros. In the 18th century the Turks had to replace the armatoloi (who very often joined the klephts) with Moslem Albanian armatoloi who ravaged the countryside of Macedonia. However, Olympus' armatoloi, even after their capitulation to Ali Pasha, never ceased fighting on land and at sea. Among them who were active there and in nearby regions were Nikotsaras, Giorgakis Olympios and the legendary family of Lazaioi. In the early 20th century, even for some time after the liberation from the Ottoman Empire (1912), robbers were active in the region - the best known of them the notorious Giagoulas, while during the German invasion in 1941 the Greek army fought significant battles along with units of New Zealanders and Australians. During the German Occupation (1941 - 1944) the mountain was one of the centers of the Greek Resistance, while a little later the Greek Civil War (1946–49) started there, in Litochoro.Wikipedia:Citation needed

Climbing expeditions

Ancient Greeks likely never tried to climb Olympus' peaks Pantheon and the Throne of Zeus (currently called Mytikas and Stefani respectively), which they considered to be the Twelve Olympians' home. But surely they reached the nearest peak, nowadays called Aghios Antonios, from where they had a view of the two peaks and where they left offerings, as recent archaeological findings indicate. In the modern era, a series of explorers tried to study the mountain and to reach, unsuccessfully, its summit. Examples include the French archaeologist Leon Heuzey (1855), the German explorer Heinrich Barth (1862), and the German engineer Edward Richter. Richter tried to reach the summit in 1911 but was abducted by Klephts, who also killed the Ottoman Gendarmes that accompanied him.

It was just one year after the liberation of Greece from Ottoman rule, on 2 August 1913, that the until then untrodden summit of Olympus was finally reached. The Swiss Frédéric Boissonnas and Daniel Baud-Bovy, aided by a hunter of wild goats from Litochoro, Christos Kakalos, were the first to reach Greece's highest peak. Kakalos, who had much experience climbing Olympus, was the first of the three to climb Mytikas. Afterwards and till his death (1976) he was the official guide of Olympus. In 1921, he and Marcel Kurz reached the second highest summit of Olympus, Stefani. Based on these explorations, Kurz in 1923 edited *Le Mont Olympe*, a book that includes the first detailed map of the summits. In 1928, the painter Vasilis Ithakisios climbed Olympus together with Kakalos, reaching a cave that he named *Shelter of the Muses*, and he spent many summers painting views of the mountain. Olympus was later photographed and mapped in detail by others, and a series of successful climbings and winter ascents of the steepest summits in difficult weather conditions took place.

Climbing Mount Olympus is a non-technical hike, except for the final section from the Skala summit to the Mytikas peak, which is a YDS class 3 rock scramble. It is estimated that 10,000 people climb Mount Olympus each year, most of them reaching only the Skolio summit. Most climbs of Mount Olympus start from the town of Litochoro, which took the name *City of Gods* because of its location at the foot of the mountain. From there a road goes to Prionia, where the hike begins at the bottom of the mountain.

Ancient and medieval sites

The whole region of Pieria's Olympus was declared archaeological and historical site for the preservation of its monumental and historical character. Five km away from the sea is Dion, sacred city of the ancient Macedons, dedicated to Zeus and the Twelve Olympians. Its prosperity lasted from the 5th century B.C. to the 5th century A.D. The excavations, continuing since 1928, have revealed numerous findings of the Macedonian, the Hellenistic and the Roman period. Currently there is a unique archaeological park of 200 hectares, with the ancient town and the sacred places of worship, outside its walls. Many statues and other invaluable items are kept in the nearby Dion's museum. Pimblia and Leivithra, two other towns in Olympus' region, are related to Orpheus and the "Orphic" mysteries. According to a tradition Orpheus, son of Apollo and Calliope (one of the Muses), taught here the mystic ceremonies of worship of Dionysus. By the sea, in a strategic position, at Macedonia's gates is located Platamon Castle, built between 7th and 10th century A.D. in the ancient town of Heracleia. To the north the ancient Pydna is located. Here, in 168 BC, the decisive battle between the Macedonians and the Romans took place. Between Pydna and Mount Olympus is a fortified bishops seat from the Bycantine aera called Louloudies.

Christian monuments

In Olympus' region there are also several Christian monuments, among them the highest-altitude chapel of Orthodox Christianity, that of Profitis Ilias, on the summit of the same name (2,803 m). It was built in the 16th century by Saint Dionysios of Olympus, who also founded the most significant monastery in the region. The Old Monastery of Dionysios (altitude 820 m) lies in Enipeas' gorge and is accessible by car from Litochoro. It was looted and burned by the Ottomans and in 1943 it was destroyed by the German invaders, who suspected it was a guerilla den. Nowadays it has been partially restored and operates as a dependency of the New Monastery of Dionysios, that is outside Litochoro. On Olympus' southern foot, in a dominant position (820 m) in Ziliana gorge, there is the Kanalon Monastery, 8 km away from Karya. It was founded in 1055 by the monks Damianos and Joakim and since 2001 it has been restored and operates as a convent. Further west, in the edge of Mavratza stream, at 1,020 m, there is the Agia Triada Sparmou Monastery, that flourished in the early 18th century, possessed great property and assisted to establish the famous Tsaritsani' school. It was abandoned in 1932, but in 2000 it was completely renovated and reopened as a male monastery, affiliated to Elassona's diocese.

Climate

Generally speaking Olympus' climate can be described as one of mediterranean type with continental influence. Its local variations is the result of the impact of the sea and the rugged relief of the region. In the lower locations (Litochoro and the foothills) the climate is typically mediterranean, i.e. hot and dry in the

Figure 116: *Christos Kakalos refuge and Profitis Ilias peak*

summer, while humid and cold in the winter. Higher it is more humid and severe, with more intense phenomena ; in these locations it often snows all over the winter, while raining and snowing is not unusual, even in the summer. The temperature varies in the winter from -10 °C to 10 °C and in the summer from 0 °C to 20 °C, while winds are an almost everyday occurrence. Generally the temperature falls 1 °C per 200 m of altitude. As the altitude rises, the phenomena are more intense and the variations of temperature and humidity are often sudden. The coastal northeast slopes of Olympus receive more rain than the continental northwest, so, as a result, there is a clear difference in vegetation. being more abundant in the first of them. Hottest month is August, while coldest is February.

The mountain's highest zone, over 2,000 metres, is snowcapped for about nine months (September to May). In some places the winds gather snow, 8–10 metres thick, ('anemosouria' in Greek), while in some deep ravines the snow is maintained all over the year (everlasting snow). For this Olympus' alpine region, recordings have been made in the 1960s in the highest-altitude weather station in Greece, that was established on the summit of Aghios Antonios (2,815 m), providing a number of interesting data for the mountain's climate. The average temperature is -5 °C in winter and 10 °C in summer. The average annual precipitation heights vary from 149 cm at Prionia (1,100 m) to 170 cm at Aghios Antonios, about half of them rainfall and hailstorms in summer and

Figure 117: *Beech forest along the path from Prionia to Spilios Agapitos refuge*

the rest snowfall in winter. The weather may change several times in the same day. In summer rainfalls are frequent, commonly as evening thunderstorms, many times accompanied by hail and strong winds. However water springs over 2,000 metres are scarce and visitors should ensure that they have always water and of course the necessary clothing for any weather conditions.

Flora

The research of Olympus' plants started in 1836, when the French botanist Aucher - Eloy studied them. According to this and later studies, the National Park of Olympus is considered one of the richest flora regions in Greece, with about 1,700 species and subspecies, that represent some 25% of Greek flora. Of them 187 are characterized as significant, 56 are Greek endemic and of them 23 are local endemic, i.e. they can be found only in Olympus, and 16 are rare in Greece or/and have there the limits of their spread within Northern Greece.

Most of those found in lower altitude are the common Mediterranean and central European species. Jankaea heldreichii, a plant relic of the Ice age, is of particular interest for the botanists. The intense diversity of the landscape, the varying orientation of the slopes and their position in relation to the sea affect locally Olympus' climate and so a local microclimate prevails, combined with the geological background and the soil favor the growth of particular vegetation types and biotopes. Generally Olympus' northeast side is densely forested, as it receives the most rainfall, while the southwest one has significantly sparser vegetation. Moreover, there is a clear sequence of the vegetation zones in accordance to altitude, in Olympus there is no such a regularity. It is due to the great microclimate variety, caused by the region's landscape.

Flora zones

In Olympus there are generally four sequent flora zones, but not clearly separated:

Mediterranean vegetation zone

In the altitude between 300 and 500 metres occurs the evergreen broadleaf trees' zone (maquis. Along with oak (Quercus ilex) and Greek strawberry tree there occur kermes oak, strawberry tree, Phillyrea latifolia, bay laurel, cedar and others. Of the deciduous species most common are flaxinus ulmus, Montpellier maple, Judas tree, terebinth, Cotinus coggygria and others.

Forest zone of beech, fir and mountain coniferous

The evergreen broadleaf trees' zone is gradually replaced by ecosystems of European black pine, that forms compact clusters, with no intermediate zone of deciduous oaks, although trees of these species occur sporadically within clusters of black pine. On the northern slopes of Xirolakos valley, at altitude between 600 and 700 metres, there is a high forest of downy oak of about 120 hectares.

The black pine dominates on the eastern and northern side of the mountain, between 500 and 1,700 metres. In this zone there is also hybrid fir in small groups and scrubs or small clumps, particularly in the lower region and in the sites Naoumi (west) and Stalamatia and Polykastro (east), where it is mixed with black pine and Bosnian pine. In this zone there is also beech. While in the neighboring mountains Pierians and Ossa it creates an extended vegetation zone, in Olympus it is restricted to small clusters, appearing as islets, mainly in more humid locations and the best soils. A particularly rich variety of trees and shrubs is found in Enipeas' gorge. One can see there elm, cherry plum, European yew, hazel, holly, cornus mas, manna ash, maple and a considerable variety of herbaceous plants. Gorges and ravines are covered by oriental planes, willows, black alders and riverside greenery.

Boreal coniferous zone

Typical species of this zone is Bosnian pine. This rare kind of pine occurs sporadically higher than 1,000 metres and gradually replaces the black pine, while over 1,400 metres it creates an almost unmixed forest. Over 2,000 metres the forest becomes sparser, reaching to 2,750 metres, thus creating the highest forest limit (highest limit of forest growth) in the Balkans, or even in Europe. Another feature of this zone is that over 2,500 metres the trees appear in a crawling form. The region, where Bosnian pine grows, is mostly dry and its slopes are rocky. There are no springs or water streams. The vegetation growing there is adapted to specific local conditions and represented by typical shrubs, graminaceous, chasmophytes etc., while the flora includes many endemic species of the Balkans.

No forest high mountains' zone (Alpine tundra)

Beyond Bosnian pine's zone follows an extensive zone, without trees, with alpine meadows, consisted by a mosaic of grassland ecosystems, depending on the topography, the slope and the orientation of the ground. In general, this alpine flora with more than 150 plant species, contains snow accumulation meadows, grassy swamps, alpine scree and rock crevices. On the meadows, the rocks and the steep slopes live most of the endemic Olympus' plants, among them some of the most beautiful wildflowers in Greece. Half of them are found only in the Balkans and 23 only in Olympus and nowhere else.

Olympus' endemic plants

1. Achillea ambrosiaca
2. Alyssum handelii
3. Asprerula muscosa
4. Aubrieta thessala
5. Campanula oreadum
6. Carum adamovicii
7. Centaurea incompleta
8. Centaurea litochorea
9. Centaurea transiens
10. Cerastrium theophrasti
11. Erysimum olympicum
12. Festuca olympica
13. Genísta sakellariadis
14. Jankaea heldreichii
15. Ligusticum olympicum
16. Melampyrum ciliatum
17. Poa thessala

Figure 118: *Salamander in Enipeas' gorge*

18. Potentilla deorum
19. Rynchosinapis nivalis
20. Silene dionysii
21. Silene oligantha
22. Veronica thessalica
23. Viola striis - notata

Fauna

Olympus' fauna, that has not been systematically studied so far, includes considerable variety and is marked by important, rare and endangered species. Large mammals, that lived formerly in the region, like deer, have disappeared. In ancient times there were lions (Pausanias), while at least until the 16th century there were bears (Life of St. Dionysios the Later). There have been recorded 32 species of mammals, including wild goat (Rυpicapra rupicapra balcanica), roe deer (Capreolus capreolus), wild boar (Sus scrofa), wildcat (Felis sylvestris), beech marten (Martes foina), red fox (vulpes vulpes) and red squirrel (Sciurus vulgaris). There have also been detected 108 species of birds (like sparrowhawk, cinereous vulture, rock partridge, white stork, rock dove, European robin, lanner falcon, peregrine falcon, tree falcon, golden eagle, short-toed snake eagle, booted eagle and hoopoe). Many of them, particularly the birds of prey, are scarce. In addition there are the common reptiles of Greek fauna (22 species like snakes, turtles, lizards, etc.) and some amphibians (8 species) in streams and seasonal ponds, as well as a great variety of insects, particularly butterflies.

National Park

Greece's highest mountain, dwelling of the Twelve Gods of antiquity, has been the first region in the country to be applied specific protective rules, by its declaration as a National Park in 1938. The aim of this declaration was "...the preservation in perpetuity of the natural environment of the region, i.e. of wild flora, fauna and natural landscape, as well as its cultural and other values...". In addition the declaration has aimed promoting scientific research along with environmental education for the public and tourist development in the region. Specific laws prohibit all forms of exploitation on the eastern side of the mountain in an area of about 4,000 hectares, that is the core of the Park. A wider region, around this core, has been designated "peripheral zone of the National Park", so that its managing and exploitation to be done so as not to adversely affect the core's protection. At present, the park has been expanded to 24,000 hectares. Administratively it belongs to Pieria's and Larissa's Prefectures and specifically to the municipalities Diou-Olympou and Katerinis (Pieria) and Tempon and Elassonas (Larissa). Its lowest altitude is 600 metres and its peak, Mytikas, at 2,918 metres. In 1981 UNESCO proclaimed Olympus "Biosphere Reserve". European Union has listed Olympus in the "Significant for Birdlife Regions of European Union". It is also registered in the list of Natura 2000 European Network as a **special protection area** and a **site of Community interest**.

Olympus' National Park's regulations

The Park is protected by specific legislation. Under the "Special Regulation" entrance to the Park is allowed only by the existing roads and traffic is allowed from sunrise to sunset only on formed paths. The visitor should also know that the following activities are not allowed :

- Entrance to children under 14 years unescorted.
- Parking in places other than the specific parking lots.
- Felling, humus transportation, rooting and collecting shrubs, plants and seeds.
- Hunting any animal by any means throughout the year.
- Collection and destruction of nests, eggs or chicks and general disturbance and destruction of fauna species.
- Damage to geological formations.
- Free movement of any animals accompanying visitors.

Access

Olympus' massif is found about in the middle of Continental Greece and is easy to approach from the national railway network on the Athens-Thessaloniki line and the secondary roads that connect towns and villages around the mountain, with the principal base for excursions being the town of Litochoro, where there is are many hotels and taverns. In addition, on Pieria's coastal zone there are many camp sites and lodgings. The nearest international airport is that of Thessaloniki, and railway stations are those of Litochoro, Katerini and Leptokarya. There is frequent service by KTEL buses and a taxi stand is in Litochoro's central square.

- By air: Makedonia Airport in Thessaloniki, 80 km away from Katerini and 150 km from Elassona.
- By train: Athens-Leptokarya (regular line), Athens-Katerini (Intercity) and Thessaloniki-Litocoro (Suburban).
- By bus: Athens-Katerini (437 km), Thessaloniki-Katerini (68 km), Katerini-Litochoro (25 km), Athens-Larissa (354 km), Larissa-Elassona, Elassona-Kokkinopilos (22 km), Elassona-Karya (36 km).
- By car:
- To Litochoro via Road P.A.TH.E. (412 km away from Athens, 93 km from Thessaloniki).
- To Elassona via National Roads Athens-Larissa (354 km) and Larissa-Elassona (38 km).
- To Karya via road Larissa-Rodia-Sykaminea-Karya (48 km, 6 km of them dirt road).
- To Karya via Road P.A.TH.E. and road Leptokarya-Karya (24 km), or Neos Panteleimonas-Kallipefki-Karya (37 km).
- To Kokkinopilos from Elassona via road Katerini-Foteina-Elassona (46 km) or via forest road Foteina-Petra-Kokkinopilos.

Refuges

- "Spilios Agapitos". The first and evener refuge of the region is at the site "Balkoni" (or "Exostis") at 2,100 metres (6,900 ft) altitude, in the center of Mavrologos and belongs to Greek Federation of Mountaineering Club (E.O.O.S). It provides 110 beds, water, electricity and telephone facilities, heating, blankets and a restaurant, managed by Maria Zolota and her husband Dionisis. It operates from May to October, 6-10 p.m.
- "Vrysopoules". The second refuge is westerly, behind Mavratzas' gorge at the site Vrysopoules (1,800 m) and is accessible also by car from location

Figure 119: *The path in the striking passage Laimou-Ghiosou (location Skourta) with high Olympus' peaks in the background*

Figure 120: *Olympus' refuge "Spilios Agapitos"*

Figure 121: *Olympus' refuge ""Christos Kakalos"*

Sparmos. It is managed by K.E.O.A.X (Army Skiers) since 1961. It provides 30 beds, a kitchen, water, electricity, central heating and a fireplace. It is open all year round, but to overnight a military license is required.
- "Christos Kakalos". It is at the southwest edge of Muses' Plateau (2,648 m), belongs to Greek Federation of Mountaineering and Climbing (E.O.O.A) that operates it from May to October and provides 18 beds, electricity, blankets, a kitchen and tank water. It is managed by one of the best experienced Greek climbers, the geologist Mihalis Stylas.
- "Stavros" ("Dimitrios Bountolas"). It is on Olympus' eastern side, 9.5 km on asphalt road away from Litochoro, at 930 metres (3,050 ft) altitude, in Dionysios Monastery forest. It belongs to the Greek Mountaineering Club of Thessaloniki, operates all year round, mainly as refreshment room and restaurant and can host 30 persons. It is managed by Doultsinou family.
- "Giosos Apostolidis". It is on Muses' Plateau (Diaselo - 2,760 m) and belongs to the Club of Greek mountaineers of Thessaloniki. It can accommodate 80 persons, it provides electricity, water, a fireplace and an equipped kitchen and it is open from June to October. It is managed by Dimitris Zorbas.
- "Petrostrouga". It is on the second, more common, path to Olympus (D10); it is the same path to reach to Muses' Plateau. This refuge is at 1,900 metres (6,200 ft) altitude, surrounded by perennial Bosnian pines.

It can accommodate 60 persons, it provides an equipped kitchen, electricity, water and a fireplace and it is open all year round. It is managed by the Hellenic Rescue Team. It provides organized medical equipment and one of the three emergency heliports in Olympus (the others at Skourta and Spilios Agapitos) and emergency wireless inside and out of the refuge.

Emergency refuges

- Aghios Antonios: emergency refuge on the summit Aghios Antonios (2,818 m). It is equipped with emergency items by the Hellenic Rescue Team. In the refuge there is wireless for communication in case of emergency.
- Kalyva tou Christaki: emergency refuge in "Megali Gourna" (2,430 m) along the Path E4, Kokinopilos - Skala. The refuge does not provide emergency items (there are only beds) but is only for protection from bad weather.
- *Kakalos*: emergency refuge at the "oropedio ton mouson"

It belongs to the Greek Mountaineering & Climbing Federation (www.eooa.gr) and is located at the eastern margin of the Plateau of Muses at an elevation of 2,650 metres (8,690 ft). It was named after Christos Kakalos the Olympus hunter and guide who together with the Swiss climbers Fred Boissonnas and Daniel Baud Bovy made the first recorded ascent to Olympus highest peak Mytikas on 2 August 1913. It has a capacity of 25 people and offers lodging, food and toilets. It is open from mid May to end of October and from December to mid April.

Coin

Mount Olympus and the national Park around it were selected as the main motif for the Greek National Park Olympus commemorative coin, minted in 2005.Wikipedia:Citation needed

On the reverse, the War of the Titans on Mount Olympus is portrayed along with flowering branches on the lower part of the coin. Above the scene is written, in Greek, "National Park Olympus".Wikipedia:Citation needed

External links

- Media related to Mount Olympus at Wikimedia Commons
- "Olympus". *Encyclopædia Britannica*. **20** (11th ed.). 1911.
- Mount Olympus website[278]
- Greek Mountain Flora[279]
- Management Agency of Olympus National Park[280]
- Laboratory of Geodesy - University of Thessaloniki:GPS measurement of the height of the peaks of Mountain Olympus[281]
- Detailed Informations about Ancient Sites, Monasteries, Museums and more.[282]

Dome of the Rock

Dome of the Rock

<indicator name="pp-default"> 🔒 </indicator>

Dome of the Rock
Qubbat As-Sakhrah قبّة الصخرة
Location within the Old City of Jerusalem

Basic information	
Location	Jerusalem
Geographic coordinates	31.7780°N 35.2354°E[283] Coordinates: 31.7780°N 35.2354°E[283]
Affiliation	Islam
Administration	Ministry of Awqaf (Jordan)
Architectural description	
Architectural type	Shrine
Architectural style	Umayyad, Abbasid, Ottoman
Date established	built 688–692, expanded 820s, restored 1020s, 1545–1566, 1721/2, 1817, 1874/5, 1959–1962, 1993.
Specifications	
Dome(s)	1
Minaret(s)	0

The **Dome of the Rock** (Arabic: قبة الصخرة *Qubbat al-Sakhrah*, Hebrew: כיפת הסלע *Kippat ha-Sela*) is an Islamic shrine located on the Temple Mount in the Old City of Jerusalem.

It was initially completed in 691 CE at the order of Umayyad Caliph Abd al-Malik during the Second Fitna, built on the site of the Roman temple of *Jupiter Capitolinus*, which had in turn been built on the site of the Second Jewish Temple, destroyed during the Roman Siege of Jerusalem in 70 CE. The original dome collapsed in 1015 and was rebuilt in 1022–23. The Dome of the Rock is in its core one of the oldest extant works of Islamic architecture.

Its architecture and mosaics were patterned after nearby Byzantine churches and palaces, although its outside appearance has been significantly changed in the Ottoman period and again in the modern period, notably with the addition of the gold-plated roof, in 1959–61 and again in 1993. The octagonal plan of the structure may also have been influenced by the Byzantine Church of the Seat of Mary (also known as *Kathisma* in Greek and *al-Qadismu* in Arabic) built between 451 and 458 on the road between Jerusalem and Bethlehem.

The site's great significance for Muslims derives from traditions connecting it to the creation of the world and to the belief that the Prophet Muhammad's Night Journey to heaven started from the rock at the center of the structure. The rock also bears great significance for Jews as the site of Abraham's attempted sacrifice of his son.

It has been called "Jerusalem's most recognizable landmark," and it is a UNESCO World Heritage Site, along with two nearby Temple Mount structures, the Western Wall, and the "Resurrection Rotunda" in the nearby Church of the Holy Sepulchre.

Figure 122: *Reconstruction of Herod's Temple as seen from the east (Holyland Model of Jerusalem, 1966)*

History

Pre-Islamic

The Dome of the Rock is situated in the center of the Temple Mount, the site of the Temple of Solomon and the Jewish Second Temple, which had been greatly expanded under Herod the Great in the 1st century BCE. Herod's Temple was destroyed in 70 CE by the Romans, and after the Bar Kokhba revolt in 135 CE, a Roman temple to *Jupiter Capitolinus* was built at the site.[284]

Jerusalem was ruled by the Christian Byzantine Empire throughout the 4th to 6th centuries. During this time, Christian pilgrimage to Jerusalem began to develop.[285] The Church of the Holy Sepulchre was built under Constantine in the 320s, but the Temple Mount was left undeveloped after a failed project of restoration of the temple under Julian the Apostate.[286]

Original construction

The Dome of the Rock is now mostly assumed to have been built by the order of Umayyad Caliph Abd al-Malik and his son and successor Al-Walid I. According to Sibt ibn al-Jawzi, construction started in 687. Construction cost was reportedly seven times the yearly tax income of Egypt.[287] A dedicatory inscription in Kufic script is preserved inside the dome. The date is recorded as AH 72 (691/2 CE), the year historians believe the construction of the original Dome was completed.[288] In this inscription, the name of al-Malik was deleted and replaced by the name of Abbasid caliph Al-Ma'mun. This alteration of the original inscription was first noted by Melchior de Vogüé in 1864.[289] Some scholars have suggested that the dome was added to an existing building, built

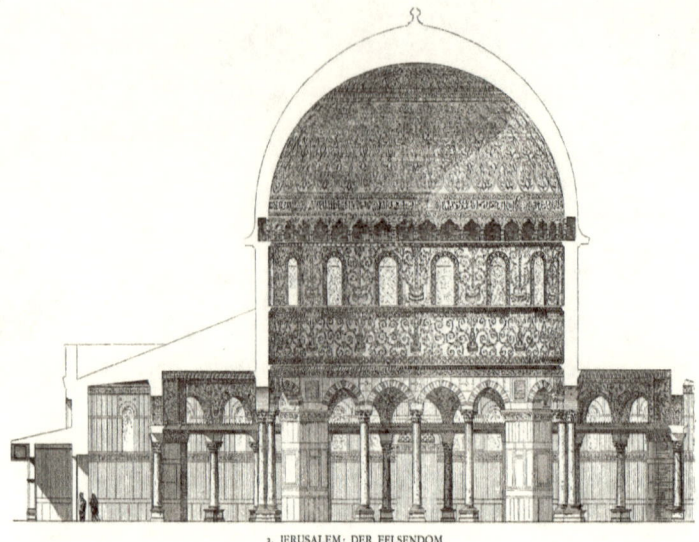

3. JERUSALEM: DER FELSENDOM.

Figure 123: *Cross section of the Dome (print from 1887, after the first detailed drawings of the Dome, made by Frederick Catherwood in 1833).*

either by Muawiyah I (r. 661–680),[290] or indeed a Byzantine building dating to before the Muslim conquest, built under Heraclius (r. 610–641).

Its architecture and mosaics were patterned after nearby Byzantine churches and palaces. The two engineers in charge of the project were Raja ibn Haywah, a Muslim theologian from Beit She'an and Yazid Ibn Salam, a non-Arab who was Muslim and a native of Jerusalem.

Shelomo Dov Goitein of the Hebrew University has argued that the Dome of the Rock was intended to compete with the many fine buildings of worship of other religions: "The very form of a rotunda, given to the *Qubbat as-Sakhra*, although it was foreign to Islam, was destined to rival the many Christian domes." K.A.C. Creswell in his book *The Origin of the Plan of the Dome of the Rock* notes that those who built the shrine used the measurements of the Church of the Holy Sepulchre. The diameter of the dome of the shrine is 20.20 m (66.3 ft) and its height 20.48 m (67.2 ft), while the diameter of the dome of the Church of the Holy Sepulchre is 20.90 m (68.6 ft) and its height 21.05 m (69.1 ft).

The structure was basically octagonal. It comprised a wooden dome, approximately 20 m (66 ft) in diameter, which was mounted on an elevated drum

Figure 124: *Depiction of the Templum Domini on the reverse side of the seal of the Knights Templar*

consisting of a circle of 16 piers and columns. Surrounding this circle was an octagonal arcade of 24 piers and columns.

Abbasids and Fatimids

The original construction was surrounded by open arcades, like the Dome of the Chain.Wikipedia:Citation neededWikipedia:Accuracy dispute#Disputed statement Under Abbasid caliph Al-Ma'mun (r. 813–833), an octagonal wall was added.Wikipedia:Citation neededWikipedia:Accuracy dispute#Disputed statement

The building was severely damaged by earthquakes in 808 and again in 846. The dome collapsed in an earthquake in 1015 and was rebuilt in 1022–23. The mosaics on the drum were repaired in 1027–28.[291]

Crusaders

For centuries Christian pilgrims were able to come and experience the Temple Mount, but escalating violence against pilgrims to Jerusalem (Al-Hakim bi-Amr Allah, who ordered the destruction of the Holy Sepulchre, was an example) instigated the Crusades.[292] The Crusaders captured Jerusalem in 1099 and the Dome of the Rock was given to the Augustinians, who turned it into a church, while the Al-Aqsa Mosque became a royal palace. The Knights Templar, active from c. 1119, identified the Dome of the Rock as the site of the Temple of Solomon and set up their headquarters in the Al-Aqsa Mosque adjacent to the Dome for much of the 12th century. The *Templum Domini*, as they called the Dome of the Rock, featured on the official seals of the Order's

Grand Masters (such as Everard des Barres and Renaud de Vichiers), and soon became the architectural model for round Templar churches across Europe.

Ayyubids and Mamluks

Jerusalem was recaptured by Saladin on 2 October 1187, and the Dome of the Rock was reconsecrated as a Muslim shrine. The cross on top of the dome was replaced by a crescent,Wikipedia:Citation needed and a wooden screen was placed around the rock below.Wikipedia:Citation needed Saladin's nephew al-Malik al-Mu'azzam Isa carried out other restorations within the building, and added the porch to the Al-Aqsa Mosque.Wikipedia:Citation needed

The Dome of the Rock was the focus of extensive royal patronage by the sultans during the Mamluk period, which lasted from 1250 until 1510.Wikipedia:Citation needed

Ottoman Empire (1517–1917)

During the reign of Suleiman the Magnificent (1520–1566) the exterior of the Dome of the Rock was covered with tiles. This work took seven years.Wikipedia:Citation needed

The interior of the dome is lavishly decorated with mosaic, faience and marble, much of which was added several centuries after its completion. It also contains Qur'anic inscriptions. Surah Ya Sin (the "Heart of the Quran") is inscribed across the top of the tile work and was commissioned in the 16th century by Suleiman the Magnificent. Al-Isra, the Surah 17 which tells the story of the *Isra* or Night Journey, is inscribed above this.

Adjacent to the Dome of the Rock, the Ottomans built the free-standing Dome of the Prophet in 1620. Large-scale renovation was undertaken during the reign of Mahmud II in 1817.

In a major restoration project undertaken in 1874–75 during the reign of the Ottoman Sultan Abdülaziz, all the tiles on the west and southwest walls of the octagonal part of the building were removed and replaced by copies that had been made in Turkey.[293]

Figure 125: *View from the north, Francis Bedford (1862)*

Figure 126: *West front in 1862. By this date many of the 16th century tiles were missing.*

Figure 127: *Interior showing mosaic decoration (1914)*

Figure 128: *Tiled façade (2013)*

Dome of the Rock

Figure 130: *1920s photograph*

Figure 129: *Interior showing rock (1915)*

Modern history

Haj Amin al-Husseini, appointed Grand Mufti by the British during the 1917 mandate of Palestine, along with Yaqub al-Ghusayn, implemented the restoration of the Dome of the Rock and the Al-Aqsa Mosque in Jerusalem.

Figure 131: *The reverse of a 1000-rials banknote from 1982.*

The Dome of the Rock was badly shaken during the 11 July 1927 Jericho earthquake, damaging many of the repairs that had taken place over previous years.

In 1955, an extensive program of renovation was begun by the government of Jordan, with funds supplied by Arab governments and Turkey. The work included replacement of large numbers of tiles dating back to the reign of Suleiman the Magnificent, which had become dislodged by heavy rain. In 1965, as part of this restoration, the dome was covered with a durable aluminium bronze alloy made in Italy that replaced the lead exterior. Before 1959, the dome was covered in blackened lead. In the course of substantial restoration carried out from 1959 to 1962, the lead was replaced by aluminum-bronze plates covered with gold leaf.

A few hours after the Israeli flag was hoisted over the Dome of the Rock in 1967 during the Six-Day War, Israelis lowered it on the orders of Moshe Dayan and invested the Muslim *waqf* (religious trust) with the authority to manage the Temple Mount / Haram al-Sharif, in order to "keep the peace".

In 1993, the golden dome covering was refurbished following a donation of USD 8.2 million by King Hussein of Jordan who sold one of his houses in London to fund the 80 kilograms of gold required.Wikipedia:Citation needed

The Dome of the Rock is depicted on the reverse of the Iranian 1000 rials banknote.[294]

Figure 132: *Sign at visitors entrance to Temple Mount*

Accessibility

The Dome is maintained by the Ministry of Awqaf in Amman, Jordan.

Until the mid-twentieth century, non-Muslims were not permitted in the area. Since 1967, non-Muslims have been permitted limited access; however non-Muslims are not permitted to pray on the Temple Mount, bring prayer books, or wear religious apparel. The Israeli police help enforce this.[295] Israel restricted access for a short time during 2012 of Palestinian residents of the West Bank to the Temple Mount. West Bank Palestinian men had to be over 35 to be eligible for a permit. Palestinian residents of Jerusalem, who hold Israeli residency cards, and Palestinians with Israeli citizenship are permitted unrestricted access.

Some Orthodox rabbis encourage Jews to visit the site, while most forbid entry to the compound lest there be a violation of Jewish law. Even rabbis who encourage entrance to the Temple Mount prohibit entrance to the actual Dome of the Rock.

Figure 133: *The Temple in Jerusalem depicted as the Dome of the Rock on the printer's mark of Marco Antonio Giustiniani, Venice 1545–52*

Religious significance

According to some Islamic scholars, the rock is the spot[296] from which the Islamic prophet Muhammad ascended to Heaven accompanied by the angel Gabriel. Further, Muhammad was taken here by Gabriel to pray with Abraham, Moses, and Jesus.[297] Other Islamic scholars believe that the Prophet ascended to Heaven from the Al-Aqsa Mosque.

Muslims believe the location of the Dome of the Rock to be the site mentioned in Sura 17 of the Qur'an, which tells the story of the Isra and Mi'raj, the miraculous Night Journey of Prophet Muhammad from Mecca to "the farthest mosque", where he leads prayers and rises to heaven to receive instructions from Allah. The Night Journey is mentioned in the Qur'an in a very brief form and is further elaborated by the hadiths. Caliph Umar ibn Al-Khattab (579–644) was advised by Ka'ab al-Ahbar, a Jewish rabbi who converted to Islam,[298] that "the farthest mosque" is identical with the site of the former Jewish Temples in Jerusalem.Wikipedia:Citation needed

The Foundation Stone and its surroundings is the holiest site in Judaism. Though Muslims now pray towards the Kaaba at Mecca, they onceWikipedia:Manual of Style/Dates and numbers faced the Temple Mount as the Jews do. Muhammad changed the direction of prayer for Muslims after a

Figure 134: *The Foundation Stone viewed from the dome. Photograph was taken between 1900 and 1920, before the removal of the surrounding iron grill.*

revelation from Allah. Jews traditionally regardedWikipedia:Manual of Style/Dates and numbers the location of the stone as the holiest spot on Earth, the site of the Holy of Holies during the Temple Period.

According to Jewish tradition, the stone is the site where Abraham prepared to sacrifice his son Isaac.

On the walls of the Dome of the Rock is an inscription in a mosaic frieze that includes an explicit rejection of the divinity of Christ, from Quran (19:33–35):

> 33. "So peace is upon me the day I was born, and the day I die, and the day I shall be raised alive!" 34. Such is Jesus, son of Mary. It is a statement of truth, about which they doubt. 35. It is not befitting to (the majesty of) Allah that He should take himself a child. Glory be to Him! when He determines a matter, He only says to it, "Be", and it is.

According to Goitein, the inscriptions decorating the interior clearly display a spirit of polemic against Christianity, whilst stressing at the same time the Qur'anic doctrine that Jesus was a true prophet. The formula *la sharika lahu* ("God has no companion") is repeated five times; the verses from Sura Maryam 19:35–37, which strongly reaffirm Jesus' prophethood to God, are quoted together with the prayer: *Allahumma salli ala rasulika wa'abdika 'Isa*

Figure 135: *Panorama of the Temple Mount, including Al-Aqsa Mosque and Dome of the Rock, from the Mount of Olives*

bin Maryam – "O Lord, send your blessings to your Prophet and Servant Jesus son of Mary." He believes that this shows that rivalry with Christendom, together with the spirit of Muslim mission to the Christians, was at work at the time of construction.

Groups such as the Temple Mount and Eretz Yisrael Faithful Movement wish to relocate the Dome to Mecca and replace it with a Third Temple.Wikipedia:Citation needed Many Israelis are ambivalent about the Movement's wishes. Some religious Jews, following rabbinic teaching, believe that the Temple should only be rebuilt in the messianic era, and that it would be presumptuous of people to force God's hand. However, some Evangelical Christians consider rebuilding of the Temple to be a prerequisite to Armageddon and the Second Coming.[299] Jeremy Gimpel, a US-born candidate for Habayit Hayehudi in the 2013 Israeli elections, caused a controversy when he was recorded telling a Fellowship Church evangelical group in Florida in 2011 to imagine the incredible experience that would follow were the Dome to be destroyed. All Christians would be immediately transported to Israel, he opined.[300]

Architectural homages

The Dome of the Rock has inspired the architecture of a number of buildings. These include the octagonal Church of St. Giacomo in Italy, the Mausoleum of Sultan Suleiman the Magnificent in Istanbul, the octagonal Moorish Revival style Rumbach Street Synagogue in Budapest, and the New Synagogue in Berlin, Germany. It was long believed by Christians that the Dome of the Rock echoed the architecture of the Temple in Jerusalem, as can be seen in Raphael's *The Marriage of the Virgin* and in Perugino's *Marriage of the Virgin*.

References

- Creswell, K.A.C. (1924). *The Origin of the Plan of the Dome of the Rock (2 Volumes)*. London: British School of Archaeology in Jerusalem. OCLC 5862604[301].

- Peterson, Andrew (1994). *Dictionary of Islamic Architecture*. London: Routledge. ISBN 0-415-06084-2
- Braswell, G. (1996). *Islam – Its Prophets, People, Politics and Power*. Nashville, TN: Broadman and Holman Publishers.
- Clermont-Ganneau, Charles (1899). "Chapter VIII The Kubbet es Sakhra"[302]. *Archaeological Researches in Palestine During the Years 1873–1874*. Volume 1. London: Committee of the Palestine Exploration Fund. pp. 179–227.
- Necipoğlu, Gülru (2008). "The Dome of the Rock as palimpsest: 'Abd al-Malik's grand narrative and Sultan Süleyman's glosses"[303] (PDF). In Necipoğlu, Gülru; Bailey, Julia. *Muqarnas: An Annual on the Visual Culture of the Islamic World*. Volume 25. Leiden: Brill. pp. 17–105. ISBN 978-900417327-9.
- Ali, A. (1946). *The Holy Qur'an – Translation and Commentary*. Bronx, NY: Islamic Propagation Centre International.
- Islam, M. Anwarul; Al-Hamad, Zaid (2007). "The Dome of the Rock: origin of its octagonal plan". *Palestine Exploration Quarterly*. **139** (2): 109–128. doi: 10.1179/003103207x194145[304].
- Christoph Luxenberg: *Neudeutung der arabischen Inschrift im Felsendom zu Jerusalem*. In: Karl-Heinz Ohlig / Gerd-R. Puin (Hg.): *Die dunklen Anfänge. Neue Forschungen zur Entstehung und frühen Geschichte des Islam*, Berlin (Verlag Hans Schiler) 2005, S. 124–147. English version: "A New Interpretation of the Arabic Inscription in Jerusalem's Dome of the Rock". In: Karl-Heinz Ohlig / Gerd-R. Puin (eds.): *The Hidden Origins of Islam: New Research into Its Early History*, Amherst, N.Y. (Prometheus Books) 2010
- Vogüé, Melchior de (1864). *Le Temple de Jérusalem : monographie du Haram-ech-Chérif, suivie d'un essai sur la topographie de la Ville-sainte*[305] (in French). Paris: Noblet & Baudry.

Further reading

- Grabar, Oleg (2006). *The Dome of the Rock*. Cambridge, Mass.: Belknap Press. ISBN 978-0-674-02313-0.
- Flood, Finbarr B. (2000). "The Ottoman windows in the Dome of the Rock and the Aqsa Mosque"[306] (PDF). In Auld, Sylvia; Hillenbrand, Robert. *Ottoman Jerusalem: The Living City: 1517–1917*. Volume 1. London: Altajir World of Islam Trust. pp. 431–463. ISBN 978-1-901435-03-0.
- Kessler, Christel (1964). "Above the ceiling of the outer ambulatory in the Dome of the Rock in Jerusalem". *Journal of the Royal Asiatic Society of Great Britain and Ireland* (3/4): 83–94. JSTOR 25202759[307].

- Kessler, Christel (1970). "'Abd Al-Malik's inscription in the Dome of the Rock: a reconsideration". *Journal of the Royal Asiatic Society of Great Britain and Ireland* (1): 2–14. JSTOR 25203167[308].
- Richmond, Ernest Tatham (1924). *The Dome of the Rock in Jerusalem: A Description of its Structure and Decoration*[309]. Oxford: Clarendon Press.
- St. Laurent, Beatrice (1998). "The Dome of the Rock and the politics of restoration"[310]. *Bridgewater Review*. **17** (2): 14–20.

External links

Wikimedia Commons has media related to *Dome of the Rock*.

- "Qubba al-Sakhra, Jerusalem"[311]. Archnet Digital Archive.
- Dome of the Rock[312] Sacred sites
- The Dome of the Rock in Jerusalem[313] Masterpieces of Islamic Architecture
- Ochs, Christoph (2010). "Dome of the Rock"[314]. *Bibledex in Israel*. Brady Haran for the University of Nottingham.
- Allen, Terry (2014). "The Marble Revetment of the Piers of the Dome of the Rock"[315]. Occidental, CA: Solipsist Press. Retrieved 26 March 2017.

Western Wall

Western Wall

Western Wall
HaKotel HaMa'aravi
A view of the Western Wall.
Shown within Jerusalem

Alternate name	Wailing Wall Kotel Al-Buraq Wall
Location	Jerusalem
Coordinates	31.7767°N 35.2345°E[316]Coordinates: 31.7767°N 35.2345°E[316]
Type	Ancient limestone wall
Part of	Temple Mount
Length	488 metres (1,601 ft)
Height	exposed: 19 metres (62 ft)
History	
Builder	Herod the Great
Material	Limestone
Founded	19 BCE
Site notes	
Condition	Preserved

The **Western Wall**, **Wailing Wall** or **Kotel** (Hebrew: הַכֹּתֶל הַמַּעֲרָבִי Wikipedia:Media helpFile:He-Kotel.ogg, translit.: *HaKotel HaMa'aravi*; Ashkenazic pronunciation: *HaKosel HaMa'arovi*; Arabic: حائط البراق, translit.: *Ḥā'iṭ al-Burāq*, translat.: the Buraq Wall, or Arabic: المبكى *al-Mabkā*: the Place of Weeping) is an ancient limestone wall in the Old City of Jerusalem. It is a relatively small segment of a far longer ancient retaining wall, known also in its entirety as the "Western Wall". The wall was originally erected as part of the expansion of the Second Jewish Temple begun by Herod the Great, which resulted in the encasement of the natural, steep hill known to Jews and Christians as the Temple Mount, in a large rectangular structure topped by a huge flat platform, thus creating more space for the Temple itself and its auxiliary buildings.

The Western Wall is considered holy due to its connection to the Temple Mount. Because of the Temple Mount entry restrictions, the Wall is the holiest place where Jews are permitted to pray, though it is not the holiest site in the Jewish faith, which lies behind it. The original, natural and irregular-shaped Temple Mount was gradually extended to allow for an ever-larger Temple compound to be built at its top. This process was finalised by Herod, who enclosed the Mount with an almost rectangular set of retaining walls, built to support extensive substructures and earth fills needed to give the natural hill a geometrically regular shape. On top of this box-like structure Herod built a vast paved esplanade which surrounded the Temple. Of the four retaining walls, the western one is considered to be closest to the former Temple, which makes it the most sacred site recognised by Judaism outside the former Temple Mount esplanade. Just over half the wall's total height, including its 17 courses located below street level, dates from the end of the Second Temple period, and is commonly believed to have been built around 19 BCE by Herod the Great, although recent excavations indicate that the work was not finished by the time Herod died in 4 BCE. The very large stone blocks of the lower courses are Herodian, the courses of medium-sized stones above them were added during the Umayyad era, while the small stones of the uppermost courses are of more recent date, especially from the Ottoman period.

The term Western Wall and its variations are mostly used in a narrow sense for the section traditionally used by Jews for prayer, and it has also been called the "Wailing Wall", referring to the practice of Jews weeping at the site over the destruction of the Temples. During the period of Christian Roman rule over Jerusalem (ca. 324–638), Jews were completely barred from Jerusalem except to attend Tisha be-Av, the day of national mourning for the Temples, and on this day the Jews would weep at their holy places. The term "Wailing Wall" was thus almost exclusively used by Christians, and was revived in the period of non-Jewish control between the establishment of British Rule in 1920 and the Six-Day War in 1967. The term "Wailing Wall" is not used by Jews, and increasingly not by many others who consider it derogatory.

In a broader sense, "Western Wall" can refer to the entire 488-metre-long (1,601 ft.) retaining wall on the western side of the Temple Mount. The classic portion now faces a large plaza in the Jewish Quarter, near the southwestern corner of the Temple Mount, while the rest of the wall is concealed behind structures in the Muslim Quarter, with the small exception of a 25 ft (8 m) section, the so-called Little Western Wall. The segment of the Western retaining wall traditionally used for Jewish liturgy, known as the "Western Wall", derives its particular importance to it having never been fully obscured by medieval buildings, and displaying much more of the original Herodian stonework than the "Little Western Wall". In religious terms, the "Little Western Wall" is presumed to be even closer to the Holy of Holies and thus to the "presence of God" (Shechina), and the underground Warren's Gate, which has been out of reach since the 12th century, even more so.

Whilst the wall was considered Muslim property as an integral part of the Haram esh-Sharif and waqf property of the Moroccan Quarter, a right of Jewish prayer and pilgrimage existed as part of the Status Quo.

The earliest source mentioning this specific site as a place of worship is from the 16th century. The previous sites used by Jews for mourning the destruction of the Temple, during periods when access to the city was prohibited to them, lay to the east, on the Mount of Olives and in the Kidron Valley below it. From the mid-19th century onwards, attempts to purchase rights to the wall

Figure 136: *Ashlar stones of the Western Wall*

and its immediate area were made by various Jews, but none was successful. With the rise of the Zionist movement in the early 20th century, the wall became a source of friction between the Jewish and Muslim communities, the latter being worried that the wall could be used to further Jewish claims to the Temple Mount and thus Jerusalem. During this period outbreaks of violence at the foot of the wall became commonplace, with a particularly deadly riot in 1929 in which 133 Jews were killed and 339 injured. After the 1948 Arab-Israeli War the Eastern portion of Jerusalem was occupied by Jordan. Under Jordanian control Jews were completely expelled from the Old City including the Jewish quarter, and Jews were barred from entering the Old City for 19 years, effectively banning Jewish prayer at the site of the Western Wall. This period ended on June 10, 1967, when Israel gained control of the site following the Six-Day War. Three days after establishing control over the Western Wall site the Moroccan Quarter was bulldozed by Israeli authorities to create space for what is now the Western Wall plaza.[317]

Etymology

Charles Wilson, 1881

Early Jewish texts referred to a "western wall of the Temple",[318] but there is doubt whether the texts were referring to the outer, retaining wall called today

Figure 137: *Panorama of the Western Wall with the Dome of the Rock (left) and al-Aqsa mosque (right) in the background*

"the Western Wall", or to the western wall of the actual Temple. The earliest Jewish use of the Hebrew term "ha-kotel ha-ma'aravi", "the Western Wall", as referring to the wall visible today, was by the 11th-century poet Ahimaaz ben Paltiel. The name "Wailing Wall", and descriptions such as "wailing place", appeared regularly in English literature during the 19th century.[319] The name *Mur des Lamentations* was used in French and *Klagemauer* in German. This term itself was a translation of the Arabic *el-Mabka*, or "Place of Weeping", the traditional Arabic term for the wall. This description stemmed from the Jewish practice of coming to the site to mourn and bemoan the destruction of the Temple.

At some time in the 19th century, the Arabs began referring to the wall as the al-Buraq Wall. This was based on the tradition that inside the wall was the place where Muhammad tethered his miraculous winged steed, al-Buraq.Wikipedia:Citation needed The tradition on which this is based only states that the Prophet, or the angel Jibra'il (Gabriel), tethered the steed at the gate of the mosque, meaning: at the gate of the Temple Mount. The location of the entry gate identified as the one used by Muhammad varied throughout the centuries, from the eastern and southern walls, to the southwest corner, and finally at the western wall, and specifically at Barclay's Gate immediately adjacent to the "Wailing Place" of the Jews.[320] Israeli archaeologist Meir Ben-Dov concluded that the Muslim association with Western Wall began in the late nineteenth century in response to renewed Jewish identification with the site.

Location and dimensions

The Western Wall commonly refers to a 187-foot (57 m) exposed section of ancient wall situated on the western flank of the Temple Mount. This section faces a large plaza and is set aside for prayer. In its entirety, however, the

Figure 138: *The Western Wall and Dome of the Rock*

above-ground portion of the Western Wall stretches for 1,600 feet (488 m), most of which is hidden behind residential structures built along its length. Other revealed sections include the southern part of the Wall which measures approximately 80 metres (262 ft) and another much shorter section known as the Little Western Wall which is located close to the Iron Gate. The wall functions as a retaining wall, supporting and enclosing the ample substructures built by Herod the Great around 19 BCE. Herod's project was to create an artificial extension to the small quasi-natural plateau on which the First and Second Temples stood, transforming it into the almost rectangular, wide expanse of the Temple Mount visible today.

At the Western Wall Plaza, the total height of the Wall from its foundation is estimated at 105 feet (32 m), with the exposed section standing approximately 62 feet (19 m) high. The Wall consists of 45 stone courses, 28 of them above ground and 17 underground. The first seven visible layers are from the Herodian period. This section of wall is built from enormous meleke limestone blocks, possibly quarried at either Zedekiah's Cave situated under the Muslim Quarter of the Old City or at Ramat Shlomo 4 kilometres (2.5 mi) northwest of the Old City. Most of them weigh between 2 and 8 short tons (1.8 and 7.3 t) each, but others weigh even more, with one extraordinary stone located slightly north of Wilson's Arch measuring 13 metres (43 ft) and weighing approximately 517 tonnes (570 short tons). Each of these ashlars is framed by fine-chiseled borders. The margins themselves measure between 5 and 20 centimetres (2 and 8 in) wide, with their depth measuring 1.5 centimetres (0.59 in). In the Herodian period, the upper 10 metres (33 ft) of wall were 1 metre (39 in) thick and served as the outer wall of the double colonnade of the Temple platform. This upper section was decorated with pilasters, the remainder of which were destroyed when the Byzantines reconquered Jerusalem from the Persians in 628.

The next four courses, consisting of smaller plainly dressed stones, date from the Umayyad period (Muslim, 8th century). Above that are 16–17 courses of small stones from the Mamluk period (Muslim, 13–16th century) and later.

Accessibility

People with disabilities

The plaza and Wall are accessible to wheelchairs and people with mobility difficulties via either the Dung Gate or Jaffa Gate.[321] Access directly from the Jewish Quarter of the Old City is via "a considerable number of steep steps". Access for cars is very restricted, "and parking is a nightmare" so disabled visitors are advised to arrive by taxi or public transportation. Guide dogs are permitted.

Transgender individuals

In January 2015 a transgender Jewish woman, Kay Long, was denied access to the Wall, first by the women's section and then by the men's section.[322,323] Long's presence was prevented by "modesty police" at women's section who are not associated with the rabbi of the Western Wall or the site administration. They are a group of female volunteers who guard the entrance to the women's section preventing entry to visitors who are not dressed to their idea of Orthodox modesty standards for women. The director of Jerusalem's Open House, a community center for the lesbian, gay, bisexual and transgender community, noted that Long's experience was not unique. "Gender separation at the Western Wall is harmful for transgender people. This is not the first story that we know of with transgender religious people that wanted to go to the Western Wall and pray and couldn't," said Elinor Sidi, who expects that the battle for access to the Western Wall for the LGBTQ community will be a long and difficult one.[324] It was later asserted that Kay Long would have been permitted in the women's section except for her clothing. "It was not an issue of her gender, but the way she was dressed."

Chotel Maarbi, or West Wall.

Figure 139: *Engraving, 1850*

History

Construction – 19 BCE

According to the Hebrew Bible, Solomon's Temple was built atop what is known as the Temple Mount in the 10th century BCE and destroyed by the Babylonians in 586 BCE,[325] and the Second Temple completed and dedicated in 516 BCE. Around 19 BCE Herod the Great began a massive expansion project on the Temple Mount. In addition to fully rebuilding and enlarging the Temple, he artificially expanded the platform on which it stood, doubling it in size. Today's Western Wall formed part of the retaining perimeter wall of this platform. In 2011, Israeli archaeologists announced the surprising discovery of Roman coins minted well after Herod's death, found under the foundation stones of the wall. The excavators came upon the coins inside a ritual bath that predates Herod's building project, which was filled in to create an even base for the wall and was located under its southern section. This seems to indicate that Herod did not finish building the entire wall by the time of his death in 4 BCE. The find confirms the description by historian Josephus Flavius, which states that construction was finished only during the reign of King Agrippa II, Herod's great-grandson. Given Josephus' information, the surprise mainly regarded the fact that an unfinished retaining wall in this area could also mean that at least parts of the splendid Royal Stoa and the monumental staircase leading up to it could not have been completed during Herod's lifetime. Also surprising was the fact that the usually very thorough Herodian builders had cut corners by filling in the ritual bath, rather than placing the foundation course directly onto the much firmer bedrock. Some scholars are doubtful of the interpretation and have offered alternative explanations, such as, for example, later repair work.

Herod's Temple was destroyed by the Romans, along with the rest of Jerusalem, in 70 CE,[326] during the First Jewish-Roman War.

Roman Empire and rise of Christianity – 100–500 CE

In the early centuries of the Common Era, after the Roman defeat of the Bar Kokhba revolt in 135 CE, Jews were banned from Jerusalem. There is some evidence that Roman emperors in the 2nd and 3rd centuries did permit them to visit the city to worship on the Mount of Olives and sometimes on the Temple Mount itself. When the empire became Christian under Constantine I, they were given permission to enter the city once a year, on the ninth day of the month of Av, to lament the loss of the Temple at the wall. The Bordeaux Pilgrim, written in 333 CE, suggests that it was probably to the perforated stone or the Rock of Moriah, "to which the Jews come every year and anoint it, bewail themselves with groans, rend their garments, and so depart". This was because an Imperial decree from Rome barred Jews from living in Jerusalem. Just once per year they were permitted to return and bitterly grieve about the fate of their people. Comparable accounts survive, including those by the Church Father, Gregory of Nazianzus and by Jerome in his commentary to Zephaniah written in 392 CE. In the 4th century, Christian sources reveal that the Jews encountered great difficulty in buying the right to pray near the Western Wall, at least on the 9th of Av. In 425 CE, the Jews of the Galilee wrote to Byzantine empress Aelia Eudocia seeking permission to pray by the ruins of the Temple. Permission was granted and they were officially permitted to resettle in Jerusalem.

Middle Ages – 500–1500

Several Jewish authors of the 10th and 11th centuries write about the Jews resorting to the Western Wall for devotional purposes.[327] Ahimaaz relates that Rabbi Samuel ben Paltiel (980-1010) gave money for oil at "the sanctuary at the Western Wall." Benjamin of Tudela (1170) wrote "In front of this place is the Western Wall, which is one of the walls of the Holy of Holies. This is called the Gate of Mercy, and hither come all the Jews to pray before the Wall in the open court." The account gave rise to confusion about the actual location of Jewish worship and some suggest that Benjamin in fact referred to the Eastern Wall along with its Gate of Mercy. While Nahmanides (d. 1270)

Figure 140: *Wailing Wall, Jerusalem, by Gustav Bauernfeind (19th century).*

did not mention a synagogue near the Western Wall in his detailed account of the temple site, shortly before the Crusader period a synagogue existed at the site. Obadiah of Bertinoro (1488) states "the Westen Wall, part of which is still standing, is made of great, thick stones, larger than any I have seen in buildings of antiquity in Rome or in other lands."[328]

Shortly after Saladin's 1187 siege of the city, in 1193, the sultan's son and successor al-Afdal established the land adjacent to the wall as a charitable trust. It was named after an important mystic Abu Madyan Shu'aib and dedicated to Moroccan settlers who had taken up residence there. Houses were built only 4 metres (13 ft) away from the wall. The first mention of the Islamic tradition that Buraq was tethered at the site is from the 14th century. A manuscript by Ibn Furkah, (d. 1328), refers to Bab al-Nab (lit. "Gate of the Prophet"),Wikipedia:Accuracy dispute#Disputed statement an old name for a gate along the southwestern wall of the Haram al-Sharif.

Ottoman period – 1517–1917

In 1517, the Turkish Ottomans conquered Jerusalem from the Mamluks who had held it since 1250 and various folktales relate Sultan Suleiman the Magnificent's quest to locate the Temple site and his order to have the area "swept and sprinkled, and the Western Wall washed with rosewater" upon its discovery.

In the late 16th century, Suleiman ordered the construction of an imposing fortress wall to be built around the entire city, which still stands today. At the time, Jews received official permission to worship at the site and Ottoman architect Mimar Sinan built an oratory for them there.[329,330] In 1625 organised prayers at the Wall are mentioned for the first time.

Over the centuries, land close to the Wall became built up. Public access to the Wall was through the Moroccan Quarter, a labyrinth of narrow alleyways. In May 1840 a firman issued by Ibrahim Pasha forbade the Jews to pave the passageway in front of the Wall. It also cautioned them against "raising their voices and displaying their books there." They were, however, allowed "to pay visits to it as of old."

Rabbi Joseph Schwarz writing in the mid-19th-century records:

> *This wall is visited by all our brothers on every feast and festival; and the large space at its foot is often so densely filled up, that all cannot perform their devotions here at the same time. It is also visited, though by less numbers, on every Friday afternoon, and by some nearly every day. No one is molested in these visits by the Mahomedans, as we have a very old firman from the Sultan of Constantinople that the approach shall not be denied to us, though the Porte obtains for this privilege a special tax, which is, however, quite insignificant.*

Over time the increased numbers of people gathering at the site resulted in tensions between the Jewish visitors who wanted easier access and more space, and the residents, who complained of the noise.[331] This gave rise to Jewish attempts at gaining ownership of the land adjacent to the Wall.

In the late 1830s a wealthy Jew named Shemarya Luria attempted to purchase houses near the Wall, but was unsuccessful, as was Jewish sage Abdullah of Bombay who tried to purchase the Western Wall in the 1850s.[332] In 1869 Rabbi Hillel Moshe Gelbstein settled in Jerusalem. He arranged that benches and tables be brought to the Wall on a daily basis for the study groups he organised and the minyan which he led there for years. He also formulated a plan whereby some of the courtyards facing the Wall would be acquired, with the intention of establishing three synagogues – one each for the Sephardim, the Hasidim and the Perushim. He also endeavoured to re-establish an ancient practice of "guards of honour", which according to the mishnah in Middot, were positioned around the Temple Mount. He rented a house near the Wall and paid men to stand guard there and at various other gateways around the mount. However this set-up lasted only for a short time due to lack of funds or because of Arab resentment. In 1874, Mordechai Rosanes paid for the repaving of the alleyway adjacent to the wall.

Figure 141: *Photograph of the Western Wall, 1870*

In 1887 Baron Rothschild conceived a plan to purchase and demolish the Moroccan Quarter as "a merit and honor to the Jewish People." The proposed purchase was considered and approved by the Ottoman Governor of Jerusalem, Rauf Pasha, and by the Mufti of Jerusalem, Mohammed Tahir Husseini. Even after permission was obtained from the highest secular and Muslim religious authority to proceed, the transaction was shelved after the authorities insisted that after demolishing the quarter no construction of any type could take place there, only trees could be planted to beautify the area. Additionally the Jews would not have full control over the area. This meant that they would have no power to stop people from using the plaza for various activities, including the driving of mules, which would cause a disturbance to worshippers. Other reports place the scheme's failure on Jewish infighting as to whether the plan would foster a detrimental Arab reaction.

In 1895 Hebrew linguist and publisher Rabbi Chaim Hirschensohn became entangled in a failed effort to purchase the Western Wall and lost all his assets. Even the attempts of the Palestine Land Development Company to purchase the environs of the Western Wall for the Jews just before the outbreak of World War I never came to fruition. In the first two months following the Ottoman Empire's entry into the First World War, the Turkish governor of Jerusalem, Zakey Bey, offered to sell the Moroccan Quarter, which consisted of about 25 houses, to the Jews in order to enlarge the area available to them for prayer. He

Figure 142: *Jews' Wailing Place, Jerusalem, 1891*

requested a sum of £20,000 which would be used to both rehouse the Muslim families and to create a public garden in front of the Wall. However, the Jews of the city lacked the necessary funds. A few months later, under Muslim Arab pressure on the Turkish authorities in Jerusalem, Jews became forbidden by official decree to place benches and light candles at the Wall. This sour turn in relations was taken up by the Chacham Bashi who managed to get the ban overturned. In 1915 it was reported that Djemal Pasha closed off the wall to visitation as a sanitary measure.

Firmans issued regarding the Wall

Year	Issued by	Content
c. 1560	Suleiman the Magnificent	Official recognition of the right of Jews to pray by the Wall.
1840	Ibrahim Pasha of Egypt	Forbidding the Jews to pave the passage in front of the Wall. It also cautioned them against "raising their voices and displaying their books there." They were however allowed "to pay visits to it as of old."
1841*	Ibrahim Pasha of Egypt	"Of the same bearing and likewise to two others of 1893 and 1909."

1889*	Abdul Hamid II	That there shall be no interference with the Jews' places of devotional visits and of pilgrimage, that are situated in the localities which are dependent on the Chief Rabbinate, nor with the practice of their ritual.
1893*		Confirming firman of 1889.
1909*		Confirming firman of 1889.
1911	Administrative Council of the Liwa	Prohibiting the Jews from certain appurtenances at the Wall.

* *These firmans were cited by the Jewish contingent at the International Commission, 1930, as proof for rights at the Wall. Muslim authorities responded by arguing that historic sanctions of Jewish presence were acts of tolerance shown by Muslims, who, by doing so, did not concede any positive rights.*

British rule – 1917–48

In December 1917, Allied forces under Edmund Allenby captured Jerusalem from the Turks. Allenby pledged "that every sacred building, monument, holy spot, shrine, traditional site, endowment, pious bequest, or customary place of prayer of whatsoever form of the three religions will be maintained and protected according to the existing customs and beliefs of those to whose faith they are sacred".

In 1919 Zionist leader Chaim Weizmann approached the British Military Governor of Jerusalem, Colonel Sir Ronald Storrs, and offered between £75,000 and £100,000 (approx. £5m in modern terms) to purchase the area at the foot of the Wall and rehouse the occupants. Storrs was enthusiastic about the idea because he hoped some of the money would be used to improve Muslim education. Although they appeared promising at first, negotiations broke down after strong Muslim opposition. Storrs wrote two decades later:

> "The acceptance of the proposals, had it been practicable, would have obviated years of wretched humiliations, including the befouling of the Wall and pavement and the unmannerly braying of the tragi-comic Arab band during Jewish prayer, and culminating in the horrible outrages of 1929"

In early 1920, the first Jewish-Arab dispute over the Wall occurred when the Muslim authorities were carrying out minor repair works to the Wall's upper courses. The Jews, while agreeing that the works were necessary, appealed to the British that they be made under supervision of the newly formed Department of Antiquities, because the Wall was an ancient relic.

In 1926 an effort was made to lease the Maghrebi *waqf*, which included the wall, with the plan of eventually buying it. Negotiations were begun in secret by the Jewish judge Gad Frumkin, with financial backing from American

Figure 143: *Jewish Legion soldiers at the Western Wall after British conquest of Jerusalem, 1917*

Figure 144: *1920. From the collection of the National Library of Israel.*

millionaire Nathan Straus. The chairman of the Palestine Zionist Executive, Colonel F. H. Kisch, explained that the aim was "quietly to evacuate the Moroccan occupants of those houses which it would later be necessary to demolish" to create an open space with seats for aged worshippers to sit on. However, Straus withdrew when the price became excessive and the plan came to nothing. The Va'ad Leumi, against the advice of the Palestine Zionist Executive, demanded that the British expropriate the wall and give it to the Jews, but the British refused.

In 1928 the Zionist Organisation reported that John Chancellor, High Commissioner of Palestine, believed that the Western Wall should come under Jewish control and wondered "why no great Jewish philanthropist had not bought it yet".

September 1928 disturbances

In 1922, a status quo agreement issued by the mandatory authority forbade the placing of benches or chairs near the Wall. The last occurrence of such a ban was in 1915, but the Ottoman decree was soon retracted after intervention of the Chacham Bashi. In 1928 the District Commissioner of Jerusalem, Edward Keith-Roach, acceded to an Arab request to implement the ban. This led to a British officer being stationed at the Wall making sure that Jews were prevented from sitting. Nor were Jews permitted to separate the sexes with a screen. In practice, a flexible modus vivendi had emerged and such screens had been put up from time to time when large numbers of people gathered to pray.

On September 24, 1928, the Day of Atonement, British police resorted to removing by force a screen used to separate men and women at prayer. Women who tried to prevent the screen being dismantled were beaten by the police, who used pieces of the broken wooden frame as clubs. Chairs were then pulled out from under elderly worshipers. The episode made international news and Jews the world over objected to the British action. Yosef Chaim Sonnenfeld, the Chief Rabbi of the ultraorthodox Jews in Jerusalem, issued a protest letter on behalf of his community, the Edah HaChareidis, and Agudas Yisroel strongly condemning the desecration of the holy site. Various communal leaders called for a general strike. A large rally was held in the Etz Chaim Yeshiva, following which an angry crowd attacked the local police station in which they believed Douglas Valder Duff, the British officer involved, was sheltering.

Commissioner Edward Keith-Roach described the screen as violating the Ottoman status quo that forbade Jews from making any construction in the Western Wall area. He informed the Jewish community that the removal had been carried out under his orders after receiving a complaint from the Supreme Muslim Council. The Arabs were concerned that the Jews were trying to extend

Figure 145: *The placing of a Mechitza similar to the one in the picture was the catalyst for confrontation between the Arabs, Jews and Mandate authorities in 1928.*

their rights at the wall and with this move, ultimately intended to take possession of the Al-Aqsa Mosque. The British government issued an announcement explaining the incident and blaming the Jewish beadle at the Wall. It stressed that the removal of the screen was necessary, but expressed regret over the ensuing events.

A widespread Arab campaign to protest against presumed Jewish intentions and designs to take possession of the Al Aqsa Mosque swept the country and a "Society for the Protection of the Muslim Holy Places" was established. The Vaad Leumi responding to these Arab fears declared in a statement that "We herewith declare emphatically and sincerely that no Jew has ever thought of encroaching upon the rights of Moslems over their own Holy places, but our Arab brethren should also recognise the rights of Jews in regard to the places in Palestine which are holy to them." The committee also demanded that the British administration expropriate the wall for the Jews.

From October 1928 onward, Mufti Amin al-Husayni organised a series of measures to demonstrate the Arabs' exclusive claims to the Temple Mount and its environs. He ordered new construction next to and above the Western Wall. The British granted the Arabs permission to convert a building adjoining the Wall into a mosque and to add a minaret. A muezzin was appointed to perform the Islamic call to prayer and Sufi rites directly next to the Wall. These were seen as a provocation by the Jews who prayed at the Wall. The Jews protested and tensions increased.

Figure 146: *British police post at the entrance to the Western Wall, 1933*

Figure 147: *British police at the Wailing Wall, 1934*

A British inquiry into the disturbances and investigation regarding the principal issue in the Western Wall dispute, namely the rights of the Jewish worshipers to bring appurtenances to the wall, was convened. The Supreme Muslim Council provided documents dating from the Turkish regime supporting their claims. However, repeated reminders to the Chief Rabbinate to verify which apparatus had been permitted failed to elicit any response. They refused to do so, arguing that Jews had the right to pray at the Wall without restrictions. Subsequently, in November 1928, the Government issued a White Paper entitled "The Western or Wailing Wall in Jerusalem: Memorandum by the Secretary of State for the Colonies", which emphasised the maintenance of the *status quo* and instructed that Jews could only bring "those accessories which had been permitted in Turkish times."

A few months later, Haj Amin complained to Chancellor that "Jews were bringing benches and tables in increased numbers to the wall and driving nails into the wall and hanging lamps on them."

1929 Palestine riots

In the summer of 1929, the Mufti Haj Amin Al Husseinni ordered an opening be made at the southern end of the alleyway which straddled the Wall. The former cul-de-sac became a thoroughfare which led from the Temple Mount into the prayer area at the Wall. Mules were herded through the narrow alley, often dropping excrement. This, together with other construction projects in the vicinity, and restricted access to the Wall, resulted in Jewish protests to the British, who remained indifferent.

On August 14, 1929, after attacks on individual Jews praying at the Wall, 6,000 Jews demonstrated in Tel Aviv, shouting "The Wall is ours." The next day, the Jewish fast of Tisha B'Av, 300 youths raised the Zionist flag and sang Hatikva at the Wall. The day after, on August 16, an organized mob of 2,000 Muslim Arabs descended on the Western Wall, injuring the beadle and burning prayer books, liturgical fixtures and notes of supplication. The rioting spread to the Jewish commercial area of town, and was followed a few days later by the Hebron massacre. 133 Jews were killed and 339 injured in the Arab riots, and in the subsequent process of quelling the riots 110 Arabs were killed by British police. This was by far the deadliest attack on Jews during the period of British Rule over Palestine.

1930 international commission

In 1930, in response to the 1929 riots, the British Government appointed a commission "to determine the rights and claims of Muslims and Jews in connection with the Western or Wailing Wall", and to determine the causes of the violence and prevent it in the future. The League of Nations approved the commission on condition that the members were not British.

The Jews requested that the Commission take the following actions:

- To give recognition to the immemorial claim that the Wailing Wall is a Holy Place for the Jews, not only for the Jews in Palestine, but also for the Jews of the whole world.
- To decree that the Jews shall have the right of access to the Wall for devotion and for prayers in accordance with their ritual without interference or interruption.
- To decree that it shall be permissible to continue the Jewish services under the conditions of decency and decorum characteristic of a sacred custom that has been carried on for many centuries without infringement upon the religious rights of others.
- To decree that the drawing up of any regulations that may be necessary as to such devotions and prayers, shall be entrusted to the Rabbinate of Palestine, who shall thus re-assume full responsibility in that matter, in discharge of which responsibility they may consult the Rabbinate of the world.
- To suggest, if the Commissioners approve of the plan, to the Mandatory Power that it should make the necessary arrangements by which the properties now occupied by the Moghrabi Waqf might be vacated, the Waqf authorities accepting in lieu of them certain new buildings to be erected upon some eligible site in Jerusalem, so that the charitable purpose, for which this Waqf was given, may still be fulfilled.

The Commission noted that 'the Jews do not claim any proprietorship to the Wall or to the Pavement in front of it (concluding speech of Jewish Counsel, Minutes, page 908).'

David Yellin, Head of the Hebrew Teachers Seminary, member of the Ottoman parliament, and one of the first public figures to join the Zionist movement openly, testified before the Commission. He stated:

> *"Being judged before you today stands a nation that has been deprived of everything that is dear and sacred to it from its emergence in its own land – the graves of its patriarchs, the graves of its great kings, the graves of its holy prophets and, above all, the site of its glorious Temple. Everything has been taken from it and of all the witnesses to its sanctity, only one vestige remains – one side of a tiny portion of a wall, which, on one side, borders the place of its former Temple. In front of this bare stone wall, that nation stands under the open sky, in the heat of summer and in the rains of winter, and pours out its heart to its God in heaven."*

Figure 148: *Members of the Anglo-American Committee of Inquiry at the Western Wall, 1946*

The Commission concluded that the wall, and the adjacent pavement and Moroccan Quarter, were solely owned by the Muslim *waqf*. However, Jews had the right to "free access to the Western Wall for the purpose of devotions at all times", subject to some stipulations that limited which objects could be brought to the Wall and forbade the blowing of the shofar, which was made illegal. Muslims were forbidden to disrupt Jewish devotions by driving animals or other means. Yitzchak Orenstein, who held the position of Rabbi of the Kotel, recorded in April 1930 that "Our master, Rabbi Yosef Chaim Sonnenfeld came to pray this morning by the *Kosel* and one of those present produced a small chair for the *Rav* to rest on for a few moments. However, no sooner had the *Rav* sat down did an Arab officer appear and pull the chair away from under him." During the 1930s, at the conclusion of Yom Kippur, young Jews persistently flouted the shofar ban each year and blew the shofar resulting in their arrest and prosecution. They were usually fined or sentenced to imprisonment for three to six months. The Shaw commission determined that the violence occurred due to "racial animosity on the part of the Arabs, consequent upon the disappointment of their political and national aspirations and fear for their economic future."

Jordanian rule – 1948–67

During the 1948 Arab-Israeli War the Old City together with the Wall was controlled by Jordan. Article VIII of the 1949 Armistice Agreement provided for Israeli Jewish access to the Western Wall.Wikipedia:Accuracy dispute#Disputed statement However, for the following nineteen years, despite numerous requests by Israeli officials and Jewish groups to the United Nations and other international bodies to attempt to enforce the armistice agreement, Jordan refused to abide by this clause. Neither Israeli Arabs nor Israeli Jews could visit their holy places in the Jordanian territories.[333] An exception was made for Christians to participate in Christmas ceremonies in Bethlehem. Some sources claim Jews could only visit the wall if they traveled through Jordan (which was not an option for Israelis) and did not have an Israeli visa stamped in their passports. Only Jordanian soldiers and tourists were to be found there. A vantage point on Mount Zion, from which the Wall could be viewed, became the place where Jews gathered to pray. For thousands of pilgrims, the mount, being the closest location to the Wall under Israeli control, became a substitute site for the traditional priestly blessing ceremony which takes place on the Three Pilgrimage Festivals.

"Al Buraq (Wailing Wall) Rd" sign

During the Jordanian rule of the Old City, a ceramic street sign in Arabic and English was affixed to the stones of the ancient wall. Attached 2.1 metres (6 ft 11 in) up, it was made up of eight separate ceramic tiles and said *Al Buraq Road* in Arabic at the top with the English "Al-Buraq (Wailing Wall) Rd" below. When Israeli soldiers arrived at the wall in June 1967, one attempted to scrawl Hebrew lettering on it. The *Jerusalem Post* reported that on June 8, Ben-Gurion went to the wall and "looked with distaste" at the road sign; "this is not right, it should come down" and he proceeded to dismantle it. This act signaled the climax of the capture of the Old City and the ability of Jews to once again access their holiest sites. Emotional recollections of this event are related by David ben Gurion and Shimon Peres.

Israeli rule – 1967–present

Following Israel's victory during the 1967 Six-Day War, the Western Wall came under Israeli control. Brigadier Rabbi Shlomo Goren proclaimed after its capture that "Israel would never again relinquish the Wall", a stance supported by Israeli Minister for Defence Moshe Dayan and Chief of Staff General Yitzhak Rabin. Rabin described the moment Israeli soldiers reached the Wall:

"There was one moment in the Six-Day War which symbolized the great victory: that was the moment in which the first paratroopers – under Gur's command – reached the stones of the Western Wall, feeling the emotion of the place; there never was, and never will be, another moment like it. Nobody staged that moment. Nobody planned it in advance. Nobody prepared it and nobody was prepared for it; it was as if Providence had directed the whole thing: the paratroopers weeping — loudly and in pain — over their comrades who had fallen along the way, the words of the Kaddish prayer heard by Western Wall's stones after 19 years of silence, tears of mourning, shouts of joy, and the singing of "Hatikvah"".

Forty-eight hours after capturing the wall, the military, without explicit government order,Wikipedia:Citation needed hastily proceeded to demolish the entire Moroccan Quarter, which stood 4 metres (13 ft) from the Wall.[334] The Sheikh Eid Mosque, which was built over one of Jerusalem's oldest Islamic schools, the Afdiliyeh, named after one of Saladin's sons, was pulled down to make way for the plaza. It was one of three or four that survived from Saladin's time.[335] 650 people consisting of 106 Arab families were ordered to leave their homes at night. When they refused, bulldozers began to demolish the buildings with people still inside, killing one person and injuring a number of others.[336,337,338]

According to Eyal Weizman, Chaim Herzog, who later became Israel's sixth president, took much of the credit for the destruction of the neighbourhood:

When we visited the Wailing Wall we found a toilet attached to it ... we decided to remove it and from this we came to the conclusion that we could evacuate the entire area in front of the Wailing Wall ... a historical opportunity that will never return ... We knew that the following Saturday [sic Wednesday], June 14, would be the Jewish festival of Shavuot and that many will want to come to pray ... it all had to be completed by then.

The narrow pavement, which could accommodate a maximum of 12,000 per day, was transformed into an enormous plaza that could hold in excess of 400,000.

Several months later, the pavement close to the wall was excavated to a depth of two and half metres, exposing an additional two courses of large stones.

A complex of buildings against the wall at the southern end of the plaza, that included Madrasa Fakhriya and the house that the Abu al-Sa'ud family had occupied since the 16th century, were spared in the 1967 destruction, but demolished in 1969.[339] The section of the wall dedicated to prayers was thus extended southwards to double its original length, from 28 to 60 metres (92 to 197 ft), while the 4 metres (13 ft) space facing the wall grew to 40 metres (130 ft).

The narrow, approximately 120 square metres (1,300 sq ft) pre-1948 alley along the wall, used for Jewish prayer, was enlarged to 2,400 square metres (26,000 sq ft), with the entire Western Wall Plaza covering 20,000 square metres (4.9 acres), stretching from the wall to the Jewish Quarter.

The new plaza created in 1967 is used for worship and public gatherings, including Bar mitzvah celebrations and the swearing-in ceremonies of newly full-fledged soldiers in the Israel Defense Forces. Tens of thousands of Jews flock to the wall on the Jewish holidays, and particularly on the fast of Tisha B'Av, which marks the destruction of the Temple and on Jerusalem Day, which commemorates the reunification of Jerusalem in 1967 and the delivery of the Wall into Jewish hands.

Conflicts over prayer at the national monument began little more than a year after Israel's victory in the Six-Day War once again made site accessible to Jews. In July 1968 the World Union for Progressive Judaism, which had planned the group's international convention in Jerusalem, appealed to the Knesset after the Ministry of Religious Affairs prohibited the organization from hosting mixed-gender services at the Wall. The Knesset committee on internal affairs backed the Ministry of Religious Affairs in disallowing the Jewish convention attendees, who had come from over 24 countries, from worshiping in their fashion. The Orthodox hold that services at the Wall should follow traditional Jewish law for segregated seating followed in synagogues, while the non-Orthodox perspective was that "the Wall is a shrine of all Jews, not one particular branch of Judaism."[340]

Robinson's Arch

At the southern end of the Western Wall, Robinson's Arch along with a row of vaults once supported stairs ascending from the street to the Temple Mount.[341] Because it does not come under the direct control of the Rabbi of the Wall or the Ministry of Religious Affairs, the site has been opened to religious groups that hold worship services that would not be approved by the Rabbi or the Ministry in the major men's and women's prayer areas against the Wall.

The need for such an area became apparent when in 1989, after repeated attacks by haredim, activists belonging to a group called Women of the Wall petitioned to secure the right of women to pray at the wall without restrictions. In a 2003 directive, Israel's Supreme Court disallowed any women from reading publicly from the Torah or wearing traditional prayer shawls at the plaza itself, but instructed the Israeli government to prepare the site of Robinson's Arch to host such events. The site was inaugurated in August 2004 and has since hosted services by Reform and Conservative groups, as well as services by the Women of the Wall. In May 2013 a judge ruled that the 2003 Israeli Supreme Court ruling prohibiting women from carrying a Torah or wearing

Figure 149: *The remains of Robinson's Arch above excavated remnants of the ancient street below.*

prayer shawls had been misinterpreted and that Women of the Wall prayer gatherings at the wall should not be deemed as disturbing the public order.[342]

In November 2010, the government approved a NIS 85m ($23m) scheme to improve access and infrastructure at the site.[343]

The Isaiah Stone, located under Robinson's Arch, has a carved inscription in Hebrew from Isaiah 66:14: הפרחנה כדשא ועצמותיכם לבכם ושש וראיתם ("And when ye see this your heart shall rejoice and your bones shall flourish like an herb").

In April 2013, Jewish Agency for Israel leader Natan Sharansky spearheaded a concept that would expand and renovate the Robinson's Arch area into an area where people may "perform worship rituals not based on the Orthodox interpretation of Jewish tradition."[344] On August 25, 2013, a new 4,480 square foot prayer platform named "Azarat Yisrael Plaza" was completed as part of this plan, with access to the platform at all hours, even when the rest of the area's archeological park is closed to visitors.[345,346] After some controversy regarding the question of authority over this prayer area, the announcement was made that it would come under the authority of a future government-appointed "pluralist council" that would include non-Orthodox representatives.[347] In January 2016, the Israeli Cabinet approved a plan to designate a new space at the Kotel that would be available for egalitarian prayer and that would not be controlled by the Rabbinate. Women of the Wall welcomed the decision,

Figure 150: *Azarat Yisrael Plaza (prayer platform), Robinson's Arch, opened August 2013*

although Sephardic Chief Rabbi Shlomo Amar of Jerusalem said creating a mixed-gender prayer section was paramount to destroying it. The Chief rabbinate said it would create an alternate plan.[348] In June 2017, it was announced that the plan approved in January 2016 had been suspended.

Wilson's Arch

In 2005, the Western Wall Heritage Foundation initiated a major renovation effort under Rabbi-of-the-Wall Shmuel Rabinovitch. Its goal was to renovate and restore the area within Wilson's Arch, the covered area to the left of worshipers facing the Wall in the open prayer plaza, in order to increase access for visitors and for prayer.[349,350]

The restoration to the men's section included a Torah ark that can house over 100 Torah scrolls, in addition to new bookshelves, a library, heating for the winter, and air conditioning for the summer. A new room was also built for the scribes who maintain and preserve the Torah scrolls used at the Wall. New construction also included a women's section,[351] overlooking the men's prayer area, so that women could use this separate area to "take part in the services held inside under the Arch" for the first time.[352]

On July 25, 2010, a Ner Tamid, an oil-burning "eternal light," was installed within the prayer hall within Wilson's Arch, the first eternal light installed in the

Figure 151: *Torah Ark inside men's section of Wilson's Arch*

area of the Western Wall.[353] According to the Western Wall Heritage Foundation, requests had been made for many years that "an olive oil lamp be placed in the prayer hall of the Western Wall Plaza, as is the custom in Jewish synagogues, to represent the menorah of the Temple in Jerusalem as well as the continuously burning fire on the altar of burnt offerings in front of the Temple," especially in the closest place to those ancient flames.

A number of special worship events have been held since the renovation. They have taken advantage of the cover, temperature control,[354] and enhanced security.[355] However, in addition to the more recent programs, one early event occurred in September 1983, even before the modern renovation. At that time U.S. Sixth Fleet Chaplain Rabbi Arnold Resnicoff was allowed to hold an unusual interfaith service—the first interfaith service ever conducted at the Wall during the time it was under Israeli control—that included men and women sitting together. The ten-minute service included the Priestly Blessing, recited by Resnicoff, who is a Kohen. A Ministry of Religions representative was present, responding to press queries that the service was authorized as part of a special welcome for the U.S. Sixth Fleet.[356,357,358]

Figure 152: *Asst. U.S. Sixth Fleet Chaplain Rabbi Arnold Resnicoff leads an unusual interfaith service*

Rabbis of the wall

After the 1967 Arab-Israeli war, Rabbi Yehuda Meir Getz was named the overseer of proceedings at the wall. After Rabbi Getz's death in 1995, Rabbi Shmuel Rabinowitz was given the position.

Theology and ritual

Judaism

Rabbinic tradition teaches that the western wall was built upon foundations laid by the biblical King Solomon from the time of the First Temple.[359] A Midrash compiled in Late Antiquity refers to a western wall of the Temple which "would never be destroyed", and Lamentations Rabbah mentions how Rome was unable to topple the western wall due to the Divine oath promising its eternal survival.[360] Another Midrash quotes a 4th-century scholar: "Rav Acha said that the Divine Presence has never departed from the Western Wall",[361] and the Zohar similarly writes that "the Divine Presence rests upon the Western Wall".[362]

Some medieval rabbis claimed that today's Western Wall is a surviving wall of the Temple itself and cautioned Jews from approaching it, lest they enter the Temple precincts in a state of impurity.[363] Many contemporary rabbis believe that the rabbinic traditions were made in reference to the Temple

Figure 153: *Prayers in the Western Wall*

Mount's Western Wall, which accordingly endows the Wall with inherent holiness. Most secular scholars believe however that these traditions originally pertained to a western wall of the Temple itself, and since the 1500s, were gradually applied to the surviving retaining Western Wall of the Mount.

Rabbi Zvi Hirsch Kaindenover discusses the mystical aspect of the Hebrew word *kotel* when discussing the significance of praying against a wall. He cites the Zohar which writes that the word *kotel*, meaning wall, is made up of two parts: "Ko", which has the numerical value of God's name, and "Tel", meaning mount, which refers to the Temple and its Western Wall.[364]

Eighteenth-century scholar Jonathan Eybeschutz writes that "after the destruction of the Temple, God removed His Presence from His sanctuary and placed it upon the Western Wall where it remains in its holiness and honour".[365] It is told that great Jewish sages, including Isaac Luria and the Radvaz, experienced a revelation of the Divine Presence at the wall.[366]

Sanctity of the Wall

Many contemporary Orthodox scholars rule that the area in front of the Wall has the status of a synagogue and must be treated with due respect. This is the view upheld by the authority in charge of the wall. As such, men and married women are expected to cover their heads upon approaching the Wall, and to dress appropriately. When departing, the custom is to walk backwards away from the Wall. On Saturdays, it is forbidden to enter the area with electronic devices, including cameras, which infringe on the sanctity of the Sabbath.

Figure 154: *Jews at the Western Wall, 1870s*

Some Orthodox Jewish codifiers warn against inserting fingers into the cracks of the Wall as they believe that the breadth of the Wall constitutes part of the Temple Mount itself and retains holiness, while others who permit doing so claim that the Wall is located outside the Temple area.[367] Wikipedia:No original research#Primary, secondary and tertiary sources

In the past, some visitors would write their names on the Wall, or based upon various scriptural verses, would drive nails into the crevices. These practices stopped after rabbis determined that such actions compromised the sanctity of the Wall. Another practice also existed whereby pilgrims or those intending to travel abroad would hack off a chip from the Wall or take some of the sand from between its cracks as a good luck charm or memento. In the late 19th century the question was raised as to whether this was permitted and a long responsa appeared in the Jerusalem newspaper *Havatzelet* in 1898. It concluded that even if according to Jewish Law it was permitted, the practices should be stopped as it constituted a desecration. More recently the *Yalkut Yosef* rules that it is forbidden to remove small chips of stone or dust from the Wall, although it is permissible to take twigs from the vegetation which grows in the Wall for an amulet, as they contain no holiness. Cleaning the stones is also problematic from a halachic point of view. Blasphemous graffiti once sprayed by a tourist was left visible for months until it began to peel away.

Figure 155: *The faithful remove their shoes upon approaching the Wall, c1880*

There was once an old custom of removing one's shoes upon approaching the Wall. A 17th-century collection of special prayers to be said at holy places mentions that "upon coming to the Western Wall one should remove his shoes, bow and recite...". Rabbi Moses Reicher wroteWikipedia:Manual of Style/Dates and numbers that "it is a good and praiseworthy custom to approach the Western Wall in white garments after ablution, kneel and prostrate oneself in submission and recite "This is nothing other than the House of God and here is the gate of Heaven." When within four cubits of the Wall, one should remove their footwear." Over the years the custom of standing barefoot at the Wall has ceased, as there is no need to remove one's shoes when standing by the Wall, because the plaza area is outside the sanctified precinct of the Temple Mount.

In Judaism, the Western Wall is venerated as the sole remnant of the Holy Temple. It has become a place of pilgrimage for Jews, as it is the closest permitted accessible site to the holiest spot in Judaism, namely the *Even ha-shetiya* or Foundation Stone, which lies on the Temple Mount. According to one rabbinic opinion, Jews may not set foot upon the Temple Mount and doing so is a sin punishable by Kareth. While almost all historians and archaeologists and some rabbinical authorities believe that the rocky outcrop in the Dome of the Rock is the Foundation Stone,[368] some rabbis say it is located directly opposite the exposed section of the Western Wall, near the El-kas fountain.[369] This spot was the site of the Holy of Holies when the Temple stood.

Figure 156: *Tisha B'Av at the Western Wall, 1970s*

Mourning over the Temple's destruction

According to Jewish Law, one is obligated to grieve and rend one's garment upon visiting the Western Wall and seeing the desolate site of the Temple.[370] Bach (17th century) instructs that "when one sees the Gates of Mercy which are situated in the Western Wall, which is the wall King David built, he should recite: Her gates are sunk into the ground; he hath destroyed and broken her bars: her king and her princes are among the nations: the law is no more; her prophets also find no vision from the Lord".[371] Some scholars write that rending one's garments is not applicable nowadays as Jerusalem is under Jewish control. Others disagree, pointing to the fact that the Temple Mount is controlled by the Muslim *waqf* and that the mosques which sit upon the Temple site should increase feelings of distress. If one hasn't seen the Wall for over 30 days, the prevailing custom is to rend one's garments, but this can be avoided if one visits on the Sabbath or on festivals.[372] According to Donneal Epstein, a person who has not seen the Wall within the last 30 days should recite: "Our Holy Temple, which was our glory, in which our forefathers praised You, was burned and all of our delights were destroyed".[373]

Figure 157: *Women at prayer, early 20th century*

Prayer at the Wall

The Sages of the Talmud stated that anyone who prays at the Temple in Jerusalem, "it is as if he has prayed before the throne of glory because the gate of heaven is situated there and it is open to hear prayer."[374] Jewish Law stipulates that the Silent Prayer should be recited facing towards Jerusalem, the Temple and ultimately the Holy of Holies,[375] as God's bounty and blessing emanates from that spot. It is generally believed that prayer by the Western Wall is particularly beneficial since it was that wall which was situated closest to the Holy of Holies. Rabbi Jacob Ettlinger writes "since the gate of heaven is near the Western Wall, it is understandable that all Israel's prayers ascend on high there... as one of the great ancient kabbalists Rabbi Joseph Gikatilla said, when the Jews send their prayers from the Diaspora in the direction of Jerusalem, from there they ascend by way of the Western Wall." A well-known *segula* (efficacious remedy) for finding one's soulmate is to pray for 40 consecutive days at the Western Wall, a practice apparently conceived by Rabbi Yisroel Yaakov Fisher.

The Scroll of Ahimaaz, a historical document written in 1050 CE, distinctly describes the Western Wall as a place of prayer for the Jews.Wikipedia:Citation needed In around 1167 CE during the late Crusader Period, Benjamin of Tudela wrote that "In front of this place is the western wall, which is one of the walls of the Holy of Holies. This is called the Gate of Mercy, and hither come all the Jews to pray before the Wall in the open court".[376] In 1625 "arranged prayers" at the Wall are mentioned for the first time by a scholar whose name has not been preserved. Scrolls of the Law were brought to the Wall on occasions of public distress and calamity, as testified to in a narrative written by Rabbi Gedaliah of Semitizi who went to Jerusalem in 1699.

> "On Friday afternoon, March 13, 1863, the writer visited this sacred spot. Here he found between one and two hundred Jews of both sexes and of all ages, standing or sitting, and bowing as they read, chanted and recited, moving themselves backward and forward, the tears rolling down many a face; they kissed the walls and wrote sentences in Hebrew upon them... The lamentation which is most commonly used is from Psalm 79:1 "O God, the heathen are come into Thy inheritance; Thy holy temple have they defiled."
>
> Rev. James W. Lee, 1863.

The writings of various travellers in the Holy Land, especially in the 18th and 19th centuries, tell of how the Wall and its environs continued to be a place of devotion for the Jews. Isaac Yahuda, a prominent member of the Sephardic community in Jerusalem recalled how men and women used to gather in a circle at the Wall to hear sermons delivered in Ladino. His great-grandmother, who arrived in Palestine in 1841, "used to go to the Western Wall every Friday afternoon, winter and summer, and stay there until candle-lighting time, reading the entire Book of Psalms and the Song of Songs...she would sit there by herself for hours." In the past women could be found sitting at the entrance to the Wall every Sabbath holding fragrant herbs and spices in order to enable worshipers to make additional blessings. In the hot weather they would provide cool water. The women also used to cast lots for the privilege of sweeping and washing the alleyway at the foot of the Wall. Throughout the ages, the Wall is where Jews have gathered to express gratitude to God or to pray for divine mercy. On news of the Normandy landings on June 6, 1944 thousands of Jews went to the Wall to offer prayers for the "success of His Majesty's and Allied Forces in the liberation of all enemy-occupied territory." On October 13, 1994, 50,000 gathered to pray for the safe return of kidnapped soldier Nachshon Wachsman. August 10, 2005 saw a massive prayer rally at the Wall. Estimates of people protesting Israel's unilateral disengagement plan ranged from 50,000 to 250,000 people.Wikipedia:Citation needed Every year on Tisha B'Av large crowds congregate at the Wall to commemorate the destruction of the Temple. In 2007 over 100,000 gathered. During the month of Tishrei 2009, a record 1.5 million people visited the site.[377]

Egalitarian and non-Orthodox prayer

While during the late 19th century, no formal segregation of men and women was to be found at the Wall,[378] conflict erupted in July 1968 when members of the World Union for Progressive Judaism were denied the right to host a mixed-gender service at the site after the Ministry of Religious Affairs insisted

Figure 158: *The separate areas for men (top) and women, seen from the walkway to the Dome of the Rock*

on maintaining the gender segregation customary at Orthodox places of worship. The progressives responded by claiming that "the Wall is a shrine of all Jews, not one particular branch of Judaism." In 1988, the small but vocal Women of the Wall launched a campaign for recognition of non-Orthodox prayer at the Wall. Their form and manner of prayer elicited a violent response from some Orthodox worshippers and they were subsequently banned from holding services at the site. In response to the repeated arrest of women, including Anat Hoffman found flouting the law, the Jewish Agency observed 'the urgent need to reach a permanent solution and make the Western Wall once again a symbol of unity among the Jewish people, and not one of discord and strife." Some commentators called for the closure of the site unless an acceptable solution to the controversy was found.[379] In 2003 Israel's Supreme Court upheld the ban on non-Orthodox worship at the Wall and the government responded by allocating Robinson's Arch for such purposes. But in 2012, critics still complained about the restrictions at the Western Wall, saying Israel had "turned a national monument into an ultra-Orthodox synagogue," and in April 2013 the Jerusalem District Court ruled that as long as there was no other appropriate area for pluralistic prayer, prayer according to non-Orthodox custom should be allowed at the Wall. This led to the expansion and renovation of the Robinson's Arch prayer area which would be placed under the authority of a Pluralist Council. In August 2013, a platform named "Azarat Yisrael Plaza"

Figure 159: *Slips of paper containing prayers in the cracks of the Wall*

was completed to facilitate non-Orthodox worship.

Prayer notes

There is a much publicised practice of placing slips of paper containing written prayers into the crevices of the Wall. The earliest account of this practice is attributed to Rabbi Chaim ibn Attar, (d. 1743).[380] More than a million notes are placed each year and the opportunity to e-mail notes is offered by a number of organisations. It has become customary for visiting dignitaries to place notes too.

Tefillin

Shortly after the Western Wall came under Israeli control in 1967, a tefillin stand was erected with permission from Rabbi Yehuda Meir Getz, the first rabbi of the Kotel. The stand offers visitors the chance to put on Tefillin, a daily Jewish ritual. In the months following the Six-Day War an estimated 400,000 Jews observed this ritual at the stand. The stand is staffed by multilingual volunteers and an estimated 100,000 visitors put on tefillin there annually.

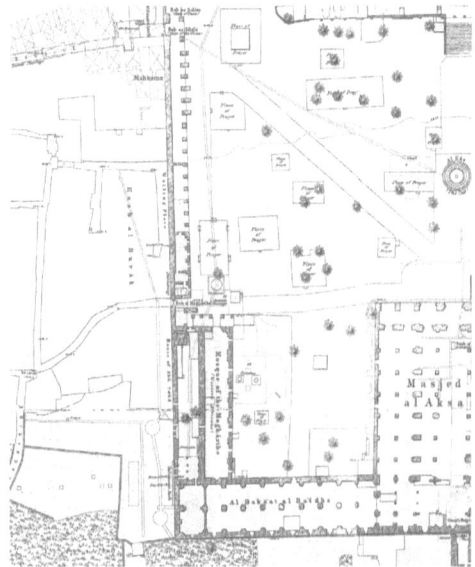

Figure 160: *South-West corner of the Haram (Wilson, 1865)*

Islam

Islamic reverence for the site is derived from the belief that the prophet Mohammed tied his miraculous steed Buraq nearby during his night journey to Jerusalem. Various places have been suggested for the exact spot where Buraq was tethered, but for several centuries the preferred location has been the al-Buraq mosque, which is just inside the wall at the south end of the present Western Wall plaza. The mosque is located above an ancient passageway, which once came out through the long-sealed Barclay's Gate whose huge lintel is still visible directly below the Maghrebi gate.

When a British Jew asked the Egyptian authorities in 1840 for permission to re-pave the ground in front of the Western Wall, the governor of Syria wrote:

> It is evident from the copy of the record of the deliberations of the Consultative Council in Jerusalem that the place the Jews asked for permission to pave adjoins the wall of the Haram al-Sharif and also the spot where al-Buraq was tethered, and is included in the endowment charter of Abu Madyan, may God bless his memory; that the Jews never carried out any repairs in that place in the past. ... Therefore the Jews must not be enabled to pave the place.[381]

Carl Sandreczki, who was charged with compiling a list of place names for Charles Wilson's Ordnance Survey of Jerusalem in 1865, reported that the

Figure 161: *Pope Francis at the Western Wall*

street leading to the Western Wall, including the part alongside the wall, belonged to the *Hosh* (court/enclosure) of *al Burâk*, "not *Obrâk*, nor *Obrat*".[382] In 1866, the Prussian Consul and Orientalist Georg Rosen wrote that "The Arabs call Obrâk the entire length of the wall at the wailing place of the Jews, southwards down to the house of Abu Su'ud and northwards up to the substructure of the Mechkemeh [Shariah court]. Obrâk is not, as was formerly claimed, a corruption of the word Ibri (Hebrews), but simply the neo-Arabic pronunciation of Bōrâk, ... which, whilst (Muhammad) was at prayer at the holy rock, is said to have been tethered by him inside the wall location mentioned above."

The name Hosh al Buraq appeared on the maps of Wilson's 1865 survey, its revised editions of 1876 and 1900, and other maps in the early 20th century.[383] In 1922, it was the street name specified by the official Pro-Jerusalem Council.

Christianity

Some scholars believe that when Jerusalem came under Christian rule in the 4th century, there was a purposeful "transference" of respect for the Temple Mount and the Western Wall in terms of sanctity to the Church of the Holy Sepulchre, while the sites around the Temple Mount became a refuse dump for Christians.[384] However, the actions of many modern Christian leaders, including Pope John Paul II and Pope Benedict XVI, who visited the Wall and

Figure 162: *A Jew praying at the Western Wall*

left prayer messages in its crevices, have symbolized for many Christians a restoration of respect and even veneration for this ancient religious site.

Views

Jewish

Most Jews, religious and secular, consider the wall to be important to the Jewish people since it was originally built to hold the Second Temple. They consider the capture of the wall by Israel in 1967 as a historic event since it restored Jewish access to the site after a 19-year gap.[385] There are, however, some haredi Jews who hold different views. Most notable are the adherents of the Satmar hasidic dynasty who retain the views espoused by their Grand Rabbi Joel Teitelbaum, who would not approach the Wall after the 1967 conquest because of his opposition to Zionism, although he did visit the site during his visits to the Holy Land in the 1920s.Wikipedia:Citation needed

In 1994, Shlomo Goren wrote that the tradition of the wall as a Jewish prayer site was only 300 years old, the Jews being compelled to pray there after being forbidden to assemble on the mount itself.

Figure 163: *Western Wall and Dome of the Rock.*

Israeli

A poll carried out in 2007 by the Jerusalem Institute for Israel Studies indicated that 96% of Israeli Jews were against Israel relinquishing the Western Wall. During a speech at Israel's Mercaz HaRav yeshivah on Jerusalem Day in 2009, Israeli Prime Minister Benyamin Netanyahu declared:

> "The flag that flies over the Kotel is the Israeli flag... Our holy places, the Temple Mount – will remain under Israeli sovereignty forever."

Muslim

In December 1973, King Faisal of Saudi Arabia stated that "Only Muslims and Christians have holy places and rights in Jerusalem". The Jews, he maintained, had no rights there at all. As for the Western Wall, he said, "Another wall can be built for them. They can pray against that". Raed Salah, leader of the northern branch of the Islamic Movement in Israel wrote that:

> "The Western Wall – all its various parts, structures and gates – are an inseparable part of the al-Aqsa compound...The Western Wall is part of Al-Aqsa's western tower, which the Israeli establishment fallaciously and sneakily calls the 'Wailing Wall'. The wall is part of the holy al-Aqsa Mosque".

Palestinian

According to the Palestinian National Authority, the Jews did not consider the Wall as a place for worship until after the Balfour Declaration was issued in 1917. The PA-appointed Mufti of Jerusalem, Sheikh Ekrima Sa'id Sabri, believes that the Wall belongs to the Muslims alone.[386] In 2000 he related that "No stone of the Al-Buraq wall has any relation to Judaism. The Jews began praying at this wall only in the nineteenth century, when they began to develop [national] aspirations." A year later he stated:

> *'There is not a single stone in the Wailing Wall relating to Jewish History. The Jews cannot legitimately claim this wall, neither religiously nor historically. The Committee of the League of Nations recommended in 1930, to allow the Jews to pray there, in order to keep them quiet. But by no means did it acknowledge that the wall belongs to them."*
>
> *—Interviewed by German magazine Die Welt, January 17, 2001*

In 2006, Dr. Hassan Khader, founder of the Al Quds Encyclopedia, told PA television that the first connection of the Jews to the Wall is "a recent one, which began in the 16th century...not ancient...like the roots of the Islamic connection".

In November 2010, an official paper published by the PA Ministry of Information denied Jewish rights to the Wall. It stated that "Al-Buraq Wall is in fact the western wall of Al-Aksa Mosque" and that Jews had only started using the site for worship after the 1917 Balfour Declaration.[387]

Yitzhak Reiter writes that "the Islamization and de-Judaization of the Western Wall are a recurrent motif in publications and public statements by the heads of the Islamic Movement in Israel."

American

While recognizing the difficulties inherent in any ultimate peace agreement that involves the status of Jerusalem, the official position of the United States includes a recognition of the importance of the Wall to the Jewish people, and has condemned statements that seek to "delegitimize" the relationship between Jews and the area in general, and the Western Wall in particular. For example, in November 2010, the Obama administration "strongly condemned a Palestinian official's claim that the Western Wall in the Old City has no religious significance for Jews and is actually Muslim property." The U.S. State Department noted that the United States rejects such a claim as "factually incorrect, insensitive and highly provocative."[388]

Figure 164: *U.S. president Donald Trump (right) visits the Western Wall, accompanied by Rabbi Shmuel Rabinovitch (center), 2017*

References

- Armstrong, Karen (April 16, 2001). "Islam's Stake"[389]. *TIME*. Retrieved October 8, 2008.
- Barclay, James Turner (1858). "Modern Jerusalem". *City of the Great King*. Challen.
- Becher, Mordechai (2005). "The Land of Israel". *Gateway to Judaism*. Mesorah Publications. ISBN 1-4226-0030-0.
- Ben-Dov, Meir; Naor, Mordechai; Aner, Ze'ev (1983). *The Western Wall*. Israel: Ministry of Defence. ISBN 965-05-0055-3.
- Bleiweiss, Robert (1997). "Tear Down the Western Wall". *Jewish Spectator*[390].
- Chertoff, Mordecai S. (1975). *Zionism: a basic reader*[391]. Herzl Press.
- Gonen, Rivka (2003). *Contested Holiness*. KTAV Publishing. ISBN 0-88125-799-0.
- Halkin, Hillel (January 21, 2001). ""Western Wall" or "Wailing Wall"?"[392]. *Forward*. Retrieved September 28, 2015.
- Idinopulos, Thomas A. (1994). *Jerusalem: A History of the Holiest City as Seen Through the Struggles of Jews, Christians, and Muslims*[393]. Ivan R. Dee, Publisher. ISBN 978-1-56663-062-7.

- Lee, James W. (1863). *Earthly Footsteps of the Man of Galilee*[394]. Retrieved May 31, 2009.
- Mock, Steven (2011). "Theories of Nations and Nationalism". *Symbols of Defeat in the Construction of National Identity*[395]. Cambridge University Press. ISBN 978-1-139-50352-5.
- Peters, F. E. (1984). *Jerusalem*. Princeton, New Jersey: Princeton University Press. pp. 357–359, 394–396.
- Shragai, Nadav (2014). ""Al-Aksa Is in Danger": The Lie that Won't Die"[396]. Jerusalem Center for Public Affairs. Retrieved September 27, 2015.
- Vilnay, Zev (2003). "How the Wall was discovered". *Legends of Palestine*. Kessinger Publishing. ISBN 0-7661-4128-4.
- Warner, Charles Dudley (1878). "Jerusalem". *In the Levant*. Houghton.
- Wilson, Charles (1881). *Picturesque Palestine*[394]. **1**. Retrieved May 31, 2009.
- *The World Book Encyclopedia*[397]. World Book. 2007. ISBN 978-0-7166-0107-4.

External links

 Wikimedia Commons has media related to *Western Wall*.

- *The Western Wall Heritage Foundation*[398]
- Jewish Virtual Library: *The Western Wall*[399]
- Chabad.org: *The Shofar and the Wall, 1930*[400]
- Historic radio broadcast of the capture of the wall by the Israel Defense Forces on June 7, 1967[401]

Photographs

- Wailing Wall to Western Wall (1960s)[402]
- Photographs of the Western Wall (Summer 2007)[403]

Google Street View

- The Western Wall on Google Street View[404]

<indicator name="good-star"> ⊕ </indicator>

Karnak Temple

Karnak

Karnak

Pillars of the Great Hypostyle Hall from the Precinct of Amun-Re

Shown within Egypt

Location	El-Karnak, Luxor Governorate, Egypt

Region	Upper Egypt
Coordinates	25°43′7″N 32°39′31″E[405] Coordinates: 25°43′7″N 32°39′31″E[405]
Type	Sanctuary
Part of	Thebes
History	
Builder	Senusret I
Periods	Middle Kingdom to Ptolemaic Kingdom
UNESCO World Heritage Site	
Official name	Ancient Thebes with its Necropolis
Type	Cultural
Criteria	i, iii, vi
Designated	1979 (3rd session)
Reference no.	87[406]
Region	Arab States

The **Karnak Temple Complex**, commonly known as **Karnak** (/ˈkɑːr.næk/[407]), comprises a vast mix of decayed temples, chapels, pylons, and other buildings. Construction at the complex began during the reign of Senusret I in the Middle Kingdom and continued into the Ptolemaic period, although most of the extant buildings date from the New Kingdom. The area around Karnak was the ancient Egyptian *Ipet-isut* ("The Most Selected of Places") and the main place of worship of the eighteenth dynasty Theban Triad with the god Amun as its head. It is part of the monumental city of Thebes. The Karnak complex gives its name to the nearby, and partly surrounded, modern village of El-Karnak, 2.5 kilometres (1.6 miles) north of Luxor.

Overview

The complex is a vast open-air museum, and the secondWikipedia:Citation needed largest ancient religious site in the world, after the Angkor Wat Temple of Cambodia. It is believed to be the secondWikipedia:Citation needed most visited historical site in Egypt; only the Giza Pyramids near Cairo receive more visits. It consists of four main parts, of which only the largest is currently open to the general public. The term Karnak often is understood as being the Precinct of Amun-Ra only, because this is the only part most visitors see. The three other parts, the Precinct of Mut, the Precinct of Montu, and the dismantled Temple of Amenhotep IV, are closed to the public. There also

Figure 165: *Great hall, Karnak. Brooklyn Museum Archives, Goodyear Archival Collection*

are a few smaller temples and sanctuaries connecting the Precinct of Mut, the Precinct of Amun-Re, and the Luxor Temple.

The Precinct of Mut is very ancient, being dedicated to an Earth and creation deity, but not yet restored. The original temple was destroyed and partially restored by Hatshepsut, although another pharaoh built around it in order to change the focus or orientation of the sacred area. Many portions of it may have been carried away for use in other buildings.

The key difference between Karnak and most of the other temples and sites in Egypt is the length of time over which it was developed and used. Construction of temples started in the Middle Kingdom and continued through to Ptolemaic times. Approximately thirty pharaohs contributed to the buildings, enabling it to reach a size, complexity, and diversity not seen elsewhere. Few of the individual features of Karnak are unique, but the size and number of features are overwhelming. The deities represented range from some of the earliest worshiped to those worshiped much later in the history of the Ancient Egyptian culture. Although destroyed, it also contained an early temple built by Amenhotep IV (Akhenaten), the pharaoh who later would celebrate a near monotheistic religion he established that prompted him to move his court and religious center away from Thebes. It also contains evidence of adaptations, using buildings of the Ancient Egyptians by later cultures for their own religious purposes.

One famous aspect of Karnak is the Hypostyle Hall in the Precinct of Amun-Re, a hall area of 50,000 sq ft (5,000 m²) with 134 massive columns arranged in 16 rows. 122 of these columns are 10 meters tall, and the other 12 are 21 meters tall with a diameter of over three meters.

The architraves on top of these columns are estimated to weigh 70 tons. These architraves may have been lifted to these heights using levers. This would be an extremely time-consuming process and also would require great balance to get to such great heights. A common alternative theory regarding how they were moved is that large ramps were constructed of sand, mud, brick or stone and that the stones were then towed up the ramps. If stone had been used for the ramps, they would have been able to use much less material. The top of the ramps presumably would have employed either wooden tracks or cobblestones for towing the megaliths.

There is an unfinished pillar in an out-of-the-way location that indicates how it would have been finished. Final carving was executed after the drums were put in place so that it was not damaged while being placed.[408,409] Several experiments moving megaliths with ancient technology were made at other locations – some of them are listed here.

In 2009 UCLA launched a website dedicated to virtual reality digital reconstructions of the Karnak complex and other resources.[410]

The sun god's shrine has light focused upon it during the winter solstice.[411]

History

The history of the Karnak complex is largely the history of Thebes and its changing role in the culture. Religious centers varied by region and with the establishment of the current capital of the unified culture that changed several times. The city of Thebes does not appear to have been of great significance before the Eleventh Dynasty and previous temple building here would have been relatively small, with shrines being dedicated to the early deities of Thebes, the Earth goddess Mut and Montu. Early building was destroyed by invaders. The earliest known artifact found in the area of the temple is a small, eight-sided temple from the Eleventh Dynasty, which mentions Amun-Re. Amun (sometimes called Amen) was long the local tutelary deity of Thebes. He was identified with the Ram and the Goose. The Egyptian meaning of Amun is, "hidden" or, the "hidden god".[412]

Figure 166: *Egypt - Gate of Pylon, Karnak. Brooklyn Museum Archives, Goodyear Archival Collection*

Major construction work in the Precinct of Amun-Re took place during the Eighteenth dynasty when Thebes became the capital of the unified Ancient Egypt.

Thutmose I erected an enclosure wall connecting the Fourth and Fifth pylons, which comprise the earliest part of the temple still standing *in situ*. Construction of the Hypostyle Hall also may have begun during the eighteenth dynasty, although most new building was undertaken under Seti I and Ramesses II.

Almost every pharaoh of that dynasty has added something to the temple site. Merneptah commemorated his victories over the Sea Peoples on the walls of the Cachette Court, the start of the processional route to the Luxor Temple.

Hatshepsut had monuments constructed and also restored the original Precinct of Mut, the ancient great goddess of Egypt, that had been ravaged by the foreign rulers during the Hyksos occupation. She had twin obelisks, at the time the tallest in the world, erected at the entrance to the temple. One still stands, as the tallest surviving ancient obelisk on Earth; the other has broken in two and toppled. Another of her projects at the site, Karnak's Red Chapel, or *Chapelle Rouge*, was intended as a barque shrine and originally, may have stood between her two obelisks. She later ordered the construction of two more obelisks to celebrate her sixteenth year as pharaoh; one of the obelisks broke during construction, and thus, a third was constructed to replace it. The broken obelisk was left at its quarrying site in Aswan, where it still remains. Known as The Unfinished Obelisk, it demonstrates how obelisks were quarried.[413]

The last major change to Precinct of Amun-Re's layout was the addition of the first pylon and the massive enclosure walls that surround the whole Precinct, both constructed by Nectanebo I.

In 323 AD, Constantine the Great recognised the Christian religion, and in 356 Constantius II ordered the closing of pagan temples throughout the empire. Karnak was by this time mostly abandoned, and Christian churches were founded among the ruins, the most famous example of this is the reuse of the Festival Hall of Thutmose III's central hall, where painted decorations of saints and Coptic inscriptions can still be seen.

European knowledge of Karnak

Thebes' exact placement was unknown in medieval Europe, though both Herodotus and Strabo give the exact location of Thebes and how long up the Nile one must travel to reach it. Maps of Egypt, based on the 2nd century Claudius Ptolemaeus' mammoth work *Geographia*, had been circling in Europe since the late 14th century, all of them showing Thebes' (Diospolis) location. Despite this, several European authors of the 15th and 16th century who visited only Lower Egypt and published their travel accounts, such as Joos van Ghistele or André Thévet, put Thebes in or close to Memphis.

The Karnak temple complex is first described by an unknown Venetian in 1589, although his account relates no name for the complex. This account, housed in the Biblioteca Nazionale Centrale di Firenze, is the first known European mention, since ancient Greek and Roman writers, about a whole range of monuments in Upper Egypt and Nubia, including Karnak, Luxor temple, Colossi of Memnon, Esna, Edfu, Kom Ombo, Philae, and others.

Karnak ("Carnac") as a village name, and name of the complex, is first attested in 1668, when two capuchin missionary brothers Protais and Charles François d'Orléans travelled though the area. Protais' writing about their travel was published by Melchisédech Thévenot (*Relations de divers voyages curieux*, 1670s–1696 editions) and Johann Michael Vansleb (*The Present State of Egypt*, 1678).

The first drawing of Karnak is found in Paul Lucas' travel account of 1704, (*Voyage du Sieur paul Lucas au Levant*). It is rather inaccurate, and can be quite confusing to modern eyes. Lucas travelled in Egypt during 1699–1703. The drawing shows a mixture of the Precinct of Amun-Re and the Precinct of Montu, based on a complex confined by the three huge Ptolemaic gateways of

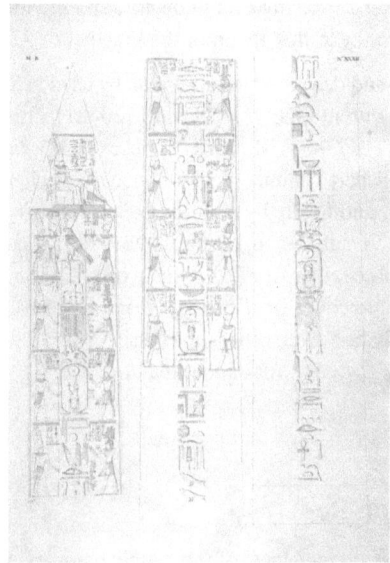

Figure 167: *Hieroglyphs from the great obelisk of Karnak, transcribed by Ippolito Rosellini in 1828*

Figure 168: *Photograph of the temple complex taken in 1914 - Cornell University Library*

Ptolemy III Euergetes / Ptolemy IV Philopator, and the massive 113 m long, 43 m high and 15 m thick, first Pylon of the Precinct of Amun-Re.

Karnak was visited and described in succession by Claude Sicard and his travel companion Pierre Laurent Pincia (1718 and 1720–21), Granger (1731), Frederick Louis Norden (1737–38), Richard Pococke (1738), James Bruce (1769), Charles-Nicolas-Sigisbert Sonnini de Manoncourt (1777), William George Browne (1792–93), and finally by a number of scientists of the Napoleon expedition, including Vivant Denon, during 1798–1799. Claude-Étienne Savary describes the complex rather detailed in his work of 1785; especially in light that it is a fictional account of a pretended journey to Upper Egypt, composed out of information from other travellers. Savary did visit Lower Egypt in 1777–78, and published a work about that too.

Main parts

Precinct of Amun-Re

This is the largest of the precincts of the temple complex, and is dedicated to Amun-Re, the chief deity of the Theban Triad. There are several colossal statues including the figure of Pinedjem I which is 10.5 meters tall. The sandstone for this temple, including all the columns, was transported from Gebel Silsila 100 miles (161 km) south on the Nile river.[414] It also has one of the largest obelisks, weighing 328 tonnes and standing 29 meters tall.[415,416]

File:Karnakpanorama.jpg

A panoramic view of the great hypostyle hall in the Precinct of Amun Re

File:Karnakfrieze1.jpg

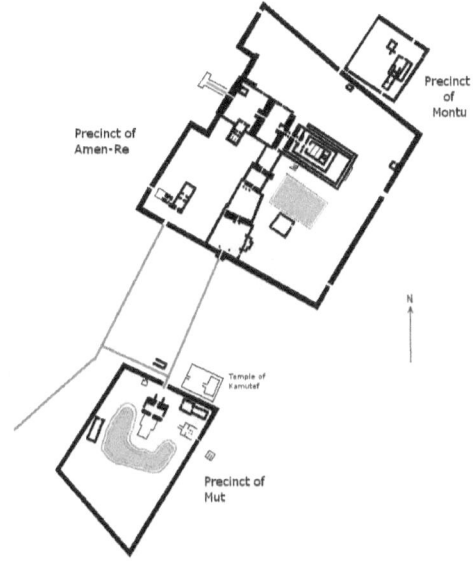

Figure 169: *Map of Karnak, showing major temple complexes and sacred crescent lake of Mut*

A panorama of a frieze in the Precinct of Amun Re

Precinct of Mut

Located to the south of the newer Amen-Re complex, this precinct was dedicated to the mother goddess, Mut, who became identified as the wife of Amun-Re in the eighteenth dynasty Theban Triad. It has several smaller temples associated with it and has its own sacred lake, constructed in a crescent shape. This temple has been ravaged, many portions having been used in other structures.

Following excavation and restoration works by the Johns Hopkins University team, lead by Betsy Bryan (see below) the Precinct of Mut has been opened to the public. Six hundred black granite statues were found in the courtyard to her temple. It may be the oldest portion of the site.

In 2006 Betsy Bryan, an archaeologist with Johns Hopkins University, excavating at the temple of Mut, presented her findings about one festival that included apparent intentional overindulgence in alcohol.[417] Participation in the festival was great, including the priestesses and the population. Historical records of tens of thousands attending the festival exist. These findings were made in the temple of Mut because when Thebes rose to greater prominence, Mut absorbed the warrior goddesses, Sekhmet and Bast, as some of her aspects. First, Mut became Mut-Wadjet-Bast, then Mut-Sekhmet-Bast (Wadjet having merged into Bast), then Mut also assimilated Menhit, another lioness goddess, and her adopted son's wife, becoming Mut-Sekhmet-Bast-Menhit, and finally becoming Mut-Nekhbet.

Temple excavations at Luxor discovered a "porch of drunkenness" built onto the temple by the pharaoh Hatshepsut, during the height of her twenty-year reign. In a later myth developed around the annual drunken Sekhmet festival, Ra, by then the sun god of Upper Egypt, created her from a fiery eye gained from his mother, to destroy mortals who conspired against him (Lower Egypt). In the myth, Sekhmet's blood-lust was not quelled at the end of battle and led to her destroying almost all of humanity, so Ra had tricked her by turning the Nile as red as blood (the Nile turns red every year when filled with silt during inundation) so that Sekhmet would drink it. The trick, however, was that the red liquid was not blood, but beer mixed with pomegranate juice so that it resembled blood, making her so drunk that she gave up slaughter and became an aspect of the gentle Hathor. The complex interweaving of deities occurred over the thousands of years of the culture.

Precinct of Montu

This portion of the site is dedicated to the son of Mut and Amun-Re, Montu, the war-god of the Theban Triad. It is located to the north of the Amun-Re complex and is much smaller in size. It is not open to the public.

Temple of Amenhotep IV (deliberately dismantled)

The temple that Akhenaten (Amenhotep IV) constructed on the site was located east of the main complex, outside the walls of the Amun-Re precinct. It was destroyed immediately after the death of its builder, who had attempted to overcome the powerful priesthood who had gained control over Egypt before his reign. It was so thoroughly demolished that its full extent and layout is currently unknown. The priesthood of that temple regained their powerful position as soon as Akhenaten died, and were instrumental in destroying many records of his existence.

In popular culture

- In *Transformers: Revenge of the Fallen* the final battle between Optimus Prime versus Megatron, The Fallen, and Starscream takes place in the hypostyle hall at Karnak.
- Agatha Christie's *Death on the Nile* takes place mainly on the steamship S.S. *Karnak*, as well as using the temple itself in one of its scenes.
- Lara Croft visited Karnak for three levels in *Tomb Raider: The Last Revelation* (Temple of Karnak, The Great Hypostyle Hall and Sacred Lake) and it was featured in the level editor package.
- In the movie *The Mummy Returns*, Karnak is one of the places Rick O'Connell and the others must go to, in order to ultimately reach the Scorpion King.
- The British symphonic metal band Bal-Sagoth have a song called *Unfettering the Hoary Sentinels of Karnak*.
- The first person shooter *PowerSlave* is set in and around Karnak.
- The first part of the modernist long poem, *Trilogy*, by H.D. is dedicated, "For Karnak 1923".
- Karnak is featured as a location for exploration in the PC game *The Sims 3: World Adventures*.
- Karnak is featured as a location in the PC game *Serious Sam*.
- Karnak is featured in the James Bond movie *The Spy Who Loved Me*.
- According to the *Stargate SG-1* episode *Serpent's Song*, Apophis' host was a scribe in the Temple of Amun at Karnak.
- In the original *Battlestar Galactica* series, For *Lost Planet of the Gods, Part II*, some shots of the pyramids at Kobol were actually filmed at the site of the Great Temple at Karnak and the Pyramids of Giza, in Egypt.
- In the Big Finish Doctor Who audio play *The Church and the Crown*, Erimemushinteperem introduces herself as princess Erimem of Karnak at the court of King Louis XIII of France.
- Karnak is the name of the Antarctic retreat of Ozymandias, one of the main characters in the 1980s comic *Watchmen* by Alan Moore and Dave Gibbons.
- In MARVEL Comics, Karnak is the name of an Inhuman.

Gallery

Figure 170: *The Sacred Lake of Precinct of Amun-Re*

Figure 171: *View of the first pylon of the temple of Amun-Re at Karnak*

Figure 172: *Ram statues at Karnak*

Figure 173: *Hypostyle hall of the Precinct of Amun-Re, as it appeared in 1838. From a tinted lithograph by David Roberts RA and Louis Hahge, 1806–1885*

Figure 174: *Ramses II*

Karnak

Figure 175: *Scarab*

Figure 176: *Egypt - Karnak. Gate and Pylon., n.d., Brooklyn Museum Archives*

Figure 177: *Egypt - Karnak. Great Statues., n.d., Goodyear. Brooklyn Museum Archives*

Further reading

- Blyth, Elizabeth (2006). *Karnak: Evolution of a Temple*. Routledge. ISBN 978-0-203-96837-6.

External links

Wikimedia Commons has media related to *Karnak temple complex*.

Wikisourcehas the text of the 1911 *Encyclopædia Britannica*article *Karnak*.

- CFEETK – Centre Franco-Égyptien d'Étude des Temples de Karnak (en)[418]
- Temple of Amun, numerous photos & schemes (comments in russian)[419]
- Karnak images[420]
- www.karnak3d.net :: "Web-book" The 3D reconstruction of the Great Temple of Amun in Karnak. Marc[421]
- *Digital Karnak UCLA*[422]
- Karnak Temple picture gallery[423] at Remains.se

Appendix

References

[1] //tools.wmflabs.org/geohack/geohack.php?pagename=Mecca&params=21_25_N_39_49_E_region:SA_type:city(1675368)

[2] Mecca Municipality http://www.holymakkah.gov.sa/. Holymakkah.gov.sa. Retrieved 3 February 2013.

[3] http://www.holymakkah.gov.sa

[4] //en.wikipedia.org/w/index.php?title=Template:Islam&action=edit

[5] Rarely, Bakkah ().

[6] Nasr, Seyyed (2005). *Mecca, The Blessed, Medina, The Radiant: The Holiest Cities of Islam*. Aperture

[7] A Saudi tower: Mecca versus Las Vegas: Taller, holier and even more popular than (almost) anywhere else, The Economist (24 June 2010), Cairo.

[8] Fattah, Hassan M. Islamic Pilgrims Bring Cosmopolitan Air to Unlikely City https://www.nytimes.com/2005/01/20/international/middleeast/20mecca.html, *The New York Times* (20 January 2005).

[9] AlSahib, AlMuheet fi Allughah, p. 303

[10] //en.wikipedia.org/w/index.php?title=Mecca&action=edit

[11] Holland, Tom; In the Shadow of the Sword; Little, Brown; 2012; Page 303: 'Otherwise, in all the vast corpus of ancient literature, there is not a single reference to Mecca – not one'

[12] The New Encyclopædia Britannica: Micropædia Volume 8. USA: Encyclopædia Britannica, Inc. 1995. p. 473.

[13] Holland, Tom; In the Shadow of the Sword; Little, Brown; 2012; Page 471

[14] Crone, Patricia; Meccan Trade and the Rise of Islam; 1987; Page 7

[15] Holland, Tom; In the Shadow of the Sword; Little, Brown; 2012; Page 303

[16] Translated by C H Oldfather, *Diodorus Of Sicily, Volume II*, William Heinemann Ltd., London & Harvard University Press, Cambridge, Massachusetts, MCMXXXV, p. 217.

[17] Jan Retsö, The Arabs in Antiquity (2003), 295–300

[18] Photius, Diodorus and Strabo (English): Stanley M. Burnstein (tr.), Agatharchides of Cnidus: On the Eritraean Sea (1989), 132–173, esp. 152–3 (§92).)

[19] *Islamic World*, p. 20

[20] Crown, Alan David (2001) *Samaritan Scribes and Manuscripts* https://books.google.com/books?id=e5iW24esf-sC&pg=PA27. Mohr Siebeck. p. 27

[21] Crone, Patricia and Cook, M. A. (1977) *Hagarism: The Making of the Islamic World*, https://books.google.com/books?id=Ta08AAAAIAAJ&pg=PA22 Cambridge University Press. p. 22.

[22] Lazarus-Yafeh, Hava (1992). *Intertwined Worlds: Medieval Islam and Bible Criticism* https://books.google.com/books?id=mzQABAAAQBAJ&pg=PA61. Princeton University Press. pp. 61–62

[23] Lapidus, p. 14

[24] Hajjah Adil, Amina, "*Prophet Muhammad*", ISCA, 1 June 2002,

[25] "Abraha." http://www.dacb.org/stories/ethiopia/_abraha.html *Dictionary of African Christian Biographies*. 2007. (last accessed 11 April 2007)

[26] Müller, Walter W. (1987) "Outline of the History of Ancient Southern Arabia" http://www.yemenweb.com/info/_disc/0000002c.htm, in Werner Daum (ed.), *Yemen: 3000 Years of Art and Civilisation in Arabia Felix*.

27

In turn citing:

28

[29] G. Lankester Harding & Enno Littman, Some Thamudic Inscriptions from the Hashimite Kingdom of the Jordan (Leiden, Netherlands – 1952), Page: 19, Inscription No. 112A

[30] Jawwad Ali, The Detailed History of Arabs before Islam (1993), Vol.4, Page: 11

31

32 " The Saud Family and Wahhabi Islam http://countrystudies.us/saudi-arabia/7.htm". Library of Congress Country Studies.
33 Cholera (pathology) http://www.britannica.com/EBchecked/topic/114078/cholera/253250/Seven-pandemics#ref=ref886683. Britannica Online Encyclopedia.
34 *Daily Telegraph* Saturday 25 November 1916, reprinted in *Daily Telegraph* Friday 25 November 2016 issue (page 36)
35 "Mecca" https://www.webcitation.org/5kx73ce9l?url=http://encarta.msn.com/encyclopedia_761577367/Mecca.html at Encarta. (Archived) 1 November 2009.
36 'The destruction of Mecca: Saudi hardliners are wiping out their own heritage' https://www.independent.co.uk/news/world/middle-east/the-destruction-of-mecca-saudi-hardliners-are-wiping-out-their-own-heritage-501647.html, The Independent, 6 August 2005. Retrieved 17 January 2011
37 Destruction of Islamic Architectural Heritage in Saudi Arabia: A Wake-up Call http://theamericanmuslim.org/tam.php/features/articles/saudi_destruction_of_muslim_historical_sites/, The American Muslim. Retrieved 17 January 2011
38 'Shame of the House of Saud: Shadows over Mecca' https//web.archive.org, The Independent, 19 April 2006 | archived from the original on 10 March, 2009
39 Express & Star http://www.expressandstar.com/days/1976-2000/1990.html. *Express & Star*. Retrieved 3 February 2013.
40
41 . ArabNews (10 November 2010)
42 Fire Breaks Out In Mecca Neighborhood Near Hajj Pilgrims http://news.outlookindia.com/items.aspx?artid=274063 . news.outlookindia.com (17 January 2005)
43 Saudi government demolishes historic Ottoman castle http://www.wsws.org/articles/2002/jan2002/fort-j28.shtml. Wsws.org (28 January 2002). Retrieved 2013-02-03.
44 WikiMapia http://wikimapia.org/1401843/ – About the Qishla and its location
45 http://www.witness-pioneer.org. Retrieved 3 February 2013.
46 IDEA Center Projects http://elabdarchitecture.com/resume.htm – Makkah Gate
47 *Mecca*. World Book Encyclopedia. 2003 edition. Volume M. p. 353
48 "المستشفيات – قائمة المستشفيات" http://www.moh.gov.sa/Sectors/Hospitals/Pages/default.aspx. moh.gov.sa.
49 Asian Football Stadiums http://www.fussballtempel.net/afc/listeafc.html – Stadium King Abdul Aziz
50 Dr Harjinder Singh Dilgeer says that Mecca was not banned to non-Muslim till nineteenth century; *Sikh History in 10 volumes*, Sikh University Press, (2010–2012), vol. 1, pp. 181–82
51 Statistical information department of the ministry of education: Statistical summary for education in Saudi Arabia http://www.moe.gov.sa/statscenter/tawzee.rar (AR)
52
53 El consorcio español firma el contrato del Ave a la Meca el 14 de enero | Economía | EL PAÍS http://www.elpais.com/articulo/economia/consorcio/espanol/firma/contrato/Ave/Meca/enero/elpepueco/20120109elpepueco_7/Tes. *El País*. (9 January 2012). Retrieved 2013-02-03.
54 "Roads" http://saudinf.com/main/g11.htm . saudinf.com.
55 "'THE ROADS AND PORTS SECTORS IN THE KINGDOM OF SAUDI ARABIA" http://www.saudia-online.com/newsnov01/news06.shtml. saudia-online.com. 5 November 2001
56 https://books.google.com/books?id=tkq3a0bXBa0C&lpg=PP1&pg=PA218
57 http://global.britannica.com/EBchecked/topic/31568/history-of-Arabia/45979/Quraysh
58 https://web.archive.org/web/20170317055002/http://www.holymakkah.gov.sa/en/Pages/default.aspx
59 http://www.saudinf.com/main/a83.htm
60 https://web.archive.org/web/20050721135336/https://etext.library.adelaide.edu.au/b/burton/richard/b97p/chapter27.html
61 //tools.wmflabs.org/geohack/geohack.php?pagename=Medina&params=24_28_N_39_36_E_region:SA_type:city(1183205)
62 http://www.stats.gov.sa/sites/default/files/ar-maddinah_1.pdf
63 Historical value of the Qur'ān and the Ḥadith https//books.google.com A.M. Khan

[64] What Everyone Should Know About the Qur'an https//books.google.com Ahmed Al-Laithy
[65] Sandra Mackey's account of her attempt to enter Mecca in
[66] http://www.perseus.tufts.edu/hopper/text?doc=Perseus%3Atext%3A2002.02.0006%3Asura%3D33%3Averse%3D13
[67] //en.wikipedia.org/w/index.php?title=Medina&action=edit
[68] However, an article in Aramco World http://www.saudiaramcoworld.com/issue/200606/Saudi by John Anthony states: "To the perhaps parochial Muslims of North Africa in fact the sanctity of Kairouan is second only to Mecca among all cities of the world." Saudi Aramco's bimonthly magazine's goal is to broaden knowledge of the cultures, history and geography of the Arab and Muslim worlds and their connections with the West; pages 30–36 of the January/February 1967 print edition The Fourth Holy City https://web.archive.org/web/20040624130307/http://www.saudiaramcoworld.com/issue/196701/the.fourth.holy.city.htm
[69] 1954 Encyclopedia Americana, vol. 18, pp.587, 588
[70] hadith found in 'Virtues of Madinah' of Sahih Bukhari http://www.searchtruth.com/book_display.php?book=30&translator=1 searchtruth.com
[71] Jewish Encyclopedia Medina http://www.jewishencyclopedia.com/view.jsp?artid=326&letter=M
[72] Peters 193
[73] "Al-Medina." *Encyclopaedia of Islam*
[74] for date see "J. Q. R." vii. 175, note
[75] See e.g., Peters 193; "Qurayza", *Encyclopaedia Judaica*
[76] Muslim sources usually referred to Himyar kings by the dynastic title of "Tubba".
[77] Guillaume 7–9, Peters 49–50
[78] Subhani, *The Message*: The Events of the First Year of Migration http://www.balagh.net/english/ahl_bayt/the_message/27.htm
[79] For alliances, see Guillaume 253
[80] Firestone 118. For opinions disputing the early date of the Constitution of Medina, see e.g., Peters 116; "Muhammad", "Encyclopaedia of Islam"; "Kurayza, Banu", "Encyclopaedia of Islam".
[81] Shelomo Dov Goitein, *The Yemenites – History, Communal Organization, Spiritual Life* (Selected Studies), editor: Menahem Ben-Sasson, Jerusalem 1983, pp. 288–299.
[82] Sahih al-Bukhari: Volume 5, Book 59, Number 287 http://www.usc.edu/schools/college/crcc/engagement/resources/texts/muslim/hadith/bukhari/059.sbt.html#005.059.287
[83] Sunan Abu Dawud: Book 14, Number 2659 http://www.usc.edu/schools/college/crcc/engagement/resources/texts/muslim/hadith/abudawud/014.sat.html#014.2659
[84] Sunan Abu Dawud: Book 14, Number 2658 http://www.usc.edu/schools/college/crcc/engagement/resources/texts/muslim/hadith/abudawud/014.sat.html#014.2658
[85] Armstrong, p. 176.
[86] Lings, p. 148.
[87] "O thou whom God hath made victorious, slay!"
[88] Quran: Al-i-Imran
[89] The Biography of Mahomet, and Rise of Islam. Chapter Fourth. http://www.answering-islam.de/Main/Books/Muir/Life2/chap4.htm Extension of Islam and Early Converts, from the assumption by Mahomet of the prophetical office to the date of the first Emigration to Abyssinia by William Muir
[90] Robert Mantran, *L'expansion musulmane* Presses Universitaires de France 1995, p. 86.
[91] Bosworth,C. Edmund: Historic Cities of the Islamic World, p. 385 – "Half-a-century later, in 654/1256, Medina was threatened by a volcanic eruption. After a series of earthquakes, a stream of lava appeared, but fortunately flowed to the east of the town and then northwards."
[92] Peters, Francis (1994). *Mecca: A Literary History of the Muslim Holy Land.* PP376-377. Princeton University Press.
[93] Mohmed Reda Bhacker (1992). *Trade and Empire in Muscat and Zanzibar: Roots of British Domination.* Routledge Chapman & Hall. P63: Following the plunder of Medina in 1810 'when the Prophet's tomb was opened and its jewels and relics sold and distributed among the Wahhabi soldiery'. P122: the Ottoman Sultan Mahmud II was at last moved to act against such outrage.

[94] Economic cities a rise http://www.fdimagazine.com/news/fullstory.php/aid/1830/Economic_cities_a_rise.html
[95] *Islamic heritage lost as Makkah modernises* http://www.islamicpluralism.org/764/islamic-heritage-lost-as-Makkah-modernises, Center for Islamic Pluralism
[96] History of the Cemetery of Jannat al-Baqi http://www.al-islam.org/shrines/baqi.htm retrieved 17 January 2011
[97] //tools.wmflabs.org/geohack/geohack.php?pagename=St._Peter%27s_Basilica&params=41_54_08_N_12_27_12_E_type:landmark_region:VA
[98] http://www.vaticanstate.va/content/vaticanstate/en/monumenti/basilica-di-s-pietro.html
[99] http://whc.unesco.org/en/list/286
[100] James Lees-Milne describes St. Peter's Basilica as "a church with a unique position in the Christian world" in .
[101]
[102] *Papal Mass* http://www.papalaudience.org/papal-mass (accessed 28 February 2012)
[103] Georgina Masson, *The Companion Guide to Rome*, (2003), pp. 615–6
[104]
[105] Helen F. North, quoted in *Secrets of Rome*, Robert Kahn, (1999) pp. 79–80
[106] Ralph Waldo Emerson, 7 April 1833
[107] Benedict XVI's theological act of renouncing the title of "Patriarch of the West" had as consequence that Catholic Roman Rite patriarchal basilicas are today officially known as Papal basilicas.
[108] *The Treaty of the Lateran* by Benedict Williamson; London: Burns, Oates, and Washbourne Limited, 1929; pages 42–66) http://www.aloha.net/~mikesch/treaty.htm. This is in contrast to the other three Papal Major Basilicas, which are within Italian territory and not the territory of the Vatican City State. (Lateran Treaty of 1929, Article 15 ()) However, the Holy See fully owns these three basilicas, and Italy is legally obligated to recognize its full ownership thereof (Lateran Treaty of 1929, Article 13 ()) and to concede to all of them "the immunity granted by International Law to the headquarters of the diplomatic agents of foreign States" (Lateran Treaty of 1929, Article 15 ()).
[109]
[110] //en.wikipedia.org/w/index.php?title=St._Peter%27s_Basilica&action=edit
[111] Frank J. Korn, *Hidden Rome* Paulist Press (2002)
[112] Quarrying of stone for the Colosseum had, in turn, been paid for with treasure looted at the Siege of Jerusalem and destruction of the temple by the emperor Vespasian's general (and the future emperor) Titus in 70 AD., Claridge, Amanda (1998). *Rome: An Oxford Archaeological Guide* (First ed.). Oxford, UK: Oxford University Press, 1998. pp. 276–282.
[113] Julius II's tomb was left incomplete and was eventually erected in the Church of St Peter ad Vincola.
[114] "Johann Tetzel", *Encyclopædia Britannica*, 2007: "Tetzel's experiences as a preacher of indulgences, especially between 1503 and 1510, led to his appointment as general commissioner by Albrecht, archbishop of Mainz, who, deeply in debt to pay for a large accumulation of benefices, had to contribute a considerable sum toward the rebuilding of St. Peter's Basilica in Rome. Albrecht obtained permission from Pope Leo X to conduct the sale of a special plenary indulgence (i.e., remission of the temporal punishment of sin), half of the proceeds of which Albrecht was to claim to pay the fees of his benefices. In effect, Tetzel became a salesman whose product was to cause a scandal in Germany that evolved into the greatest crisis (the Reformation) in the history of the Western church."
[115] Hillerbrand, Hans J. "Martin Luther: Indulgences and salvation," *Encyclopædia Britannica*, 2007.
[116] Bramante's plan,
[117] Raphael's plan,
[118] Peruzzi's plan,
[119] Sangallo's plan,
[120] Michelangelo's plan,
[121] Eneide Mignacca, *Michelangelo and the architecture of St. Peter's Basilica*, lecture, Sydney University, (1982)

[122] This claim has recently been made for Yamoussoukro Basilica, the dome of which, modelled on St. Peter's, is lower but has a taller cross.
[123] The dome of Florence Cathedral is depicted in a fresco at Santa Maria Novella that pre-dates its building by about 100 years.
[124] * *Galassi Alghisii Carpens., apud Alphonsum II. Ferrariae Ducem architecti, opus* https://books.google.com/books?id=qP5PAAAAcAAJ&printsec=frontcover&dq=Alghisi&hl=en&sa=X&ei=quiyUPqrHeffyQGW_IE4&ved=0CDkQ6AEwAw, by Galasso Alghisi, Dominicus Thebaldius (1563). page 44/147 of Google PDF download.
[125] http://www.biblegateway.com/passage/?search=Matthew%2016:18-19:18&version=4
[126] BBC, *Rare Michelangelo sketch for sale*, Friday, 14 October 2005, http://news.bbc.co.uk/2/hi/entertainment/4343488.stm accessed: 9 February 2008
[127] Another view of the façade statues. From left to right: ① Thaddeus, ② Matthew, ③ Philip, ④ Thomas, ⑤ James the Elder, ⑥ John the Baptist (technically a 'precursor' and not an apostle); ⑦ Christ (centre, the only one with a halo); ⑧ Andrew, ⑨ John the Apostle, ⑩ James the Younger, ⑪ Bartholomew, ⑫ Simon and ⑬ Matthias. ()
[128] The word "stupendous" is used by a number of writers trying to adequately describe the enormity of the interior. These include James Lees-Milne and Banister Fletcher.
[129] The obelisk was originally erected at Heliopolis by an unknown pharaoh of the Fifth dynasty of Egypt (c. 2494 BC – 2345 BC).
[130] The statue was damaged in 1972 by Lazlo Toft, a Hungarian-Australian, who considered that the veneration shown to the statue was idolatrous. The damage was repaired and the statue subsequently placed behind glass.
[131] Source: the respective biographical entries on Essay of a General List of Cardinals http://www.fiu.edu/~mirandas/essay.htm by Salvador Miranda with corrections provided by Werner Maleczek, *Papst und Kardinalskolleg von 1191 bis 1216*, Wien 1984 for the period before 1190 until 1254
[132] "Since Nicholas V twenty-seven popes over a span of 178 years had imagined this day. They had already spent 46 800 052 ducats (...) And still the building was not done. The basic construction was complete, but the last genius (Bernini) to put his signature on the Basilica was just beginning his work." in .
[133] //www.jstor.org/stable/988425
[134] //www.worldcat.org/oclc/19640446
[135] //doi.org/10.2307%2F988425
[136] //www.jstor.org/stable/990755
[137] //doi.org/10.2307%2F990755
[138] //www.jstor.org/stable/3258914
[139] //www.worldcat.org/oclc/39642638
[140] //doi.org/10.2307%2F3258914
[141] //www.jstor.org/stable/767006
[142] //doi.org/10.2307%2F767006
[143] https://archive.org/details/historyofarchite00flet
[144] //www.worldcat.org/issn/0022-1953
[145] //www.jstor.org/stable/204124
[146] //doi.org/10.2307%2F204124
[147] http://penelope.uchicago.edu/Thayer/E/Gazetteer/Places/Europe/Italy/Lazio/Roma/Rome/_Texts/Lanciani/LANPAC/3*.html
[148] http://www.stpetersbasilica.info/Docs/JLM/SaintPeters-1.htm
[149] //www.worldcat.org/oclc/1393052
[150] //www.worldcat.org/issn/0079-0958
[151] //www.jstor.org/stable/1567138
[152] //doi.org/10.2307%2F1567138
[153] //www.worldcat.org/oclc/2208913
[154] http://news.nationalgeographic.com/news/2001/11/1118_vaticanmain.html
[155] https://web.archive.org/web/20140610233733/http://bernini2013.org/truth-unveiled-by-time/urban-viiis-bell-towers/
[156] http://bernini2013.org/truth-unveiled-by-time/urban-viiis-bell-towers/

[157] http://www.vaticanstate.va/content/vaticanstate/en/monumenti/basilica-di-s-pietro.html#
[158] http://www.vatican.va/various/basiliche/san_pietro/vr_tour/index-en.html
[159] http://www.stpetersbasilica.info
[160] http://news.nationalgeographic.com/2015/07/150720-Vatican-360-Degree-Tour-Saint-Peters-Basilica
[161] https://maps.google.com/maps?q=vatican&ll=41.901806,12.455138&spn=0.004081,0.007298&t=h&hl=en
[162] //tools.wmflabs.org/geohack/geohack.php?pagename=Mahabodhi_Temple&params=24.696004_N_84.991358_E_
[163] http://whc.unesco.org/en/list/1056
[164] Harle, 201; Michell, 228-229
[165] Harle, 201; Michell, 228-229
[166] Harle, 201; Michell, 228-229
[167] J.iv.233 (puthuvinābhi)
[168] J.iv.229
[169] DA.ii.412
[170] DA.ii.425; BuA.248
[171] Buddhist Architecture, Huu Phuoc Le, Grafikol, 2010 p.240 https://books.google.com/books?id=9jb364g4BvoC&pg=PA240
[172] Buddhist Architecture, Huu Phuoc Le p.240 https://books.google.com/books?id=9jb364g4BvoC&pg=PA240
[173] A Global History of Architecture, Francis D. K. Ching, Mark M. Jarzombek, Vikramaditya Prakash, John Wiley & Sons, 2017 p.570ff https://books.google.com/books?id=SPqKDgAAQBAJ&pg=PT570
[174] "Sowing the Seeds of the Lotus: A Journey to the Great Pilgrimage Sites of Buddhism, Part I" by John C. Huntington. *Orientations*, November 1985 pg 61
[175] Mahâbodhi, or the great Buddhist temple under the Bodhi tree at Buddha-Gaya, Alexander Cunningham, 1892 https://archive.org/stream/cu31924008747788
[176] Buddhist Architecture, Huu Phuoc Le, Grafikol, 2010 p.240 https://books.google.com/books?id=9jb364g4BvoC&pg=PA240
[177] Didactic Narration: Jataka Iconography in Dunhuang with a Catalogue of Jataka Representations in China, Alexander Peter Bell, LIT Verlag Münster, 2000 p.15ff https://books.google.com/books?id=77hHrXX4COgC&pg=PA15
[178] "The railing of Sanchi Stupa No.2, which represents the oldest extensive stupa decoration in existence, (and) dates from about the second century B.C.E" Constituting Communities: Theravada Buddhism and the Religious Cultures of South and Southeast Asia, John Clifford Holt, Jacob N. Kinnard, Jonathan S. Walters, SUNY Press, 2012 p.197 https://books.google.com/books?id=PnnG8sclrdYC&pg=PA197
[179] British Library Online Gallery http://www.bl.uk/onlinegallery/onlineex/apac/photocoll/a/019pho000001003u00065000.html
[180] Coedès, George (1968). Walter F. Vella, ed. The Indianized States of Southeast Asia. trans.Susan Brown Cowing. University of Hawaii Press.
[181] India Revisited by Sri Edwin Arnold http://rankotviharaya.org/profile.html
[182] Dipak K. Barua, "Buddha Gaya Temple: its history"
[183] Amendment allows non-Hindu to head Bodh Gaya temple committee http://www.thehindu.com/news/national/other-states/amendment-allows-nonhindu-to-head-bodh-gaya-temple-committee/article4974856.ece, The Hindu, August 1, 2013
[184] Buddhists seek control over Mahabodhi temple management http://www.buddhistchannel.tv/index.php?id=42,6138,0,0,1,0 IANS. March 28, 2008. Retrieved March 29, 2008.
[185] Scandal gnaws at Buddha's holy tree in India http://www.buddhistchannel.tv/index.php?id=42,5857,0,0,1,0. Denyer, Simon. Reuters News Service. February 3, 2008. Retrieved March 27, 2008.
[186] No damage to Bodhi tree: Govt http://www.dnaindia.com/report.asp?NewsID=1043040. Singh, Sanjay. July 21, 2006. Retrieved March 27, 2008.
[187] http://www.bodhgayatemple.com/images/pdf/Annual%20Puja%20List%202017-18.pdf

[188] https://books.google.com/?id=jWhMCAAAQBAJ&pg=PT339&lpg=PT339&dq=Surai+Sasai#v=onepage&q=Surai%20Sasai&f=false
[189] http://www.jstor.org/stable/1466173
[190] http://crossasia-journals.ub.uni-heidelberg.de/index.php/iaf/article/view/989/967
[191] http://ncert.nic.in/NCERTS/l/kefa106.pdf
[192] http://www.mahabodhi.com/
[193] http://www.trodly.com/destination/5004/mahabodhi-temple
[194] http://www.bodhgayanews.net/
[195] http://whc.unesco.org/pg.cfm?cid=31&id_site=1056
[196] http://www.buddhistplacesinindia.com/bodhgaya-temple-in-bihar.aspx
[197] //tools.wmflabs.org/geohack/geohack.php?pagename=Golden_Temple&params=31_37_12_N_74_52_37_E_region:IN-PB_type:landmark
[198] Arvind-Pal Singh Mandair 2013, pp. 41-42.
[199] http://new.sgpc.net/sriharmandirsahib/
[200] The Editors of Encyclopaedia Britannica 2014.
[201] Louis E. Fenech & W. H. McLeod 2014, p. 33.
[202] Pardeep Singh Arshi 1989, pp. 5-7.
[203] Pashaura Singh & Louis E. Fenech 2014, pp. 431-432.
[204] Trudy Ring, Noelle Watson & Paul Schellinger 2012, pp. 28-29.
[205] Pashaura Singh & Louis E. Fenech 2014, pp. 30-31.
[206] Louis E. Fenech & W. H. McLeod 2014, p. 146.
[207] Henry Walker 2002, pp. 95-98.
[208] Arvind-Pal Singh Mandair 2013, pp. 38-40.
[209] Christopher Shackle & Arvind Mandair 2013, pp. xv-xvi.
[210] Arvind-Pal Singh Mandair 2013, pp. 42–43.
[211] Louis E. Fenech & W. H. McLeod 2014, p. 67.
[212] Singh 2011, pp. 34-35.
[213] Dr. Madanjit Kaur "The Golden Temple: Past and Present" Dept. of Guru Nanak Studies, Guru Nanak Dev University Press, 1983, p. 11
[214] Pashaura Singh & Louis E. Fenech 2014, pp. 435-436.
[215]
[216] Louis E. Fenech, Martyrdom in the Sikh Tradition, Oxford University Press, pp. 118-121
[217] Louis E. Fenech & W. H. McLeod 2014, pp. 146-147.
[218] Pardeep Singh Arshi 1989, pp. 22–25.
[219] , Quote: "The Golden Temple (...) By 1776, the present structure, a harmonious blending of Mughal and Rajput (Islamic and Hindu) architectural styles was complete."
[220] Pardeep Singh Arshi 1989, pp. 97–116.
[221] Pardeep Singh Arshi 1989, pp. 68–73.
[222] Singh 2011, p. 80.
[223] W. Owen Cole 2004, p. 10.
[224] Golden temple's hi-tech basement info center http//www.hindustantimes.com
[225] Golden temple story comes alive http://www.tribuneindia.com/news/amritsar/golden-temple-s-story-comes-alive-at-its-plaza/340292.html
[226] Singh 2011, pp. 81-82.
[227] NG Barrier and Nazar Singh (2015), Singh Sabha Movement http://www.learnpunjabi.org/eos/index.aspx, Encyclopedia of Sikhism, Harbans Singh (Editor in Chief), Punjab University
[228] Arvind-Pal Singh Mandair 2013, pp. 85-86.
[229] Louis E. Fenech & W. H. McLeod 2014, pp. 273-274.
[230] Pashaura Singh & Louis E. Fenech 2014, pp. 28–29, 73–76.
[231] , Quote: "Brahmin priests and their idols had been associated with the Golden Temple for at least a century and had over these years received the patronage of pious Hindus and Sikhs. In the 1890s these practices came under increasing attack by reformist Sikhs."
[232] Pashaura Singh & Louis E. Fenech 2014, pp. 433-434.
[233] https://www.britannica.com/topic/Harmandir-Sahib
[234] http://www.learnpunjabi.org/eos/index.aspx
[235] https://books.google.com/books?id=rcmfAAAAMAAJ

[236] https://books.google.com/books?id=ohYwDwAAQBAJ&pg=PT18
[237] https://books.google.com/books?id=xajcAwAAQBAJ
[238] https://books.google.com/books?id=7xIT7OMSJ44C
[239] https://books.google.com/books?id=voerPYsAB5wC
[240] https://books.google.com/books?id=VvoJV8mw0LwC
[241] https://books.google.com/books?id=7YwNAwAAQBAJ
[242] https://books.google.com/books?id=vdhLAQAAQBAJ
[243] https://books.google.com/books?id=h40AAwAAQBAJ
[244] https://books.google.com/books?id=ddgO-DldmSwC
[245] https://web.archive.org/web/20131116080518/http://new.sgpc.net/
[246] https://dmoztools.net/Regional/Asia/India/Punjab/Localities/Amritsar/Society_and_Culture/Religion/Golden_Temple/
[247] http://www.columbia.edu/itc/mealac/pritchett/00routesdata/1500_1599/sikhism/goldenphotosearly/goldenphotosearly.html
[248] //tools.wmflabs.org/geohack/geohack.php?pagename=Pashupatinath_Temple&params=27_42_35_N_85_20_55_E_type:landmark_region:NP
[249] http://www.pashupati.org.np//
[250] //en.wikipedia.org/w/index.php?title=Template:Hinduism&action=edit
[251] Robertson McCarta and Nelles Verlag: Nelles Guide to Nepal, First Edition, 1990, page 94
[252] Encyclopaedia of Saivism https://books.google.com/books?id=N4xIBNmhpXcC&dq=pashupatinath&source=gbs_navlinks_s, Swami P. Anand, Swami Parmeshwaranand, Publisher Sarup & Sons, , , page 206
[253] http://www.npsin.in/mandir/Shri-Pashupatinath-Mandir
[254] http://www.pashupatinathtemple.org
[255] http://www.muktinathdarshan.com/tripDetail/232-Pashupatinath-Darshan.html
[256] http://nepal.tv/watch/pashupatinath
[257] http://www.nepalopedia.com/virtual-tour/Pashupati
[258] //tools.wmflabs.org/geohack/geohack.php?pagename=Mount_Kailash&params=31_4_0_N_81_18_45_E_region:CN-54_type:mountain
[259] Monier-Williams Sanskrit Dictionary, page 311 column 3 http://www.sanskrit-lexicon.uni-koeln.de/cgi-bin/monier/serveimg.pl?file=/scans/MWScan/MWScanjpg/mw0311-kesaragrAma.jpg
[260] Entry for कैलास: http://dsal.uchicago.edu/cgi-bin/philologic/getobject.pl?c.2:1:1523.apte in Apte Sanskrit-English Dictionary
[261] Sarat Chandra Das (1902). *Tibetan-English Dictionary with Sanskrit Synonyms*. Calcutta, India: Bengal Secretariat Book Depot, page 32 https://archive.org/stream/tibetanenglishdi00dassuoft#page/32/mode/1up.
[262] Albinia (2008), p. 288. abc
[263] //en.wikipedia.org/w/index.php?title=Template:Saivism&action=edit
[264]
[265] *The Sacred Mountain*, pp. 39, 33, 35, 225, 280, 353, 362–363, 377–378
[266] *The Sacred Mountain*, pp. 31, 33, 35
[267] The World's Most Mysterious Places Published by Reader's Digest pg.85
[268] *The Sacred Mountain*, pp. 25–26
[269] Geology and Geography of the Mt. Kailash area and Indus River headwaters in south-western Tibet http://www.shangri-la-river-expeditions.com/wchinageo/indushwgeo/kailash&indushwgeo.html Pete Winn , Science Director Earth Science Expeditions. Accessed January 2014.
[270] Plate Tectonic & northern Pacific http://plate-tectonic.narod.ru/chinageo1photoalbum.html Accessed January 2014.
[271] *The Sacred Mountain*, p. 120
[272] *The Sacred Mountain*, p. 116
[273] *The Sacred Mountain*, p. 129
[274] https://www.youtube.com/watch?v=njJmHg1z5aY
[275] //tools.wmflabs.org/geohack/geohack.php?pagename=Mount_Olympus&params=40_05_08_N_22_21_31_E_type:mountain_scale:100000

[276] Jones, Daniel (2003) [1917], Peter Roach, James Hartmann and Jane Setter, eds., *English Pronouncing Dictionary*, Cambridge: Cambridge University Press, ISBN 3-12-539683-2
[277] https//books.google.com
[278] http://www.musesnet.gr/etimes/MOUNT%20OLYMPUS.htm
[279] http://www.greekmountainflora.info/Olympos/Olympos%20Olympus.html
[280] http://www.olympusfd.gr/us/Default.asp
[281] http://gserver.civil.auth.gr/glab/indexen-research.htm#f12
[282] http://olympos.bitballoon.com
[283] //tools.wmflabs.org/geohack/geohack.php?pagename=Dome_of_the_Rock&params=31.7780_N_35.2354_E_type:landmark
[284] Chisholm, Hugh, ed. (1911). "Aelia Capitolina". Encyclopædia Britannica (11th ed.). Cambridge University Press. p. 256. Lester L. Grabbe (2010). An Introduction to Second Temple Judaism: History and Religion of the Jews in the Time of Nehemiah, the Maccabees, Hillel, and Jesus. A&C Black. p. 29.
[285] Davidson, Linda Kay and David Martin Gitlitz *Pilgrimage: From the Ganges to Graceland : an Encyclopedia* https//books.google.com Volume 1, ABC-CLIO, Inc, Santa Barbara, CA 2002, p. 274.
[286] "Julian thought to rebuild at an extravagant expense the proud Temple once at Jerusalem, and committed this task to Alypius of Antioch. Alypius set vigorously to work, and was seconded by the governor of the province, when fearful balls of fire, breaking out near the foundations, continued their attacks, till the workmen, after repeated scorchings, could approach no more: and he gave up the attempt." Ammianus Marcellinus, *Res Gestae*, 23.1.2–3.
[287] Jacob Lassner: *Muslims on the sanctity of Jerusalem: preliminary thoughts on the search for a conceptual framework*. In: *Jerusalem Studies in Arabic and Islam*. Band 31 (2006), p. 176.
[288] Necipoğlu 2008, p. 22.
[289] Vogüé 1864, p. 85 https://archive.org/stream/letempledejrusal00vogm#page/85/mode/1up
[290] Olge Grabar: *The Meaning of the Dome of the Rock*.
[291] Necipoğlu 2008, p. 31.
[292] Stark, Rodney. *God's Battalions; a Case for the Crusades*. Harper Collins, NY, 2009, pp. 84–85.
[293] Clermont-Ganneau 1899, p. 179 https://archive.org/stream/archaeologicalre01cler#page/179/mode/1up
[294] Central Bank of Iran http://www.cbi.ir/default_en.aspx. Banknotes & Coins: 1000 Rials http://www.cbi.ir/page/1979.aspx. – Retrieved on 24 March 2009.
[295] Jerusalem's Holy Places and the Peace Process http://www.washingtoninstitute.org/templateC04.php?CID=6 Marshall J. Breger and Thomas A. Idinopulos, Washington Institute for Near East Policy, 1998.
[296] Braswell, G. *Islam – Its Prophets, People, Politics and Power*. Nashville, TN: Broadman and Holman Publishers. 1996. p. 14
[297] Ali, A. *The Holy Qur'an – Translation and Commentary*. Bronx, NY: Islamic Propagation Centre International. 1946. pp. 1625–31
[298] Yakub of Syria (Ka'b al-Ahbar) Last Jewish Attempt at Islamic Leadership http://www.alsadiqin.org/en/index.php?title=Yakub_of_Syria_(Ka'b_al-Ahbar)_Last_Jewish_Attempt_at_Islamic_Leadership Committee for Historical Research in Islam and Judaism, © 2004–2012, accessed July 2013. "He continued to follow Rabbinic tradition such that later Islamic historians questioned whether he ever 'converted' to Islam."
[299] Stephen Spector, *Evangelicals and Israel:The Story of American Christian Zionism*, Oxford University Press, 2008 p. 202.
[300] Andrew Esensten U.S.-born Knesset candidate, Jeremy Gimpel, and his Dome of the Rock 'joke' http://www.haaretz.com/weekend/anglo-file/u-s-born-knesset-candidate-jeremy-gimpel-and-his-dome-of-the-rock-joke.premium-1.494616, *Haaretz* 20 January 2013.
[301] //www.worldcat.org/oclc/5862604
[302] https://archive.org/stream/archaeologicalre01cler#page/179/mode/1up
[303] https://archnet.org/system/publications/contents/6779/original/DPC3643.pdf?1384802697
[304] //doi.org/10.1179%2F003103207x194145
[305] https://archive.org/details/letempledejrusal00vogm

[306] http://www.nyu.edu/gsas/dept/fineart/people/faculty/flood_PDFs/Ottoman%20windows.pdf
[307] //www.jstor.org/stable/25202759
[308] //www.jstor.org/stable/25203167
[309] https://archive.org/details/in.ernet.dli.2015.533956
[310] http://vc.bridgew.edu/cgi/viewcontent.cgi?article=1422&context=br_rev
[311] https://archnet.org/sites/2814
[312] http://www.sacredsites.com/1st30/domeof.html
[313] http://www.ne.jp/asahi/arc/ind/2_meisaku/28_jerusalem/jer_eng.htm
[314] http://www.bibledex.com/israel/dome_of_the_rock.html
[315] http://www.sonic.net/~tallen/palmtree/dor.piers/dor.piers.htm
[316] //tools.wmflabs.org/geohack/geohack.php?pagename=Western_Wall&params=31.7767_N_35.2345_E_type:landmark
[317] "One of the best documented endowments, one that embraced the entire quarter of Western Muslims or Maghrebis".
[318] Shir ha-Shirim Rabbah, ch. 2–8
[319] "Wailing Wall" appears, for example, in J.J. Reynolds, *Jewish Advocate for the Young* (1859). H. Bonar, *Days and Nights in the East* (1866) and J.R. Macduff, *Memories of Olivet* (1868), and many later works.
[320] "Dr. Shmuel Berkovitz, a scholar of the holy places in the Land of Israel, found that until the eleventh century, Muslim scholars disagreed as to the location of the tethering of Muhammad's steed and pointed to different places on Al-Haram al-Sharif."
[321] http://www.israelinsideout.com/Things-to-do-in-Jerusalem/the-kotel-wailingwestern-wall.html
[322] Transgender woman denied entry to Western Wall http://www.ynetnews.com/articles/0,7340,L-4612205,00.html YNET News, January 6, 2015
[323] Transgender woman prevented from accessing Western Wall http://www.haaretz.com/jewish-world/jewish-world-news/1.635838 Haaretz, January 7, 2015
[324] 'Transgendered woman barred from Western Wall prayer http://www.timesofisrael.com/transgendered-woman-barred-from-western-wall-prayer/ Times of Israel, January 7, 2015
[325] Date is adjusted in some Jewish texts to read 422 BCE. See Chronology of the Bible.
[326] Date is adjusted in some Jewish texts to read 68 CE. See Chronology of the Bible.
[327] David M. Gitlitz & Linda Kay Davidson "Pilgrimage and the Jews" (Westport: CT: Praeger, 2006)40-.
[328] Adler preferred the generic translation "western wall" rather than "Western Wall".
[329] "In the 16th century, Ottoman Sultan Suleiman the Magnificent permitted the Jews to make the Western Wall their official holy place and had his court architect Sinan build an oratory for them there."
[330] "It is possible that official recognition of the right of Jews to pray by the Wall was granted already in the second half of the sixteenth century by a *firman* (official decree) issued by Suleiman the Magnificent. This firman may have been related to the efforts of the Ottoman ruler to lure Jews to Palestine as a counterbalance to the Arab population, which had rebelled against the new rulers, who were Turkish rather than Arabs."
[331]
[332] Baruch, Yuval. The Mughrabi Gate Access – the Real Story http://www.antiquities.org.il/article_Item_eng.asp?sec_id=17&sub_subj_id=468. Israel Antiquities Authority
[333] Martin Gilbert, Jerusalem in the Twentieth Century (New York: John Wiley & Sons, 1996, p254.
[334] Joost R. Hiltermann, 'Teddy Kollek and the Native Question,' in Annelies Moors, Toine van Teeffelen, Sharif Kanaana, Ilham Abu Ghazaleh (eds.) *Discourse and Palestine: Power, Text and Context*, https://books.google.com/books?id=FsjgmSPiWvsC&pg=PA55 Het Spinhuis, 1995 pp.55-65, p.55-6
[335] Nir Hasson, 'Rare photograph reveals ancient Jerusalem mosque destroyed in 1967,' http://www.haaretz.com/news/national/rare-photograph-reveals-ancient-jerusalem-mosque-destroyed-in-1967.premium-1.436593 at Haaretz, June 15, 2012.

[336] Ari Shavit, 'Jerusalem-born thinker Meron Benvenisti has a message for Israelis: Stop whining,' http://www.haaretz.com/weekend/magazine/jerusalem-born-thinker-meron-benvenisti-has-a-message-for-israelis-stop-whining.premium-1.469447 at Haaretz, October 11, 2012.

[337] Gershom Gorenberg, *The End of Days: Fundamentalism and the Struggle for the Temple Mount.* Oxford University Press, 2002 p.102.

[338] Henry Cattan, *The Palestine Question,* Taylor & Francis, 1988 p.256.

[339] Reinventing Jerusalem:Israel's Reconstruction of the Jewish Quarter after 1967, Simone Ricca https//books.google.com, pp. 67–113

[340] From the Archive: First rumblings in the battle for pluralism at the Western Wall http://www.jta.org/2015/04/24/news-opinion/the-telegraph/from-the-archive-when-the-western-wall-battles-began JTA, April 24, 2015.

[341] Jewish Virtual Library https://www.jewishvirtuallibrary.org/jsource/Archaeology/Robinsons_Arch.html, retrieved March 26, 2011.

[342] Court Rules for Women in Western Wall Dispute https://www.nytimes.com/2013/04/12/world/middleeast/israeli-court-rules-for-women-at-western-wall.html New York Times, April 11, 2013

[343] Israel approves $23 million plan to renovate near Western Wall http://www.haaretz.com/news/national/israel-approves-23-million-plan-to-renovate-near-western-wall-1.325927, *Haartez,* (November 21, 2010).

[344] Guttman, Nathan and Jane Eisner. "Kotel Egalitarian Prayer Plan Set in Motion by Dramatic Western Wall Compromise." http://forward.com/articles/174588/kotel-egalitarian-prayer-plan-set-in-motion-by-dra/?p=all *The Jewish Daily Forward.* April 10, 2013. April 11, 2013.

[345] Jaffay, Nathan, "Is Western Wall Prayer Platform a Step Forward For Women – or Back?" http://forward.com/articles/183130/is-western-wall-prayer-platform-step-forward-for-w/?p=all,, *The Jewish Daily Forward,* August 30, 2013. Retrieved June 15, 2014.

[346] Pollack, Suzanne, *Separate — but not equal* http://washingtonjewishweek.com/5015/separate-but-not-equal/, *Washington Jewish Week,* August 28, 2013. Retrieved June 16, 2014.

[347] "Pluralist Council Will Oversee Robinson's Arch at Western Wall" http://forward.com/articles/193988/pluralist-council-will-oversee-robinsons-arch-at-w/, *Jewish Daily Forward* (from Jewish Telegraphic Agency press release), published March 6, 2014. Retrieved June 15, 2014.

[348] Jerusalem chief rabbi: Mixed-gender plaza akin to razing Western Wall http://www.timesofisrael.com/jerusalem-rabbi-mixed-gender-plaza-akin-to-razing-western-wall/ Times of Israel, March 6, 2016

[349] English.thekotel.org TheKotel.org http://english.thekotel.org/today/article.asp?ArticleID=3, retrieved March 11, 2011.

[350] iaa-conservation.org http://www.iaa-conservation.org.il/Projects_Item_eng.asp?id=49&subject_id=10&site_id=3, retrieved March 11, 2011.

[351] The Kotel, note about May 25, 2006. http://english.thekotel.org/today/Event.asp?EventId=803&CatId=2, retrieved March 11, 2011.

[352] English.TheKotel.org http://english.thekotel.org/today/Event.asp?EventId=628&CatId=4, retrieved March 24, 2011.

[353] Thekotel.org, note for July 25, 2010 http://english.thekotel.org/today/Event.asp?EventId=2715&CatId=4, retrieved March 12, 2011.

[354] The Kotel.org, note on February 3, 2006. http://english.thekotel.org/today/Event.asp?EventId=131&CatId=4, retrieved March 13, 2011.

[355] TheKotel.org, Lag B'omer 2009 http://english.thekotel.org/today/article.asp?ArticleID=80, retrieved March 13, 2011.

[356] *Jerusalem Post*, Sep 5, 1983, and *Jerusalem Post* International Edition, Sep 11–17, 1983, "U.S. Navy Chaplain Conducts Western Wall Interfaith Litany"

[357] *St Petersburg Times* http://www.sptimes.com/News/122901/news_pf/NorthPinellas/Lion__lamb_reside_in_.shtml, retrieved March 25, 2011

[358] Borschel-Dan, Amanda, "The Day Israel Gave Its Blessing to Egalitarian Prayer at Western Wall," The Times of Israel, Jun 30, 2017 http://www.timesofisrael.com/the-day-in-1983-when-the-israeli-government-gave-its-blessing-to-a-mixed-gender-prayer-service-at-the-western-wall

[359] Frishman, Avraham; *Kum Hisalech Be'aretz,* Jerusalem 2004

[360] Lamentations Rabbah 1:32
[361] Exodus Rabbah 2:2
[362] Zohar Mishpatim 116
[363] See Radvaz 692
[364] *Kav ha-Yashar* Ch. 50
[365] *Ya'arot Devash* Vol. 1, Ch. 4
[366] See also *Kav ha-Yashar* Ch. 93 and *Shem Ha-gedolim* for a similar account with Rabbi Avraham Ha-levi of Safed.
[367] See *Avnei Nezer* Yoreh Deah 450
[368] Radbaz Responsa 691: "Under the dome on the Temple Mount, which the Arabs call El-Sakhrah, without a doubt, is the location of the Foundation Stone."; Ya'ari, Avraham: *Igrot Eretz Yisrael* by Obadiah ben Abraham, Ramat Gan 1971: "I sought the place of the Foundation Stone where the Ark of the Covenant was placed, and many people told me it is under a tall and beautiful dome which the Arabs built in the Temple precinct."
[369] Sternbuch, Moishe *Teshuvos Ve-hanhagos* Vol. 3, Ch. 39: "In truth they have erred, thinking that the stone upon they built their dome was in fact the Foundation Stone, however, most possibly, the Stone is located further to the south in the open space opposite the exposed section of the Western Wall."
[370] Moed Katan 26a; Orach Chaim 561; Yoreh Deah 340
[371] *Bayit Chadash* to Orach Chaim 561. He contends that the city itself is in such a state of disrepair that once a person has reached the hills surrounding Jerusalem, he can immediately view the Western Wall.
[372] Minchas Shlomo Vol. 1, Ch. 73. See also: Tearing keriah for Jerusalem http://www.rjconline.org/hib52.htm; Ask the Rabbi: Kosel Keriah http://www.ksy.org.il/AskTheRabbi.asp?QID=89
[373] Epstein, Donneal. Halachos for the Traveler https//books.google.com, Feldheim 2000, Pg. 70.
[374] Pirke De-Rabbi Eliezer 35
[375] *Kitzur Shulchan Aruch* 18:10. The *Kaf hachaim* (Orach Chaim 94:1:4 citing Radvaz Vol. 2; Ch. 648) rules that if a Jew was forced onto the Temple Mount and the time of prayer arrived while he's standing between the Western Wall and the place of the Holy of Holies, "he should pray facing towards the Holy of Holies even though his back will be facing the Western Wall."
[376] Adler N. M. (1907) *The Itinerary of Benjamin of Tudela* London; page 23.
[377] Judith Weil. "Kosel Visitors record", *Jewish Tribune*, October 22, 2010.
[378] The Women's Wall http://tabletmag.com/jewish-news-and-politics/130878/the-womens-wall Tablet Magazine, April 30, 2013
[379] Bleiweiss, Robert. "Tear Down the Western Wall". *Jewish Spectator*, 1997. p.3: "There is no quick or easily acceptable way to change this sorry situation, so the blighted thing probably ought to be torn down before its continued presence leads to the irreparable splitting of the Jews and perhaps even civil war and the end of the state of Israel."
[380] Sperling, Avraham Yitzchak (1999). *Sefer Tamei Ha-minhagim U'mekorei Ha-dinim*; Inyanei Hilula D'Rashbi, p. 270. Jerusalem: Shai Le-morah Publishing.
[381] . Arabic text in
[382] reproduced in
[383] ; Wilson 1876 http://www.jnul.huji.ac.il/dl/maps/jer/html/jer202.htm; Wilson 1900 http://jnul.huji.ac.il/dl/maps/jer/html/jer318.htm; August Kümmel 1904 http://jnul.huji.ac.il/dl/maps/jer/html/jer093.htm; Karl Baedeker 1912 http://www.lib.utexas.edu/maps/historical/history_middle_east.html;
[384] USCatholic.org http://www.uscatholic.org/church/2009/08/sensitivity-training?page=0,1, retrieved March 27, 2011.
[385] Wein, Berel. *Triumph of Survival*; Section VIII – The Modern Jew 1958–1988, pg. 451.
[386] On Jewish rights to the Western Wall in Jerusalem http://iris.org.il/quotes/quote49.htm, Voice of Palestine, June 12, 1998.
[387] Khaled Abu Toameh. Jews have no right to Western Wall, PA 'study' says http://www.jpost.com/Israel/Article.aspx?id=196329, *Jerusalem Post*, (November 22, 2010).
[388] Cleveland.com http://www.cleveland.com/world/index.ssf/2010/11/us_condemns_palestinian_claim.html, retrieved March 27, 2011.
[389] http://www.time.com/time/2001/jerusalem/islam.html

[390] https://books.google.com/books?id=GmcuAQAAIAAJ
[391] https://books.google.com/books?id=uj68AAAAIAAJ
[392] https://www.jewishvirtuallibrary.org/jsource/History/wallname.html
[393] https://books.google.com/books?id=QnugAAAAMAAJ
[394] http://www.lifeintheholyland.com/wailing_wall_1800s.htm
[395] https://books.google.com/books?id=Xb-9J4KoT6EC&pg=PA35
[396] http://jcpa.org/al-aksa-libel-advocate-mufti-haj-amin-al-husseini/#sthash.znaRozE6.dpuf
[397] https://books.google.com/books?id=eDrYAAAAMAAJ
[398] http://english.thekotel.org/default.asp
[399] https://www.jewishvirtuallibrary.org/jsource/Judaism/walltoc.html
[400] http://www.chabad.org/library/article.asp?AID=2246
[401] http://isracast.com/Transcripts/060605a_trans.htm
[402] http://lifeintheholyland.com/wailing_wall_1960s.htm
[403] http://www.ianandwendy.com/Israel/Jerusalem/Western_Wall/slideshow.htm
[404] https//maps.google.com
[405] //tools.wmflabs.org/geohack/geohack.php?pagename=Karnak&params=25_43_7_N_32_39_31_E_type:landmark
[406] http://whc.unesco.org/en/list/87
[407] "Karnak" http://dictionary.reference.com/browse/karnak. *Merriam-Webster's Collegiate Dictionary, Eleventh Edition.* Merriam-Webster, 2007. p. 1550
[408] Egypt: Engineering an empire engineering feats
[409] Lehner, Mark The Complete Pyramids, London: Thames and Hudson (1997) pp.202–225 .
[410] "Ancient Egypt Brought To Life With Virtual Model Of Historic Temple Complex", Science Daily, 30 April 2009, retrieved 12 June 2009 http://www.sciencedaily.com/releases/2009/04/090429172224.htm
[411] Brian Handwerk (December 21, 2015) Everything You Need to Know About the Winter Solstice http://news.nationalgeographic.com/2015/12/151221-winter-solstice-explained-pagans/ National Geographic
[412] Stewert, Desmond and editors of the Newsweek Book Division "The Pyramids and Sphinx" 1971 pp. 60–62
[413] *The Unfinished Obelisk* https://www.pbs.org/wgbh/nova/egypt/dispatches/990316.html by Peter Tyson March 16, 1999 NOVA online adventure
[414] Time Life Lost Civilizations series: Ramses II: Magnificence on the Nile (1993) pp. 53–54
[415] Walker, Charles, 1980 "Wonders of the Ancient World" pp24–7
[416] "The Seventy Wonders of the Ancient World", edited by Chris Scarre (1999) Thames & Hudson, London
[417] "Sex and booze figured in Egyptian rites" http://www.nbcnews.com/id/15475319/#.V3MUP0_UnYg nbcnews.com, Oct 30, 2006
[418] http://www.cfeetk.cnrs.fr/uk/
[419] http://www.bellabs.ru/Egypt/Karnak.html
[420] http://www.picturechoice.org/egypt/karnak_temple.html
[421] http://www.karnak3d.net
[422] http://dlib.etc.ucla.edu/projects/Karnak
[423] http://remains.se/picturem.php?ObjectID=129&Browse=AREA

Article Sources and Contributors

The sources listed for each article provide more detailed licensing information including the copyright status, the copyright owner, and the license conditions.

Mecca *Source:* https://en.wikipedia.org/w/index.php?oldid=808148866 *License:* Creative Commons Attribution-Share Alike 3.0 *Contributors:* 2003szm, 7804j, Abuhamza1979, Adilx7523, Adnan.saad99, AdventurousSquirrel, Agtx, Alhadramy Alkendy, Anandmoorti, Anonymous from the 21st century, Anthony Appleyard, Aperiarcam, ApprenticeFan, Aqm2k, Arjayay, Arshu05, AsceticRose, AstroLynx, BU Rob13, Ballymore1, Bellerophon5685, Bender235, Beyond My Ken, Bones Jones, Booyahhayoob, Brianga, CLCStudent, CambridgeBayWeather, Campista1891, Charliethump, Chewings72, Chris the speller, Chrism, Cls14, ClueBot NG, Collounsbury, CommonsDelinker, Crumpled Fire, Cyberbot II, Cynulliad3, D.Nino, DVdm, Dcirovic, DeCausa, Deville, Diannaa, Dissident93, DivermanAU, DivineAlpha, Dominator1453, Ducks are cool, Dunditschia, Ebonelm, El C, Elspamo4, Emir of Wikipedia, EricEnfermero, Explosionmannn, Eyesnore, Fagairolles 34, Fauzan, Flyer22 Reborn, FreeatlastChitchat, Frietjes, Gap9551, General Ization, Gilliam, GorgeCustersSabre, Hairy Dude, IamNotU, Ispor, J 1982, Jamamasjid1, Jandalhandler, JasonJaber42, JayB91, Jimmy fallon, John N Smith, JosueGSMST, K9re11, KUMAR SANU SINGH, Keith D, Kelisi, Khestwol, KylieTastic, Leocomix, Lighthead, LlywelynII, Londoner82, M2545, MHLTALBERT, Magioladitis, Mar4d, Marchino61, Materialscientist, MelbourneStar, Mikequfv, Milowent, Mrceleb2007, Muhammad Abul Fazal, NMaia, Naef Alduhaim, Natg 19, New.pangaea, Non-dropframe, Nurealam10, Omirocksthisworld, Onel5969, Optakeover, Paketumrohdena, Pappig, Paris1127, Peaceworld111, Pleiotrop3, Ramendoctor, Ras67, Rich Farmbrough, Rjwilmsi, Ronhjones, Rowan5j, Rupert loup, Sager502, SantiLak, Saud zakir, Scientus, Scott2357, Selfhatingmuslim, Selsdon, Serols, Shafqatazeem, Sheila Ki Jawani, Shimlaites, Siddharth Kumarr, Sinneral, Skinsmoke, Sodicadl, Srich32977, Srnec, Ssbbplayer, Stevietheman, Storkk, Tarook97, Tessaract2, This lousy T-shirt, Timsdad, Tobby72, Typhoon, Ulric1313, UnforgivablyPotatoes, Vayuyatra, Vijay8808, WOSlinker, Wavelength, Westfield2015, Widr, Wikid77, WitherOrNot, Wjwetzel, Worldbruce, Wtmitchell, XerxesII, Yasou3, ZFT, Zedgefan, 135 anonymous edits 1

Medina *Source:* https://en.wikipedia.org/w/index.php?oldid=806519407 *License:* Creative Commons Attribution-Share Alike 3.0 *Contributors:* 2003szm, ALIwaince, Ahab E. Gapheer, Alaa Alfarooqi, Alexander Domanda, Alhadramy Alkendy, Andy M. Wang, Anibahk, Anonymous from the 21st century, Anthony Appleyard, Asad Baig, AsceticRose, AstroLynx, Azgs, Bender235, Caballero1967, CambridgeBayWeather, Casliber, Cherkash, Chris the speller, ClueBot NG, Collounsbury, Colonies Chris, Coltsfan, CommonsDelinker, Coyau, Cyberbot II, Cynulliad3, DA1, DVdm, Dale Arnett, Darorcilmir, Davidbena, Dawn Bard, DeCausa, DemocraticLuntz, Dendrite1, Dolescum, Dominator1453, Dongar Kathorekar, Edward321, El C, Emir of Wikipedia, Epicgenius, Excirial, Faizhaider, Fardeeen008, Fertejol, Foreignshore, Gaius Cornelius, Grand Hustle Ent, Guajara3718, Hamid awan, Hejazi Israeli, I dream of horses, Ian.thomson, Ibnnaeem, Imminent77, Info-Screen, J 1982, Jackmcbarn, JaconaFrere, JahlilMA, Jamamasjid1, John N Smith, Johnuniq, Kaiketsu, Katieh5584, Keldan17, KhalilAziz, Khestwol, Killaswaggdougi, King Eliot, Krano, KylieTastic, Lagger.boyie, Loriendrew, M2545, Mahmudmasri, Makin1, Marc.soave, Marek69, Marvel Hero, Materialscientist, MeanMotherJr, Midas02, Mikemoral, Misconceptions2, Monochrome Monitor, MrHumanPersonGuy, Mtahaalam, MuhannadDarwish, NeilN, Novusuna, Omni Flames, Omnipaedista, PBS-AWB, Park3r, Peaceworld111, Peaksnary, PhilKnight, Photo3Qom3, PohranicniStraze, QianCheng, Qzd, R'n'B, Rahibsaleem, Rendichoda, Rich Farmbrough, Rubbish computer, Sayowais, Sburke, SheikhJunaidAhmed, Sheila Ki Jawani, Spicemix, SpyButeo, Symphonic Spenguin, Tarook97, The Last Arietta, Triplingual, Vandergay, Waghlis, Wavelength, Werldwayd, Wheeltapper, Whoop whoop pull up, Winner 42, Xtremedood, Yamaguchi先生 , Zeddesszii, أخوها, عربي-٣١, 169 anonymous edits 31

St. Peter's Basilica *Source:* https://en.wikipedia.org/w/index.php?oldid=800676762 *License:* Creative Commons Attribution-Share Alike 3.0 *Contributors:* 115ash, Acroterion, Adriano.93, Ahwiv, Ajfweb, Alessandro57, Alistair Wettin, Alvesgaspar, Amandajm, AmateurEditor, Antique Rose, Arado, Awesomeness3183, B A Andersen, Barjimoa, Bender235, Bmclaughlin9, CarloMartinelli, CarlosPn, Charles01, Chicbyaccident, Clivemacd, ClueBot NG, Cpetty9979, Craigus84, CuriousMind01, DVdm, DarylNickerson, Daveschmitzca, Dcirovic, Disembodied Soul, Dl2000, Dma777, Dnalor 01, Doug Weller, Drmies, Eccekevin, Egsan Bacon, Electricsheep82, Emiliovillegas24, Ergo Sum, Esoglou, Ethan Doyle White, Filiep, Finn Froding, Fiora fontana, Flyer22 Reborn, Frietjes, Geraldo Perez, Giraffedata, Good Olfactory, Graham11, Grover cleveland, Gyrofrog, Haldraper, Ham II, Hammersoft, HappyJake, Hbh2014, Hornmaster111, Howcheng, InedibleHulk, Isogood, J 1982, JB82, JJMC89, Jobas, John of Reading, Johnbod, Johnpacklambert, JonRidinger, Joobo, Joseph2302, Juan M Romero, Kansas Bear, Keith D, Kind Tennis Fan, Lightlowemon, Livioandronico2013, Lotje, MAlanH, Makcimfarrell, Mandarax, Mapzahn, Marcus Cyron, Marek69, Materialscientist, Moosehadley, Mr Stephen, MusikAnimal, Neptune's Trident, Oldstone James, Oshwah, Ospalh, Patapsco913, Pax:Vobiscum, Philipfolta, Podz00, Polmandc, President Rhapsody, Prestinius, Randy Kryn, RazorCrackers, Redheadrambler, Rich Farmbrough, Rjwilmsi, Rockypedia, Rococo1700, RomanSpa, Shellwood, Shgür Datsügen, Sillyfolkboy, Simplexity22, SnodyYT, Srnec, Srschu273, Stephan Schulz, SuddenFrost, Suthari, Tom.Reding, Trackteur, Vyvek, Widr, WilliamDigiCol, Zyxw, 143 anonymous edits 51

Mahabodhi Temple *Source:* https://en.wikipedia.org/w/index.php?oldid=807232519 *License:* Creative Commons Attribution-Share Alike 3.0 *Contributors:* Abhewday, Actionist, AddWittyNameHere, Ajyrds, Algarve1233, Amanhanda, Ankush 89, Apparition11, ArionVII, Arthena, Arthur Rubin, Arzun, Ashishbhatnagar72, Askalan, AxelBoldt, Bannyk, Bellerophon, Betterusername, Bgwhite, Bhooshannpy, Biglovinb, Boing! said Zebedee, Bonkers The Clown, BrainMarble, CFynn, Cihan, ClueBot NG, ConanBaltar, Concord113, Conradjagan, Cpt.a.haddock, Dapsv～enwiki, Dave.Dunford, Dharmalion76, Digital User, Dimadick, Discospinster, Doug Weller, Dsvyas, E2eamon, EJlol, Engine Gone Loco, Ermahgerd9, Eu.stefan, FaisalAbbasid, Fixer88, Fuhghettaboutit, Furrykef, Gfosankar, Greg Pandatshang, GregorB, Ground Zero, Gryffindor, Hamish59, Helpsome, Holothurion, Hugo999, Human3015, Indianets, JJMC89, Jaraalbe, Jarble, JimRenge, Jllm06, John of Reading, Johnbod, Jonathansammy, JorisvS, Jweaver28, KRRK, Kafziel, Knverma, Kosher Fan, KylieTastic, Larry Rosenfeld, Lee, MER-C, MIKHEIL, Malaiya, Mike Peel, Mild Bill Hiccup, Mogism, Morrisjm, My name is not dave, Nat Krause, Night w, Ninly, Nizil Shah, Oddbodz, Onel5969, PhnomPencil, Physchim62, Podzemnik, Prabhath lk, Prof saxx, Professoremeritus, Prowikipedians, Quartzd, Quinton Feldberg, Rajupalli, Randy Kryn, Rayabhari, Rebekahw7, Redtigerxyz, Ricardo Frantz, Ricky81682, Rjwilmsi, Ronakshah1990, Sbblr geervaanee, SeeingMole, Shadowjams, Sjlain, Skbhat, Spasemunki, Swingoswingo, Sylvain1972, Tachs, Takeaway, Tanthalas39, Tartarus, The Anomebot2, TheLeopard, TimBentley, Todowd, Torquemama007, Tpbradbury, UnconditionalLight, Utcursch, VASANTH S.N., Varunsin, VictoriaGrayson, Vipulksoni, VoABot II, WWGB, Wantsallanger, Wayne Slam, Werieth, Whitebox, WhitehatGuru, Wiae, Widr, Wiki-uk, WikiOriginal-9, Wikiman5676, Winston786, Woodega, Xufanc, Yanajin33, YeOldeGentleman, ZappaOMati, Zzuuzz, पाटलिपुत्र, 125 anonymous edits 103

Golden Temple *Source:* https://en.wikipedia.org/w/index.php?oldid=808099377 *License:* Creative Commons Attribution-Share Alike 3.0 *Contributors:* Abductive, Ahecht, Anishpp3, AnonymousResearcher, Apuldram, Arjunprasad.95, Arjunsingh001, Bender235, Bhadani, Bishonen, Bongwarrior, CAPTAIN RAJU, Cahk, Chrissymad, Classicwiki, ClueBot NG, Conradjagan, Death pilani, Denisarona, Dharahara, Divyang49, Evil Little Genius, Filpro, Fixer88, Flyer22 Reborn, Geobeedude, Gorthian, Grayfell, Gsingh, Guanaco, Gurbar Akaal, Horseless Headman, Human3015, IRISZOOM, IceDragon64, IdreamofJeanie, IronGargoyle, Jeppiz, Jim1138, Johnpacklambert, Js82, Jsu～enwiki, Kahtar, Khairaarsh, Khalsa Intelligence, Kheeva, Khushu05, Kintetsubuffalo, Kkm010, KylieTastic, Lapota1234567890, LeopoldMarsh, Lotje, MBlaze Lightning, Manjinder3, Materialscientist, Ms Sarah Welch, Muon, Nutty Pro, OCNative, Oluwa2Chainz, Omiey71, Oshwah, P2prules, Patient Zero, Peeta Singh, Pincrete, Ravneetn13, Ruby B, Rupert loup, SanataniWarrior, Savraj67, Sb2001, Serols, Shellwood, Shyamsunder, Siddharthajoshi, Singh.Nirbhai, Singh8778, Singhsardarji, Sisu55, SkyWarrior, SpacemanSpiff, Sportzak, Srednuas Lenoroc, Sridarbarsahib, Sukanta Pal, Sunnya343, Tachs, Tammana-B, Thomas.W, TonyBallioni, Trinity4156, Vikram Mahant, Vsmith, Widr, Willard84, Winner 42, 202 anonymous edits 125

Pashupatinath Temple *Source:* https://en.wikipedia.org/w/index.php?oldid=805445756 *License:* Creative Commons Attribution-Share Alike 3.0 *Contributors:* *Treker, A. Parrot, Acagastya, Adirlanz, Aditya Mahar, AlanM1, Alcmaeonid, Ambar wiki, Anandmoorti, AnnThapa, Ascii002, Ashim nep, Atrivo, B Jambulingam, Baibhavpandey, BaralSir, Belbasesuraj, Bender235, Bgwhite, Bijay chaurasia, Bijaya2043, Bineetojha, Black Falcon, Blurpeace, Bsvarun, Capankajsmilyo, Chandpr, Chipkali rakshas, Chris the speller, Clarkcj12, ClueBot NG, DARIO SEVERI, Dawnseeker2000, Diannaa, Dipendra2007, Doug Weller, Dr. Blofeld, DynamoDegsy, Emperyan, EoGuy, Favre1fan93, Flyer22 Reborn, Gareth Griffith-Jones, Gilliam, Glane23, Gz33, HMSLavender, Happysailor, HowZatt17, I dream of horses, Icarusgeek, Irrigator, JaGa, Jiayq, John of Reading, Jungbdr, Just a guy from the KP, Justaperfectday, K kisses, Krish Dulal, KylieTastic, Lakshmikanthdas, Learnerktm, Lifebonzza, Lotje, Magioladitis, Mandesa31, Manto17, Materialscientist, Mhockey, Mogism, Murali Mohan Ji, MusikAnimal, Nepalichoro255, Nepallapen12, Niceguyedc, Nizil Shah, NottNott, Novusuna, Nyttend, Oshwah, Parabolooidal, Paudel.ashok, PawanJha91, Plasticspork, Plastikspork, Pnr26j, Prakashgovind1, Prof saxx, Profpremrajpushpakaran, Queenmomcat, R'n'B, Racer Omega, Rao Ravindra, Raunak Maskay, Regstuff, Rohitmds, Rrburke, Rs.mukhiya, Rusahang, Shrawanroy, Shrofshrs, Shyamsunder, SnzvDulal, Sole Soul, SparklingPessimist, Ssriram mt, SumerianPrince, Sundar1, Surfer43, Surya Prakash.S.A., UY Scuti, Vnaynb, Widr, WikHead, Wiki-uk, 212 anonymous edits 141

Mount Kailash *Source:* https://en.wikipedia.org/w/index.php?oldid=806849209 *License:* Creative Commons Attribution-Share Alike 3.0 *Contributors:* 29prathewsh, Aarp65, Aayush18, Abecedare, Ajayprakashyadav, AlanM1, Alexandernachaj, Anandmoorti, Anders k, Ankush 89, Anna Frodesiak, Anthony Appleyard, Arjayay, Avinit90, Avoided, B Jambulingam, BabelStone, Beetstra, Bender235, Bermicourt, Bgwhite, Biplab Anand, Bsvarun, Cattus, ClueBot NG, Coinmanj, D4iNa4, DBigXray, Dawnseeker2000, Deli nk, Denisarona, Derek R Bullamore, Drift chambers, Droll, DuncanHill, Elephantachaun, Ericoides, Eshwar.om, Filjil, Florian Blaschke, Flyer22 Reborn, Foreverknowledge, Frietjes, Gogo Dodo, Helpsome, Hemant Dabral, Hi2lok, Hike395, Hjin2020, Hmains, Hu12, Hunnjazal, I am One of Many, IronGargoyle, Jagadeesh puthukkudi, Jim1138, JimRenge, Jinomp, Jishnu123, Johanna-Hypatia, John Hill, Josan420, Kautuk1, Keithonearth, King Prithviraj II, Kkm010, Krish Dulal, Kuldeepofficial, KylieTastic, LADave, Lifebonzza, Lotsaprob, Lumos3, MKar, MRD2014, Madhuprakasan, Mandards, Mannerheimo, Marchoctober, Materialscientist, Mgiganteus1, Muchness, Mukuruthi, Myasuda, NC4PK, Naniwako, Niceguyedc, NoGhost, Ogress, Oshwah, Owain Knight, Pappig, Piz Beaucannon, Pratyk321, Pseudois, Pushkarkr, RTPking, Racerx11, Rahul RJ Jain, Rao Ravindra, Redtigerxyz, Richard-of-Earth, Rossen4, SFK2, Sanjoydey33, ShotgunMavericks, Smrgeog, Spicemix, Spnepal,

Suhas.msh, ThaneFreedomScholar, The Interior, Tmangray, Veerensha, Viewfinder, Vsmith, WannaBeEditor, WikiDan61, Willard84, Ymblanter, ไพด์จีชบ, เพียรพุทธ, 臧湾, 209 anonymous edits 159

Mount Olympus *Source:* https://en.wikipedia.org/w/index.php?oldid=804545184 *License:* Creative Commons Attribution-Share Alike 3.0 *Contributors:* Abductive, Amortias, Anaxial, Atsunaga, Bamyers99, Barosaurus Lentus, Baxtlog, Bermicourt, Bgwhite, CAPTAIN RAJU, CLCStudent, Chackerian, Chrissymad, ClueBot NG, Coretheapple, Cplakidas, Crow, Cwp3004, DatGuy, David Edgar, Dawnseeker2000, Dcirovic, Derek R Bullamore, Dewritech, Doc James, Donner60, Doprendek, Dricherby, EditSafe, Enkinisi, Espoo, Esszet, Favonian, Flobbadob, Flyer22 Reborn, Force Radical, Fraggle81, FreeatlastChitchat, George Ho, Gilliam, Giraffedata, Glide08, Gobonobo, Gorthian, Guliolopez, Hike395, Hmains, Hobbitschuster, Hoskibs4397, I dream of horses, J. 'mach' wust, Jllm06, John of Reading, Josh3580, Joy, Juergen Weidner, JustAMuggle, KGirlTrucker81, KH-1, Khirurg, Kontam, Kys12, Lambiam, Leschnei, LilHelpa, Ljuba brank, Lor, Lourdes, LukeSurl, Manul, Marcocapelle, Markussep, Mboesch, Mgpolitis, Michael Glass, Money money tickle parsnip, Mr. Smart LION, Muntele, N0n3up, Niceguyedc, Nlaskaridis, North Shoreman, OcarinaOfTime, Operator873, Oshwah, PBS, Paul August, Perlareyes1, Peter238, Philip Trueman, Pkbwcgs, Presidentman, Prinsgezinde, RA0808, Racerx11, RedWolf, RetroReapa, Rms125a@hotmail.com, Santi-Lak, Shellwood, Simon Peter Hughes, SirFoz, Sjpapa, Snowman325, Suede Cat, Tgeorgescu, Tre6616, Troller2169, Ulric1313, VicGuy, Vieque, Vsmith, WOSlinker, Wbm1058, Wiae, Willarocks, YeOldeGentleman, Ü, 200 anonymous edits 169

Dome of the Rock *Source:* https://en.wikipedia.org/w/index.php?oldid=806688044 *License:* Creative Commons Attribution-Share Alike 3.0 *Contributors:* Aa77zz, Ahecht, Alonso de Mendoza, AmateurEditor, Arminden, Arthur Holland, Ashterot, Ayratayrat, BD2412, Babymissfortune, Bellerophon5685, Bender235, Benlisquare, Biplab Anand, Cakerzing, Calidrago, CambridgeBayWeather, Carnby, Chicbyaccident, Chiswick Chap, Clue-Bot NG, Colonies Chris, Continentaleurope, Dawnseeker2000, Dbachmann, Doug Weller, Dovev, Download, EdJohnston, Eik Corell, Ender's Shadow Snr, Error, Evanbango03, Frietjes, Gaia Octavia Agrippa, Galatz, GeneralizationsAreBad, GregKaye, Gurra.79, Hertz1888, Hillbillyholiday, Islamftw, Jab843, Jacob D, Jayakumar RG, Jmorley13, Johnbod, K6ka, Khalidar, Korossyl, Koryhearn, KylieTastic, LahmacunKebab, Lispenard, MPS1992, MShabazz, Makeandtoss, Malik Shabazz, Marcocapelle, MarnetteD, Md ict, Mech Aaron, Meerkat77, Michael Tango, Monochrome Monitor, Monosig, Moonraker12, Nahleezy, Narky Blert, Naytz, NewEnglandYankee, Oculi, Onef9day, Oshwah, Ost316, Pccjf0, Quinto Simmaco, Red58bill, Rich Farmbrough, Rtan248, Rupert Nichol, Samsara, SantiLak, Sean.hoyland, Serols, ShulMaven, Starbuck121, Sweepy, The Almighty Drill, TheEpTic, Tpbradbury, Uncle Milty, User2534, Vegaswikian, Wailnakib, WereSpielChequers, Wrestlingring, Wtmitchell, Zero0000, المقدسي عماد الدین, 161 anonymous edits 189

Western Wall *Source:* https://en.wikipedia.org/w/index.php?oldid=807298430 *License:* Creative Commons Attribution-Share Alike 3.0 *Contributors:* 2016kotel, Ahwiv, Aliyahbook, AmYisroelChai, Angel defender, Aperiarcam, Arminden, AwfullyBrittish, BD2412, BedrockPerson, Bender235, Benjamín Núñez González, Bgwhite, Brandmeister, Brycehughes, Chesdovi, ClueBot NG, CogitoErgoSum14, Cognita, Dapilars, Davidbena, Dbfirs, Dcirovic, Debresser, Dweller, E.M.Gregory, Emeryradio, Equinox, Fitindia, Fixingstuff44, Funnyhat, Galatz, Greyshark09, Guanaco, Harfarhs, Hertz1888, J 1992, JaneSwifty, Jaquestheripper, JaventheAlderick, Jim1138, Korosuke, Ladam11, MShabazz, Magioladitis, Malik Shabazz, Marcocapelle, Marek69, Materialscientist, Maureendepresident, Mk17b, Mrbrklyn, MuzikJunky, Mx. Granger, Nahleezy, NearTheZoo, NewEnglandYankee, Nishidani, Noon, Nurealam10, Ofishy12, Onceinawhile, OscillationDesk, Oshwah, Petelowery, Philip Trueman, Poliocretes, Quebec99, Ritchie333, ST15RMwikipedia, Satellizer, Sepsis II, Shellwood, Shnyusasl.deaf, Skookum1, Skknuniq, Jpc4031, Khazar2, Khruner, Kkkz, Koektrommel, Kwiki, Level C, Luke.oscar, Luppy-GT, Magioladitis, Marek69, Markh, Martin451, MartinPoulter, Matteo717, McGeddon, Meno25, Merlin-UK, Metal Oracle, Mike Rosoft, Mimihitam, Minecraft1234567890, Moe Epsilon, MrOllie, MuskAnimal, N5iln, NPrice, Nascar1996, NawlinWiki, Nethac DIU, Nokota~enwiki, Omnipaedista, Oshwah, Patiwat, PericlesofAthens, Philip Trueman, Phuntazztique, Piledhigheranddeeper, Pmsyyz, Pratyya Ghosh, RalfHuels, Razimantv, Reach Out to the Truth, RobertEves92, Robina Fox, Rybec, Sardanaphalus, Saturday, Shadow24, Shlomke, Shreibman, ShreiberBike, Slumbe20, Slazenger, Snow Blizzard, Ss charley, Stubborntinyight, TMC1982, Tkam, Terrymacro, TheXenomorph1, Theartofthemuses, Thebestofall007, Thirdright, Thor Dockweiler, Tim!, Timsdad, Tracield, Twthmoses, Vegaswikian, VoABot II, Widr, WikiHannibal, Wikislemur, Yngvadottir, Yoxi, Ysgala, Zacherystaylor, Zollo9999, 197 anonymous edits 249

287

Image Sources, Licenses and Contributors

The sources listed for each image provide more detailed licensing information including the copyright status, the copyright owner, and the license conditions.

Image *Source:* https://en.wikipedia.org/w/index.php?title=File:Makkah_Montage.jpg *Contributors:* User:MrJoker07 1
Image *Source:* https://en.wikipedia.org/w/index.php?title=File:Flag_of_Saudi_Arabia.svg *License:* Public Domain *Contributors:* Alkari, Ancintosh, Anime Addict AA, AnonMoos, Bobika, Brian Ammon, CommonsDelinker, Cycn, Denelson83, Duduziq, Ekabhishek, Er Komandante, Fabioravanelli, File Upload Bot (Magnus Manske), Fry1989, Gazimagomedov, Herbythyme, Homo lupus, INeverCry, Itsemurhaja, Jeff G., Klemen Kocjancic, Lokal Profil, Love Krittaya, Love monju, Mattes, Menasim, Meno25, Mnmazur, Mohammed alkhater, Nard the Bard, Nightstallion, Palosirkka, Pitke, Pmsyyz, Ranveig, Ratatosk, Reisio, Ricordisamoa, Sainv, Sarang, SiBr4, Wouterhagens, Zscout370, Zyido, 16 anonymous edits 1
Image *Source:* https://en.wikipedia.org/w/index.php?title=File:Allah3.svg *License:* Public Domain *Contributors:* http://commons.wikimedia.org/wiki/File:Allah.svg 2
Image *Source:* https://en.wikipedia.org/w/index.php?title=File:Allah-green.svg *License:* Public Domain *Contributors:* User:AnonMoos, User:Darwinek, User:Guanaco, User:Mattes, User:Ttog 2
Figure 1 *Source:* https://en.wikipedia.org/w/index.php?title=File:Mecca_from_Jabal_Nur.JPG *License:* Public Domain *Contributors:* Adiput (talk) 5
Figure 2 *Source:* https://en.wikipedia.org/w/index.php?title=File:OldmapofMecca.jpg *License:* Public Domain *Contributors:* Ashashyou, Elonka, Gryffindor, JMCC1, Juiced lemon, LX, M2545, Timeshifter, WJBscribe, WhisperToMe 5
Figure 3 *Source:* https://en.wikipedia.org/w/index.php?title=File:Jabal_Nur.JPG *License:* Public Domain *Contributors:* Adiput (talk) 9
Figure 4 *Source:* https://en.wikipedia.org/w/index.php?title=File:First_Saudi_State_Big.png *License:* Creative Commons Attribution-Sharealike 3.0 *Contributors:* Ameen Mohammad 11
Figure 5 *Source:* https://en.wikipedia.org/w/index.php?title=File:Adriaan-Reland-Verhandeling-van-de-godsdienst-der-Mahometaanen_MG_0723.tif *Contributors:* Ahm masum, Aschroet, Hansmuller, HyperGaruda, Steinsplitter 12
Figure 6 *Source:* https://en.wikipedia.org/w/index.php?title=File:Mecca-1850.jpg *License:* Public Domain *Contributors:* Ammar shaker, Ashashyou, Diannaa, Look2See1, M2545, Thomas doerfer, 6 anonymous edits 13
Figure 7 *Source:* https://en.wikipedia.org/w/index.php?title=File:Mecca1880s.jpg *License:* Public Domain *Contributors:* Elspamo4, OgreBot 2 13
Figure 8 *Source:* https://en.wikipedia.org/w/index.php?title=File:Makkah-1910.jpg *Contributors:* the Matson Collection, 1910 (LOC) 14
Figure 9 *Source:* https://en.wikipedia.org/w/index.php?title=File:Mecca_view.jpg *License:* Creative Commons Zero *Contributors:* Ashashyou, Officer, Paulbe, Shaibalahmar, مائع 14
Figure 10 *Source:* https://en.wikipedia.org/w/index.php?title=File:La_mecque_pelerinage.png *License:* GNU Free Documentation License *Contributors:* Bilou~commonswiki, Flappiefh, HyperGaruda, Itu, Karlfk, MGA73bot2, OgreBot 2, W like wiki, 1 anonymous edits 16
Figure 11 *Source:* https://en.wikipedia.org/w/index.php?title=File:Masjid_al-Haram_panorama.JPG *License:* Creative Commons Attribution 3.0 *Contributors:* Abdelrhman 1990, Mathonius, OgreBot 2, 1 anonymous edits 21
Figure 12 *Source:* https://en.wikipedia.org/w/index.php?title=File:ISS-44_Mecca,_Saudi_Arabia.jpg *License:* Public Domain *Contributors:* Badzil, Elisfkc, Ras67 21
Figure 13 *Source:* https://en.wikipedia.org/w/index.php?title=File:Entry-Gate-of-Mecca-on-Jaddah-Makkah-Highway_2.jpg *Contributors:* User:Rowan5j 21
Figure 14 *Source:* https://en.wikipedia.org/w/index.php?title=File:Abraj-al-Bait-Towers.JPG *License:* Creative Commons Attribution-Sharealike 3.0 *Contributors:* King of Hearts, W like wiki 22
Figure 15 *Source:* https://en.wikipedia.org/w/index.php?title=File:Downtown_Makkah_Azizia.jpg *Contributors:* User:King Eliot 23
Figure 16 *Source:* https://en.wikipedia.org/w/index.php?title=File:Mecca.JPG *License:* Creative Commons Attribution-Sharealike 3.0 *Contributors:* User:Ariandra 03 24
Figure 17 *Source:* https://en.wikipedia.org/w/index.php?title=File:KAAirport-NT.JPG *License:* Public Domain *Contributors:* Ammar shaker . 28
Figure 18 *Source:* https://en.wikipedia.org/w/index.php?title=File:Mecca_Metro_Route_Map.png *License:* Creative Commons Attribution-Sharealike 3.0 *Contributors:* Angnation 29
Figure 19 *Source:* https://en.wikipedia.org/w/index.php?title=File:Entry-Gate-of-Mecca-on-Jaddah-Makkah-Highway.jpg *Contributors:* User:Rowan5j 29
Image *Source:* https://en.wikipedia.org/w/index.php?title=File:Flag_of_Turkmenistan.svg *License:* Public Domain *Contributors:* User:Vzb83 . 29
Image *Source:* https://en.wikipedia.org/w/index.php?title=File:Flag_of_Turkey.svg *License:* Public Domain *Contributors:* User:Dbenbenn 29
Image *Source:* https://en.wikipedia.org/w/index.php?title=File:Inside_Masjid.n.Nabavi_-_panoramio.jpg *License:* Creative Commons Attribution-Sharealike 3.0 *Contributors:* HyperGaruda 31
Image *Source:* https://en.wikipedia.org/w/index.php?title=File:HAC_2010_MEDINE_MESCIDI_NEBEVI_-_panoramio.jpg *License:* Creative Commons Attribution 3.0 *Contributors:* HyperGaruda 31
Image *Source:* https://en.wikipedia.org/w/index.php?title=File:Jannat.ul.Baqi_-_Madina_-_panoramio.jpg *License:* Creative Commons Attribution-Sharealike 3.0 *Contributors:* HyperGaruda 31
Image *Source:* https://en.wikipedia.org/w/index.php?title=File:Mount_Uhud.JPG *License:* Public Domain *Contributors:* BotMultichill, BotMultichillT, Chyah 31
Image *Source:* https://en.wikipedia.org/w/index.php?title=File:Mohamad_shrine_9_-_panoramio.jpg *License:* Creative Commons Attribution 3.0 *Contributors:* HyperGaruda 31
Figure 20 *Source:* https://en.wikipedia.org/w/index.php?title=File:Dome_of_Prophet's_Mosque_-_Medina.jpg *License:* Creative Commons Attribution-Sharealike 3.0 *Contributors:* User:Abdul Hafeez Bakhsh 34
Figure 21 *Source:* https://en.wikipedia.org/w/index.php?title=File:مسجد-قبان-يدعم.PNG *License:* Public Domain *Contributors:* Chyah, HyperGaruda, M2545, XXXshatha, 1 anonymous edits 36
Figure 22 *Source:* https://en.wikipedia.org/w/index.php?title=File:Battle_of_Badr.png *License:* Creative Commons Attribution *Contributors:* GifTagger 38
Figure 23 *Source:* https://en.wikipedia.org/w/index.php?title=File:Mount_Uhud.JPG *License:* Public Domain *Contributors:* BotMultichill, BotMultichillT, Chyah 40
Figure 24 *Source:* https://en.wikipedia.org/w/index.php?title=File:Madina_Munavara.JPG *License:* Public Domain *Contributors:* Airelle, Fatbuu1000, M2545, OgreBot 2 42
Figure 25 *Source:* https://en.wikipedia.org/w/index.php?title=File:Modern_Medina.JPG *License:* Public domain *Contributors:* BotMultichill, BotMultichillT, Chyah, Funfood, M2545, OgreBot 2 43
Figure 26 *Source:* https://en.wikipedia.org/w/index.php?title=File:Madina_Haram_at_evening.jpg *License:* Public Domain *Contributors:* Ahmed Medineli 47
Figure 27 *Source:* https://en.wikipedia.org/w/index.php?title=File:Louvre_-_carreaux_ottomans_07.jpg *License:* Public Domain *Contributors:* User:Coyau 47
Figure 28 *Source:* https://en.wikipedia.org/w/index.php?title=File:Terminal_Lama_Bandar_Udara_Internasional_Pangeran_Muhammad_bin_Abdul_Aziz_Madinah.jpg *License:* Creative Commons Attribution-Sharealike 3.0 *Contributors:* User:Imam Khairul Annas 48
Image *Source:* https://en.wikipedia.org/w/index.php?title=File:Commons-logo.svg *License:* logo *Contributors:* Anomie, Callanecc, CambridgeBayWeather, Jo-Jo Eumerus, RHaworth 49
Image *Source:* https://en.wikipedia.org/w/index.php?title=File:Wikivoyage-Logo-v3-icon.svg *License:* Creative Commons Attribution-Sharealike 3.0 *Contributors:* User:AleXXw 49
Image *Source:* https://en.wikipedia.org/w/index.php?title=File:Wikisource-logo.svg *License:* Creative Commons Attribution-Sharealike 3.0 *Contributors:* ChrisiPK, Guillom, INeverCry, Jarekt, JuTa, Leyo, Lokal Profil, MichaelMaggs, NielsF, Rei-artur, Rocket000, Romaine, Steinsplitter 49
Image *Source:* https://en.wikipedia.org/w/index.php?title=File:Basilica_di_San_Pietro_in_Vaticano_September_2015-1a.jpg *Contributors:* User:Alvesgaspar 51
Figure 29 *Source:* https://en.wikipedia.org/w/index.php?title=File:Saint_Peter's_Basilica_at_night.jpg *Contributors:* User:PetarM 54
Figure 30 *Source:* https://en.wikipedia.org/w/index.php?title=File:PonteSantAngeloRom.jpg *Contributors:* User:Rabax63 55
Figure 31 *Source:* https://en.wikipedia.org/w/index.php?title=File:Petersdom_bei_Nacht_Via_della_Conciliazione_in_Rome.jpg *Contributors:* Schlurcher (talk) 55
Figure 32 *Source:* https://en.wikipedia.org/w/index.php?title=File:0_Place_Saint-Pierre_-_Vatican_(4).JPG *License:* Creative Commons Attribution-Sharealike 3.0 *Contributors:* Jean-Pol GRANDMONT 56
Image *Source:* https://en.wikipedia.org/w/index.php?title=File:Vatican_StPeter_Square.jpg *License:* GNU Free Documentation License *Contributors:* François Malan 57

Figure 33 *Source:* https://en.wikipedia.org/w/index.php?title=File:Konzilseroeffnung_2.jpg *License:* Public Domain *Contributors:* Peter Geymayer 58

Figure 34 *Source:* https://en.wikipedia.org/w/index.php?title=File:Worlds_tallest_buildings,_1884.jpg *License:* Public Domain *Contributors:* George F. Cram (1842-1928) ... 59

Figure 35 *Source:* https://en.wikipedia.org/w/index.php?title=File:Crepescular_rays_in_saint_peters_basilica.JPG *License:* GNU Free Documentation License *Contributors:* Athaenara, Jagro, OgreBot 2, Robert Laymont, Till.niermann ... 60

Figure 36 *Source:* https://en.wikipedia.org/w/index.php?title=File:Basilica_di_San_Pietro_1450.jpg *License:* Public Domain *Contributors:* AnRo0002, Anthony Appleyard, Clio20, Closeapple, DenghiùComm, G.dallorto, Gryffindor, Leinad-Z∼commonswiki, Lewenstein, Lusitana, Mac9, Saperaud∼commonswiki, Un1c0s bot∼commonswiki, ZxxZxxZ, 1 anonymous edits ... 62

Figure 37 *Source:* https://en.wikipedia.org/w/index.php?title=File:SaintPierre.svg *License:* Public Domain *Contributors:* SaintPierre4.JPG: derivative work: Malyszkz (talk) ... 64

Figure 38 *Source:* https://en.wikipedia.org/w/index.php?title=File:SaintPierreRaphael.JPG *License:* Public Domain *Contributors:* Caton, Joanbanjo, Jodo, Merchbow∼commonswiki, Myrabella, Robert Laymont, TomAlt ... 64

Figure 39 *Source:* https://en.wikipedia.org/w/index.php?title=File:L'Architecture_de_la_Renaissance_-_Fig._13.PNG *Contributors:* Aristoi, Coyau, Elekhh, Rd232 ... 65

Figure 40 *Source:* https://en.wikipedia.org/w/index.php?title=File:Vatican_Altar_2.jpg *License:* Creative Commons Attribution-Sharealike 3.0 *Contributors:* Patrick Landy (FSU Guy (talk)) ... 66

Figure 41 *Source:* https://en.wikipedia.org/w/index.php?title=File:Roma_S.Pietro_in_Vaticano_(zzf).jpg *License:* Public Domain *Contributors:* Donato Bramante ... 68

Figure 42 *Source:* https://en.wikipedia.org/w/index.php?title=File:Roma_S.Pietro_in_Vaticano_(zzg).jpg *License:* Public Domain *Contributors:* Original uploader was Etienne (Li) at it.wikipedia ... 69

Figure 43 *Source:* https://en.wikipedia.org/w/index.php?title=File:Petersdom_von_Engelsburg_gesehen.jpg *License:* Public Domain *Contributors:* User:WolfgangStuck ... 70

Figure 44 *Source:* https://en.wikipedia.org/w/index.php?title=File:Michdome.jpg *License:* Public Domain *Contributors:* Gilliam, Good Olfactory, J M Rice, 2 anonymous edits ... 71

Figure 45 *Source:* https://en.wikipedia.org/w/index.php?title=File:Dome_of_Saint_Peter's_Basilica_(Interior).jpg *Contributors:* User:Livioandronico2013 ... 73

Figure 46 *Source:* https://en.wikipedia.org/w/index.php?title=File:Saint_peter_basilica_2.jpg *Contributors:* Grabado, Isogood ... 74

Figure 47 *Source:* https://en.wikipedia.org/w/index.php?title=File:StPetersplan_OttoLeuger1904.jpg *License:* Public Domain *Contributors:* DenghiùComm, Ham II, Kolossos, Mapmarks, TTaylor ... 75

Figure 48 *Source:* https://en.wikipedia.org/w/index.php?title=File:0_Basilique_Saint-Pierre_-_Rome_(2).JPG *License:* Creative Commons Attribution-Sharealike 3.0 *Contributors:* Jean-Pol GRANDMONT ... 76

Figure 49 *Source:* https://en.wikipedia.org/w/index.php?title=File:San_Pietro_in_Vaticano_4.jpg *License:* Creative Commons Attribution-ShareAlike 3.0 Unported *Contributors:* Vincent de Groot - http://www.videgro.net ... 77

Figure 50 *Source:* https://en.wikipedia.org/w/index.php?title=File:Vatican-StPierre-Intérieur1.jpg *License:* Creative Commons Attribution 2.5 *Contributors:* Jean-Christophe BENOIST ... 78

Figure 51 *Source:* https://en.wikipedia.org/w/index.php?title=File:The_Chair_of_Saint_Peter_adjusted.JPG *License:* Creative Commons Attribution-Sharealike 3.0 *Contributors:* Vitold Muratov ... 80

Figure 52 *Source:* https://en.wikipedia.org/w/index.php?title=File:Interiorvaticano8baldaquino.jpg *License:* Creative Commons Attribution-Sharealike 2.5 *Contributors:* Ricardo André Frantz (User:Tetraktys) ... 81

Figure 53 *Source:* https://en.wikipedia.org/w/index.php?title=File:Cathedrapetri+gloria.jpg *License:* Creative Commons Attribution-Sharealike 3.0 *Contributors:* Ricardo André Frantz (User:Tetraktys) ... 82

Figure 54 *Source:* https://en.wikipedia.org/w/index.php?title=File:Basilica_di_San_Pietro_(notte).jpg *License:* Creative Commons Attribution 3.0 *Contributors:* User:Евгений Пивоваров, User:Евгений Пивоваров ... 83

Figure 55 *Source:* https://en.wikipedia.org/w/index.php?title=File:Fountain_of_Carlo_Maderno_night.jpg *License:* Creative Commons Attribution-Sharealike 3.0 *Contributors:* user:Max_Ryazanov ... 84

Figure 56 *Source:* https://en.wikipedia.org/w/index.php?title=File:St_Peter's_Square,_Vatican_City_-_April_2007.jpg *License:* Creative Commons Attribution-ShareAlike 3.0 Unported *Contributors:* Diliff ... 86

Figure 57 *Source:* https://en.wikipedia.org/w/index.php?title=File:Crypt_air_vent.jpg *License:* Creative Commons Attribution-Sharealike 3.0 *Contributors:* User:Ctny ... 86

Figure 58 *Source:* https://en.wikipedia.org/w/index.php?title=File:Saint_Helena.jpg *License:* Public Domain *Contributors:* Use the force ... 89

Figure 59 *Source:* https://en.wikipedia.org/w/index.php?title=File:Saint_Longinus.jpg *License:* Public Domain *Contributors:* Use the force ... 89

Figure 60 *Source:* https://en.wikipedia.org/w/index.php?title=File:Saint_Andreas.jpg *License:* Public Domain *Contributors:* Use the force ... 90

Figure 61 *Source:* https://en.wikipedia.org/w/index.php?title=File:Saint_veronica.jpg *License:* Public Domain *Contributors:* Use the force ... 90

Figure 62 *Source:* https://en.wikipedia.org/w/index.php?title=File:Pilgrim_at_St_Peter_Enthroned.jpg *Contributors:* Ethan_Doyle_White ... 91

Figure 63 *Source:* https://en.wikipedia.org/w/index.php?title=File:Rome_basilica_st_peter_004_adjusted.JPG *License:* Public Domain *Contributors:* Mattana ... 92

Figure 64 *Source:* https://en.wikipedia.org/w/index.php?title=File:0_Monument_funéraire_du_pape_Alexandre_VII_-_St-Pierre_-_Vatican_(1).jpg *License:* Creative Commons Attribution 3.0 *Contributors:* Jean-Pol GRANDMONT ... 93

Figure 65 *Source:* https://en.wikipedia.org/w/index.php?title=File:Rome_basilica_st_peter_011c_adjusted.jpg *License:* Public Domain *Contributors:* Mattana (Crop of original picture; lighting balanced) ... 93

Figure 66 *Source:* https://en.wikipedia.org/w/index.php?title=File:Michelangelo's_Pietà,_St_Peter's_Basilica_(1498–99).jpg *Contributors:* User:Juan M Romero ... 94

Figure 67 *Source:* https://en.wikipedia.org/w/index.php?title=File:Cardinals_at_StPeters.jpg *License:* Public Domain *Contributors:* User:Queenofthewilis ... 95

Figure 68 *Source:* https://en.wikipedia.org/w/index.php?title=File:Francis_Inauguration_fc06.jpg *License:* Creative Commons Attribution-Sharealike 3.0 *Contributors:* User:Fczarnowski ... 96

Figure 69 *Source:* https://en.wikipedia.org/w/index.php?title=File:Rom,_Vatikan,_Petersdom_-_Silhouette_bei_Sonnenuntergang_3.jpg *License:* Creative Commons Attribution-Sharealike 3.0 *Contributors:* User:Dnalor 01 ... 98

Image *Source:* https://en.wikipedia.org/w/index.php?title=File:Mahabodhitemple.jpg *License:* Creative Commons Attribution-Sharealike 2.5 *Contributors:* Bpilgrim ... 103

Image *Source:* https://en.wikipedia.org/w/index.php?title=File:Blue_pencil.svg *License:* Public Domain *Contributors:* User:VasilievVV and user:Jarekt ... 103

Figure 70 *Source:* https://en.wikipedia.org/w/index.php?title=File:Worshipper_at_Mahabodhi_Temple_Bodh_Gaya_India.jpg *License:* Creative Commons Attribution 2.0 *Contributors:* FlickreviewR, Fowler&fowler, Roland zh, Wiki-uk ... 105

Figure 71 *Source:* https://en.wikipedia.org/w/index.php?title=File:Bodhgaya_3639641913_f4c5f73689_t.jpg *License:* Creative Commons Attribution-Sharealike 2.0 *Contributors:* Ken Wieland from Philadelphia, USA ... 106

Figure 72 *Source:* https://en.wikipedia.org/w/index.php?title=File:Pipal_tree_temple_of_Bodh_Gaya_depicted_in_Sanchi_Stupa_1_Eastern_Gateway.jpg *License:* Creative Commons Attribution 3.0 *Contributors:* User:Gangulybiswarup ... 107

Figure 73 *Source:* https://en.wikipedia.org/w/index.php?title=File:Diamond_throne_discovery.jpg *License:* Public Domain *Contributors:* पाटलिपुत्र 108

Figure 74 *Source:* https://en.wikipedia.org/w/index.php?title=File:Bodh_Gaya_pillar_reconstitution_from_archaeology_and_from_artistic_relief.jpg *Contributors:* User:G41rn8 ... 109

Figure 75 *Source:* https://en.wikipedia.org/w/index.php?title=File:Bodhgaya_ei06-16.jpg *Contributors:* User:G41rn8 ... 110

Figure 76 *Source:* https://en.wikipedia.org/w/index.php?title=File:Bodhgaya_ei06-29.jpg *Contributors:* User:G41rn8 ... 110

Figure 77 *Source:* https://en.wikipedia.org/w/index.php?title=File:Bodh_Gaya_railing_adoration_of_the_wheel_of_the_Law.jpg *Contributors:* User:G41rn8 ... 111

Figure 78 *Source:* https://en.wikipedia.org/w/index.php?title=File:Bodh_Gaya_railings_Indian_Museum_Calcutta.jpg *License:* Creative Commons Attribution 3.0 *Contributors:* User:Gangulybiswarup ... 111

Figure 79 *Source:* https://en.wikipedia.org/w/index.php?title=File:Bodh_Gaya_railings_corner.jpg *License:* Creative Commons Attribution 3.0 *Contributors:* User:Gangulybiswarup ... 111

Figure 80 *Source:* https://en.wikipedia.org/w/index.php?title=File:Bodh_Gaya_pillar_original_Indian_Museum_Calcutta.jpg *License:* Creative Commons Attribution 3.0 *Contributors:* User:Gangulybiswarup ... 112

Figure 81 *Source:* https://en.wikipedia.org/w/index.php?title=File:Bodh_Gaya_post_relief_2.jpg *License:* Creative Commons Attribution 2.0 *Contributors:* पाटलिपुत्र ... 112

Figure 82 *Source:* https://en.wikipedia.org/w/index.php?title=File:Bodh_Gaya_Sunga_pillar.jpg *License:* Public Domain *Contributors:* पाटलिपुत्र 113

Figure 83 *Source:* https://en.wikipedia.org/w/index.php?title=File:Bodh_Gaya_Sunga_railing.jpg *License:* Public Domain *Contributors:* पाटलिपुत्र 113
Figure 84 *Source:* https://en.wikipedia.org/w/index.php?title=File:Bodh_Gaya_Sunga_railings_4.jpg *License:* Public Domain *Contributors:* पाटलिपुत्र 114
Figure 85 *Source:* https://en.wikipedia.org/w/index.php?title=File:Bodh_Gaya_Sunga_railing_5.jpg *License:* Public Domain *Contributors:* पाटलिपुत्र 114
Figure 86 *Source:* https://en.wikipedia.org/w/index.php?title=File:Bodh_Gaya_Sunga_railings_3.jpg *License:* Public Domain *Contributors:* पाटलिपुत्र 115
Figure 87 *Source:* https://en.wikipedia.org/w/index.php?title=File:Winter_India_(1903)_(14783119433).jpg *Contributors:* BoringHistoryGuy, FlickreviewR 2, Fæ, Hilohello, पाटलिपुत्र 115
Figure 88 *Source:* https://en.wikipedia.org/w/index.php?title=File:Bodh_gaya_before_restoration.jpg *License:* Public Domain *Contributors:* Hekerui, JMCC1, Ranjithsutari, Wiki-uk, Zhuyifei1999 117
Figure 89 *Source:* https://en.wikipedia.org/w/index.php?title=File:Mucalinda_protecting_Buddha.jpg *Contributors:* User:WhitehatGuru 118
Figure 90 *Source:* https://en.wikipedia.org/w/index.php?title=File:Mahabodhi-restored.jpg *License:* Public Domain *Contributors:* Belasd, G.dallorto, Nat Krause, Oo91, Podzemnik, Ras67, Roland zh, Wiki-uk, 2 anonymous edits 118
Figure 91 *Source:* https://en.wikipedia.org/w/index.php?title=File:Bodh_Gaya_railing_pillar.jpg *Contributors:* User:G41rn8 119
Figure 92 *Source:* https://en.wikipedia.org/w/index.php?title=File:Bodh_Gaya_quadriga_relief.jpg *Contributors:* पाटलिपुत्र 120
Figure 93 *Source:* https://en.wikipedia.org/w/index.php?title=File:Mahabodhi.jpg *License:* GNU Free Documentation License *Contributors:* AnRo0002, Belasd, MGA73bot2, Podzemnik, Roger roger, Wiki-uk 121
Image *Source:* https://en.wikipedia.org/w/index.php?title=File:Hamandir_Sahib_(Golden_Temple).jpg *License:* Creative Commons Attribution-Sharealike 3.0 *Contributors:* Oleg Yunakov 125
Figure 94 *Source:* https://en.wikipedia.org/w/index.php?title=File:A_night_view_of_people_waiting_for_darsana_into_Golden_Temple_India_Sikhism.jpg *License:* Creative Commons Attribution-Sharealike 2.0 *Contributors:* ビッグアップジャパン from EARTH, EARTH 127
Figure 95 *Source:* https//en.wikipedia.org *License:* Public Domain *Contributors:* Bukk, Gryffindor, Gurbar Akaal, OgreBot 2, Sinbad the sailor, Soranoch 128
Figure 96 *Source:* https://en.wikipedia.org/w/index.php?title=File:1880_photograph_of_the_Golden_Temple,_Darbar_Sahib,_sacred_pool_and_nearby_buildings,_Amritsar.jpg *Contributors:* Ms Sarah Welch 131
Figure 97 *Source:* https://en.wikipedia.org/w/index.php?title=File:The_Golden_temple_map.jpg *License:* Public domain *Contributors:* MGA73bot2, Ms Sarah Welch, OgreBot 2, Paterm 132
Image *Source:* https://en.wikipedia.org/w/index.php?title=File:Sarovar_and_the_Golden_Temple.jpg *License:* Creative Commons Attribution-Sharealike 2.0 *Contributors:* Ken Wieland 132
Image *Source:* https://en.wikipedia.org/w/index.php?title=File:Golden_Temple,_Amristar.jpg *Contributors:* User:Manshi Bhanushali 132
Image *Source:* https://en.wikipedia.org/w/index.php?title=File:Akal_Takht_illuminated,_in_Harmandir_Sahib_complex,_Amritsar.jpg *License:* Creative Commons Attribution 2.0 *Contributors:* Giridhar Appaji Nag Y from Bangalore, India 133
Image *Source:* https://en.wikipedia.org/w/index.php?title=File:Guru_Ka_Dwar.jpg *Contributors:* User:Twinkle.luthra 133
Figure 98 *Source:* https://en.wikipedia.org/w/index.php?title=File:1860s_photo_of_the_Amritsar_Golden_Temple_with_the_British_style_Gothic_Clock_Tower.jpg *Contributors:* Ms Sarah Welch 134
Figure 99 *Source:* https://en.wikipedia.org/w/index.php?title=File:Dukh_Bhanjani_Ber_tree_and_entrance_gate_near_the_Langar_at_the_Golden_Temple.jpg *Contributors:* User:Devoshri 135
Figure 100 *Source:* https://en.wikipedia.org/w/index.php?title=File:Ceiling_of_the_Golden_Temple_in_gold_and_precious_stones.JPG *License:* Creative Commons Attribution 3.0 *Contributors:* SM14 136
Image *Source:* https://en.wikipedia.org/w/index.php?title=File:2017_sukhasan_ritual_palki_palanquin_for_Guru_Granth_Sahib_every_night,_Golden_temple_Amritsar.jpg *Contributors:* User:Ms Sarah Welch 137
Image *Source:* https://en.wikipedia.org/w/index.php?title=File:Sikh_pilgrim_at_the_Golden_Temple_(Harmandir_Sahib)_in_Amritsar,_India.jpg *License:* Creative Commons Attribution-Share Alike *Contributors:* Paulrudd 137
Image *Source:* https://en.wikipedia.org/w/index.php?title=File:108_Night_View_Of_Pasupatinath_Temple.jpg *Contributors:* User:Bijay chaurasia 141
Image *Source:* https://en.wikipedia.org/w/index.php?title=File:Om_symbol.svg *License:* Public Domain *Contributors:* User:Rugby471 142
Image *Source:* https://en.wikipedia.org/w/index.php?title=File:Aum_Om_red.svg *Contributors:* Cathy Richards, Ms Sarah Welch, Sarang 142
Figure 101 *Source:* https://en.wikipedia.org/w/index.php?title=File:Pashupatinath_Temple,_UNESCO_World_Heritage_Site.jpg *Contributors:* User:Manto17 143
Image *Source:* https://en.wikipedia.org/w/index.php?title=File:Pashupati_dec_20_2009.jpg *License:* Copyrighted free use *Contributors:* Thapa.laxman 145
Figure 102 *Source:* https://en.wikipedia.org/w/index.php?title=File:Pashupati_temple_surroundings.JPG *License:* Creative Commons Attribution-Sharealike 3.0 *Contributors:* User:Araz cafle 146
Figure 103 *Source:* https://en.wikipedia.org/w/index.php?title=File:Priest_of_Pashupatinath_Temple_of_Kathmandu-2009.jpg *Contributors:* User:Ashim nep 147
Figure 104 *Source:* https://en.wikipedia.org/w/index.php?title=File:NP-pashu-terrasse.jpg *License:* Creative Commons Attribution-Sharealike 3.0,2.5,2.0,1.0 *Contributors:* Balou46, MGA73bot2, OgreBot 2 149
Figure 105 *Source:* https://en.wikipedia.org/w/index.php?title=File:2015_Earthquake_in_Nepal-Pashupatinath_Temple_Area_(12).JPG *Contributors:* User:Nabin K. Sapkota 151
Image *Source:* https://en.wikipedia.org/w/index.php?title=File:Pashupatinath_Temple_and_its_premises,_Nepal_3.jpg *Contributors:* User:Belbasesuraj 152
Image *Source:* https://en.wikipedia.org/w/index.php?title=File:Pashupatinath_temple.JPG *License:* Creative Commons Attribution 2.5 *Contributors:* Ondřej Žváček 152
Image *Source:* https://en.wikipedia.org/w/index.php?title=File:Pasupatinath_Temple,_Front_gate-IMG_3501.jpg *Contributors:* User:Bijay chaurasia 152
Image *Source:* https://en.wikipedia.org/w/index.php?title=File:Pashupatinath_Cremation.jpg *License:* Creative Commons Attribution 2.5 *Contributors:* BotMultichill, File Upload Bot (Magnus Manske), MGA73bot2, Mayer Bruno, OgreBot 2, Parabolooidal, Roland zh, Soranoch, Till.niermann 153
Image *Source:* https://en.wikipedia.org/w/index.php?title=File:Pashupatinath_Temple_Tending_a_ghat.jpg *Contributors:* Benjamint444 153
Image *Source:* https://en.wikipedia.org/w/index.php?title=File:Nepal_-_Kathmandu_-_017_-_Sadhus_at_Pashupatinath_Temple_(5793637308).jpg *License:* Creative Commons Attribution 2.0 *Contributors:* McKay Savage from London, UK 153
Image *Source:* https://en.wikipedia.org/w/index.php?title=File:A_glimpse_at_the_temple.jpg *Contributors:* User:Sushan116 154
Image *Source:* https://en.wikipedia.org/w/index.php?title=File:Shiva_Ratri.jpg *License:* Public Domain *Contributors:* Bhutri 154
Image *Source:* https://en.wikipedia.org/w/index.php?title=File:Western_entrance_of_Pasupatinath_Temple,_Front_Gate-IMG_3466.jpg *Contributors:* User:Bijay chaurasia 154
Image *Source:* https://en.wikipedia.org/w/index.php?title=File:Pashupati_Temple-IMG_0030.jpg *Contributors:* User:Bijaya2043 155
Image *Source:* https://en.wikipedia.org/w/index.php?title=File:Pashupati_Temple-IMG_0031.jpg *Contributors:* User:Bijaya2043 155
Image *Source:* https://en.wikipedia.org/w/index.php?title=File:Pashupati_temple-G0237311.jpg *Contributors:* User:Bijaya2043 155
Image *Source:* https://en.wikipedia.org/w/index.php?title=File:Pashupati_Temple-IMG_0061.jpg *Contributors:* User:Bijaya2043 156
Image *Source:* https://en.wikipedia.org/w/index.php?title=File:Pashupatinath_temple,kathmandu,Nepal.jpg *Contributors:* User:Pravasshh 157
Image *Source:* https://en.wikipedia.org/w/index.php?title=File:Kailash_north.JPG *License:* Creative Commons Attribution 2.5 *Contributors:* Ondřej Žváček 159
Image *Source:* https://en.wikipedia.org/w/index.php?title=File:SaivismFlag.png *Contributors:* 5anan27, De728631, Jeff G., Yann 161
Figure 106 *Source:* https://en.wikipedia.org/w/index.php?title=File:Hindukailash.JPG *License:* Public Domain *Contributors:* Platonides, Redtigerxyz, Roland zh, Un1c0s bot∼commonswiki, Vivek Sarje, 1 anonymous edits 162
Figure 107 *Source:* https://en.wikipedia.org/w/index.php?title=File:KailashTanka.JPG *License:* Public Domain *Contributors:* Gryffindor, Miuki, Redtigerxyz, Roland zh, Rédacteur Tibet 163
Figure 108 *Source:* https://en.wikipedia.org/w/index.php?title=File:Chortens_andKailash.jpg *License:* Creative Commons Attribution-Share Alike *Contributors:* Yasunori Koide 164
Figure 109 *Source:* https://en.wikipedia.org/w/index.php?title=File:Mt_Kailash_sat.jpg *License:* GNU Free Documentation License *Contributors:* Badzil, BaldBoris, Common Good, File Upload Bot (Magnus Manske), MGA73bot2, OgreBot 2, Zolo 165
Figure 110 *Source:* https://en.wikipedia.org/w/index.php?title=File:2005_Kailash_with_moon_Tibet.jpg *License:* Creative Commons Attribution-Share Alike *Contributors:* Yasunori Koide 166
Image *Source:* https://en.wikipedia.org/w/index.php?title=File:Mytikas.jpg *License:* Creative Commons Attribution 2.0 *Contributors:* stefg74 from Larisa, Greece 169

Figure 111 *Source:* https://en.wikipedia.org/w/index.php?title=File:Mytikas_from_Skala.jpg *License:* Creative Commons Attribution 2.0 *Contributors:* stefg74 from Larisa, Greece ... 171
Figure 112 *Source:* https://en.wikipedia.org/w/index.php?title=File:Olymp-nasa1.jpg *License:* Public Domain *Contributors:* NASA ... 172
Figure 113 *Source:* https://en.wikipedia.org/w/index.php?title=File:Olympus15.jpg *Contributors:* User:Nlaskaridis ... 173
Figure 114 *Source:* https://en.wikipedia.org/w/index.php?title=File:Petra_Olympus.jpeg *Contributors:* User:Cristos Vlahos ... 173
Figure 115 *Source:* https://en.wikipedia.org/w/index.php?title=File:Oropediolympou.jpg *License:* Attribution *Contributors:* Cristo Vlahos. ... 174
Figure 116 *Source:* https://en.wikipedia.org/w/index.php?title=File:Olympus17.jpg *Contributors:* User:Nlaskaridis ... 178
Figure 117 *Source:* https://en.wikipedia.org/w/index.php?title=File:Olympus26.jpg *Contributors:* User:Nlaskaridis ... 179
Figure 118 *Source:* https://en.wikipedia.org/w/index.php?title=File:Salamander-olympus.jpg *License:* Creative Commons Attribution 3.0 *Contributors:* Cristo Vlahos ... 182
Figure 119 *Source:* https://en.wikipedia.org/w/index.php?title=File:Skourta.jpg *License:* Attribution *Contributors:* Cristo Vlahos. ... 185
Figure 120 *Source:* https://en.wikipedia.org/w/index.php?title=File:Katafygiolympou.jpg *License:* Attribution *Contributors:* Cristo Vlahos. ... 185
Figure 121 *Source:* https://en.wikipedia.org/w/index.php?title=File:Olympus13.jpg *Contributors:* User:Nlaskaridis ... 186
Image *Source:* https://en.wikipedia.org/w/index.php?title=File:Padlock-blue.svg *Contributors:* User:AzaToth, User:Eleassar ... 189
Image *Source:* https://en.wikipedia.org/w/index.php?title=File:Israel-2013(2)-Jerusalem-Temple_Mount-Dome_of_the_Rock_(SE_exposure).jpg *License:* Attribution *Contributors:* User:Godot13 ... 189
Figure 122 *Source:* https://en.wikipedia.org/w/index.php?title=File:TempleMount_HolylandModel.JPG *License:* Public Domain *Contributors:* Berthold Werner ... 191
Figure 123 *Source:* https://en.wikipedia.org/w/index.php?title=File:Dehio_10_Dome_of_the_Rock_Section.jpg *Contributors:* Aschroet, Fb78, Молох, 1 anonymous edits ... 192
Figure 124 *Source:* https://en.wikipedia.org/w/index.php?title=File:Seal_of_Templars.jpg *License:* Public Domain *Contributors:* Thomas Andrew Archer, Charles Lethbridge Kingsford ... 193
Figure 125 *Source:* https://en.wikipedia.org/w/index.php?title=File:Dome_of_the_Rock,_from_Governor's_House,_Francis_Bedford_1862.jpg *License:* Public Domain *Contributors:* Aa77zz ... 195
Figure 126 *Source:* https://en.wikipedia.org/w/index.php?title=File:Dome_of_the_Rock,_West_Front,_Francis_Bedford_1862.jpg *License:* Public Domain *Contributors:* Aa77zz ... 195
Figure 127 *Source:* https://en.wikipedia.org/w/index.php?title=File:MosqueOfOmar1914.jpg *License:* Public Domain *Contributors:* Dogears, Jarekt, Lambtron, Mattes, Schimmelreiter, Молох, 3 anonymous edits ... 196
Figure 128 *Source:* https://en.wikipedia.org/w/index.php?title=File:Israel-2013-Jerusalem-Temple_Mount-Dome_of_the_Rock-Detail_01.jpg *License:* Attribution *Contributors:* User:Godot13 ... 196
Figure 129 *Source:* https://en.wikipedia.org/w/index.php?title=File:Inside_the_Dome_of_the_Rock.jpg *Contributors:* MATSON ERIC ... 196
Figure 130 *Source:* https://en.wikipedia.org/w/index.php?title=File:Jerusalem_Dome_Rock.JPG *License:* Public Domain *Contributors:* Anonimski, Hedwig in Washington, Jeff G., Judithcomm, OgreBot 2 ... 197
Figure 131 *Source:* https://en.wikipedia.org/w/index.php?title=File:1000_IRR_1982_Back.jpg *Contributors:* Chyah, Ephraim33, Judithcomm, Ks-M9, Travelbird, مانفی ... 198
Figure 132 *Source:* https://en.wikipedia.org/w/index.php?title=File:Hebrew_domeEntrance_sign.jpg *License:* Creative Commons Attribution-Sharealike 2.5 *Contributors:* Bantosh ... 199
Figure 133 *Source:* https://en.wikipedia.org/w/index.php?title=File:Dome_of_the_Rock,_1546.jpg *License:* Public Domain *Contributors:* Chesdovi ... 200
Figure 134 *Source:* https://en.wikipedia.org/w/index.php?title=File:The_rock_of_the_Dome_of_the_Rock_Corrected.jpg *Contributors:* Aa77zz, BomBom, BotMultichill, Chesdovi, Copytopic1, Earthsound, Electron, Goltz20707, Hertz1888, Jbribeiro1, Judithcomm, Msisson, MushiHoshiIshi, Nachcommonsverschieber, Postdlf, Rcbutcher, 1 anonymous edits ... 201
Figure 135 *Source:* https://en.wikipedia.org/w/index.php?title=File:Panorámica_de_Jerusalén_desde_el_Monte_de_los_Olivos.jpg *License:* Creative Commons Attribution-Share Alike *Contributors:* Bienchido ... 202
Image *Source:* https://en.wikipedia.org/w/index.php?title=File:Westernwall2.jpg *License:* Creative Commons Attribution-Share Alike *Contributors:* Golasso ... 205
Image *Source:* https://en.wikipedia.org/w/index.php?title=File:Loudspeaker.svg *License:* Public Domain *Contributors:* User:Dbenbenn, User:Optimager, User:Tsca, User:Dbenbenn, User:Optimager, User:Tsca, User:Dbenbenn, User:Optimager, User:Tsca ... 206
Figure 136 *Source:* https://en.wikipedia.org/w/index.php?title=File:Jerusalem_Western_Wall_stones.jpg *License:* Creative Commons Attribution 3.0 *Contributors:* Gilabrand at en.wikipedia ... 208
Figure 137 *Source:* https://en.wikipedia.org/w/index.php?title=File:Klagemauer.JPG *License:* Creative Commons Attribution-Sharealike 3.0 Germany *Contributors:* Sheepdog85 ... 209
Figure 138 *Source:* https://en.wikipedia.org/w/index.php?title=File:The_Western_Wall_and_Dome_of_the_rock_in_the_old_city_of_Jerusalem.jpg *License:* Creative Commons Attribution-Sharealike 3.0 *Contributors:* User:Yourway-israel ... 210
Figure 139 *Source:* https://en.wikipedia.org/w/index.php?title=File:Kotel_engraving_1850.jpg *License:* Public Domain *Contributors:* Rabbi Joseph Schwarz. ... 212
Figure 140 *Source:* https://en.wikipedia.org/w/index.php?title=File:Wailing_Wall_by_Gustav_Bauernfeind.png *License:* Public Domain *Contributors:* Botaurus, Chesdovi, FA2010, Geagea, Scewing ... 214
Figure 141 *Source:* https://en.wikipedia.org/w/index.php?title=File:Koisel_1870.jpg *License:* Public Domain *Contributors:* Inyan, Netanel h, 1 anonymous edits ... 216
Figure 142 *Source:* https://en.wikipedia.org/w/index.php?title=File:Jew's_Wailing_Place,_Jerusalem.jpg *Contributors:* User:Kimberlyblaker 217
Figure 143 *Source:* https://en.wikipedia.org/w/index.php?title=File:Jewish_legion_hakotel_1917.jpg *License:* Public Domain *Contributors:* Chesdovi, Ekki01, Geagea, Masur, Netanel h, Pieter Kuiper, TVJunkie, Ub ... 219
Figure 144 *Source:* https://en.wikipedia.org/w/index.php?title=File:Historical_images_of_the_Western_Wall_-_1920_C_SR_016b.JPG *License:* Public Domain *Contributors:* National Library of Israel ... 219
Figure 145 *Source:* https://en.wikipedia.org/w/index.php?title=File:Kotel_jerusalem.jpg *License:* Creative Commons Attribution 2.0 *Contributors:* Juan Reyero ... 221
Figure 146 *Source:* https://en.wikipedia.org/w/index.php?title=File:Western_Wall_Jerusalem_1933.jpg *License:* Public Domain *Contributors:* Geagea, Oyoyoy ... 222
Figure 147 *Source:* https://en.wikipedia.org/w/index.php?title=File:British_police_wailing_wall1.jpg *License:* Public Domain *Contributors:* Verlag Wien (Transfered by /מתניהOriginal uploaded by Golf Bravo) ... 222
Figure 148 *Source:* https://en.wikipedia.org/w/index.php?title=File:Anglo-American_Committee_at_the_Western_Wall.jpg *License:* Public Domain *Contributors:* Aviados, Djampa, Geagea, Renamed user akdllvjbhlnbjfl ... 225
Figure 149 *Source:* https://en.wikipedia.org/w/index.php?title=File:The_remains_of_Robinson's_Arch_on_the_western_side_of_the_Temple_Mount.jpg *License:* Creative Commons Attribution 2.0 *Contributors:* Brian Jeffery Beggerly from S'pore (Singapore), Singapore ... 229
Figure 150 *Source:* https://en.wikipedia.org/w/index.php?title=File:Azarat_Yisrael_Plaza.jpg *License:* Creative Commons Attribution-Sharealike 3.0 *Contributors:* User:NearTheZoo ... 230
Figure 151 *Source:* https://en.wikipedia.org/w/index.php?title=File:Jerusalem_Western_Wall_BW_2.JPG *License:* Public Domain *Contributors:* Berthold Werner ... 231
Figure 152 *Source:* https://en.wikipedia.org/w/index.php?title=File:USNAVY_Kotel_Service.jpg *License:* Public Domain *Contributors:* Unknown U.S. Navy photographer from U.S. Sixth Fleet, accompanying Chapain Resnicoff to site. ... 232
Figure 153 *Source:* https://en.wikipedia.org/w/index.php?title=File:Muro_de_las_Lamentaciones,_Jerusalén,_Israel,_2017.gif *Contributors:* User:Benjamín Núñez González ... 233
Figure 154 *Source:* https://en.wikipedia.org/w/index.php?title=File:Jews_at_Western_Wall_by_Felix_Bonfils,_1870s.jpg *Contributors:* Asclepias, Chesdovi, Geagea, Marcus Cyron, Scewing, Triggerhippie4, 1 anonymous edits ... 234
Figure 155 *Source:* https://en.wikipedia.org/w/index.php?title=File:Wall_of_Solomon,_c1880.jpg *License:* Public Domain *Contributors:* Print published by Boussod and Valadon, after the original drawing by Alexandre Bida (1813-1895). ... 235
Figure 156 *Source:* https://en.wikipedia.org/w/index.php?title=File:PikiWiki_Israel_3432_9_av_kotel.JPG *License:* Creative Commons Attribution 2.5 *Contributors:* SAIMI ... 236
Figure 157 *Source:* https://en.wikipedia.org/w/index.php?title=File:Women_at_western_wall.jpg *Contributors:* Taken either by the American Colony Photo Department or its successor the Matson Photo Service ... 237
Figure 158 *Source:* https://en.wikipedia.org/w/index.php?title=File:Men's_and_women's_prayer_areas_at_the_Western_Wall,_seen_from_walkway_to_the_Dome_of_the_Rock.jpg *License:* GNU Free Documentation License *Contributors:* Daniel Case ... 239
Figure 159 *Source:* https://en.wikipedia.org/w/index.php?title=File:Prayer_Papers_in_the_Western_Wall.jpg *License:* Creative Commons Attribution 2.0 *Contributors:* Yarin Kirchen from Stamford ... 240
Figure 160 *Source:* https://en.wikipedia.org/w/index.php?title=File:WilsonHoshAlBurak.png *License:* Public Domain *Contributors:* Ashashyou, Themightyquill, Zero0000, 'שילוני ... 241
Figure 161 *Source:* https://en.wikipedia.org/w/index.php?title=File:Franciscus_kotel.jpg *License:* Creative Commons Attribution-Sharealike 3.0 *Contributors:* ישראל משטרת דוברות ... 242

Figure 162 *Source:* https://en.wikipedia.org/w/index.php?title=File:A_man_prays_at_the_Western_Wall_in_Jerusalem.jpg *License:* Creative Commons Attribution 3.0 *Contributors:* David Shankbone 243
Figure 163 *Source:* https://en.wikipedia.org/w/index.php?title=File:Jerusalem_Dome_of_the_rock_BW_12.JPG *License:* Public Domain *Contributors:* Berthold Werner 244
Figure 164 *Source:* https://en.wikipedia.org/w/index.php?title=File:President_Trump_visit_to_Israel,_May_2017_DSC_3714OSD_(34019020653).jpg *License:* Creative Commons Attribution 2.0 *Contributors:* Matty Stern/ U.S. Embassy Tel Aviv 246
Image *Source:* https://en.wikipedia.org/w/index.php?title=File:Symbol_support_vote.svg *License:* Public Domain *Contributors:* Anomie, Fastily, Jo-Jo Eumerus 247
Image *Source:* https://en.wikipedia.org/w/index.php?title=File:Karnak-Hypostyle3.jpg *License:* Creative Commons Attribution-Sharealike 3.0,2.5,2.0,1.0 *Contributors:* Kurohito 249
Figure 165 *Source:* https://en.wikipedia.org/w/index.php?title=File:S03_06_01_018_image_2382.jpg *License:* Public Domain *Contributors:* DenghiùComm, JMCC1, Theartofthemuses 251
Figure 166 *Source:* https://en.wikipedia.org/w/index.php?title=File:S03_06_01_018_image_2398.jpg *License:* Public Domain *Contributors:* DenghiùComm, JMCC1, Theartofthemuses 253
Figure 167 *Source:* https://en.wikipedia.org/w/index.php?title=File:Monumenti_dell'Egitto_e_della_Nubia-plate-0032.jpg *Contributors:* JMCC1, MartinPoulter 255
Figure 168 *Source:* https://en.wikipedia.org/w/index.php?title=File:Temple_Complex_at_Karnak.jpg *License:* Creative Commons Attribution 3.0 *Contributors:* Cornell University Library 255
Image *Source:* https://en.wikipedia.org/w/index.php?title=File:Karnakpanorama.jpg *License:* Public Domain *Contributors:* Blalonde 256
Image *Source:* https://en.wikipedia.org/w/index.php?title=File:Karnakfrieze1.jpg *License:* Public Domain *Contributors:* Blalonde 256
Image *Source:* https://en.wikipedia.org/w/index.php?title=File:Temple-Karnak.jpg *License:* Creative Commons Attribution 3.0 *Contributors:* Focusredsea 257
Figure 169 *Source:* https://en.wikipedia.org/w/index.php?title=File:Karnak_Temple_Map.jpg *License:* Public Domain *Contributors:* Apocheir, Borvan53, JMCC1, Kajk, Oesermaatra0069~commonswiki, Vonvon, 2 anonymous edits 257
Figure 170 *Source:* https://en.wikipedia.org/w/index.php?title=File:Great_Lake_at_Karnak_Temple.jpg *License:* Creative Commons Attribution-Sharealike 3.0 *Contributors:* timsdad 260
Figure 171 *Source:* https://en.wikipedia.org/w/index.php?title=File:Parvis_Karnak.jpg *License:* Public Domain *Contributors:* User:Neithsabes 260
Figure 172 *Source:* https://en.wikipedia.org/w/index.php?title=File:KarnakTemple@LuxorEgypt_rams_2007feb9-08_byDanielCsorfoly.JPG *License:* Public Domain *Contributors:* Daniel Csörföly 260
Figure 173 *Source:* https://en.wikipedia.org/w/index.php?title=File:Karnacs2.jpg *License:* Public Domain *Contributors:* A.Savin, Durova, Ephraim33, Hekerui, JMCC1, Kozuch, Martin H., MattWade, Pmsyyz, Takabeg, TheRealHuldra, Wronkiew, باسم, 1 anonymous edits 261
Image *Source:* https://en.wikipedia.org/w/index.php?title=File:SFEC_EGYPT_KARNAK_2006-001.JPG *License:* GNU Free Documentation License *Contributors:* Steve F-E-Cameron (Merlin-UK) 261
Figure 174 *Source:* https://en.wikipedia.org/w/index.php?title=File:Statue_of_Ramesses_II_in_Karnak_Temple_in_Luxor_Egypt.JPG *Contributors:* User:MusikAnimal 261
Image *Source:* https://en.wikipedia.org/w/index.php?title=File:SFEC_EGYPT_KARNAK_2006-003.JPG *License:* GNU Free Documentation License *Contributors:* Steve F-E-Cameron (Merlin-UK) 262
Image *Source:* https://en.wikipedia.org/w/index.php?title=File:SFEC_EGYPT_KARNAK_2006-004.JPG *License:* GNU Free Documentation License *Contributors:* Steve F-E-Cameron (Merlin-UK) 262
Image *Source:* https://en.wikipedia.org/w/index.php?title=File:SFEC_EGYPT_KARNAK_2006-005.JPG *License:* GNU Free Documentation License *Contributors:* Steve F-E-Cameron (Merlin-UK) 263
Image *Source:* https://en.wikipedia.org/w/index.php?title=File:SFEC_EGYPT_KARNAK_2006-006.JPG *License:* GNU Free Documentation License *Contributors:* Steve F-E-Cameron (Merlin-UK) 263
Image *Source:* https://en.wikipedia.org/w/index.php?title=File:SFEC_EGYPT_KARNAK_2006-007.JPG *License:* GNU Free Documentation License *Contributors:* Steve F-E-Cameron (Merlin-UK) 264
Image *Source:* https://en.wikipedia.org/w/index.php?title=File:SFEC_EGYPT_KARNAK_2006-008.JPG *License:* GNU Free Documentation License *Contributors:* Steve F-E-Cameron (Merlin-UK) 264
Image *Source:* https://en.wikipedia.org/w/index.php?title=File:SFEC_EGYPT_KARNAK_2006-009.JPG *License:* GNU Free Documentation License *Contributors:* Steve F-E-Cameron (Merlin-UK) 265
Image *Source:* https://en.wikipedia.org/w/index.php?title=File:SFEC_EGYPT_KARNAK_2006-010.JPG *License:* GNU Free Documentation License *Contributors:* Steve F-E-Cameron (Merlin-UK) 265
Image *Source:* https://en.wikipedia.org/w/index.php?title=File:SFEC_EGYPT_KARNAK_2006-011.JPG *License:* GNU Free Documentation License *Contributors:* Steve F-E-Cameron (Merlin-UK) 266
Image *Source:* https://en.wikipedia.org/w/index.php?title=File:SFEC_EGYPT_KARNAK_2006-012.JPG *License:* GNU Free Documentation License *Contributors:* Steve F-E-Cameron (Merlin-UK) 266
Image *Source:* https://en.wikipedia.org/w/index.php?title=File:SFEC_EGYPT_KARNAK_2006-013.JPG *License:* GNU Free Documentation License *Contributors:* Steve F-E-Cameron (Merlin-UK) 267
Image *Source:* https://en.wikipedia.org/w/index.php?title=File:SFEC_EGYPT_KARNAK_2006-014.JPG *License:* GNU Free Documentation License *Contributors:* Steve F-E-Cameron (Merlin-UK) 267
Image *Source:* https://en.wikipedia.org/w/index.php?title=File:SFEC_EGYPT_KARNAK_2006-015.JPG *License:* GNU Free Documentation License *Contributors:* Steve F-E-Cameron (Merlin-UK) 267
Image *Source:* https://en.wikipedia.org/w/index.php?title=File:SFEC_EGYPT_KARNAK_2006-016.JPG *License:* GNU Free Documentation License *Contributors:* Steve F-E-Cameron (Merlin-UK) 268
Image *Source:* https://en.wikipedia.org/w/index.php?title=File:SFEC_EGYPT_KARNAK_2006-017.JPG *License:* GNU Free Documentation License *Contributors:* Steve F-E-Cameron (Merlin-UK) 268
Image *Source:* https://en.wikipedia.org/w/index.php?title=File:SFEC_EGYPT_KARNAK_2006-018.JPG *License:* GNU Free Documentation License *Contributors:* Steve F-E-Cameron (Merlin-UK) 268
Figure 175 *Source:* https://en.wikipedia.org/w/index.php?title=File:S_F-E-CAMERON_EGYPT_2005_KARNAK_00954.JPG *License:* Creative Commons Attribution-Sharealike 3.0,2.5,2.0,1.0 *Contributors:* Steve F-E-Cameron (Merlin-UK) 269
Figure 176 *Source:* https://en.wikipedia.org/w/index.php?title=File:S10.08_Karnak,_image_9922.jpg *License:* Public Domain *Contributors:* JMCC1, Smbalmuth 269
Figure 177 *Source:* https://en.wikipedia.org/w/index.php?title=File:Lantern_Slide_Collection,_Karnak.jpg *Contributors:* Brooklyn Museum . 270

License

Creative Commons Attribution-Share Alike 3.0
//creativecommons.org/licenses/by-sa/3.0/

Index

Abbasid architecture, 190
Abbasid Caliphate, 10
ABC-CLIO, 30
Abd Allah ibn al-Zubayr, 11
Abd-Allah ibn Ubayy, 37
Abd al-Malik ibn Marwan, 190, 191
Abdülaziz, 194
Abdul Hamid II, 218
Abdul Majeed bin Abdulaziz Al Saud, 4
Abdul Muttalib, 8
Abha, 47
Abhisheka, 150
Above sea level, 44
Abraha, 6, 7
Abraham, 9, 36, 200
Abrahamic religions, 9
Abraham in Islam, 2
Abraj Al Bait, 3, 22
Abraj Al-Bait, 1
Abraj Al Bait Towers, 15, 20
Abu Bakr, 15, 33, 41
Abu Madyan, 214, 241
Abu Sufyan ibn Harb, 38
Abū-Tāhir Al-Jannābī, 11
Acer monspessulanum, 180
Achillea ambrosiaca, 181
Acts of the Apostles, 60
Adhan, 221
Adi Granth, 126, 129
Aedicula, 61
Aegean Sea, 174
Aelia Eudocia, 213
Afghanistan, 26
Africa, 26

Āgama (Hinduism), 148

Aghori, 154
Agia Triada Monastery, Sparmos, 171, 177
Agios Dionysios Monastery, Olympus, 177
Agostino Cornacchini, 77, 87, 88
Agrippa II, 212
Ahimaaz ben Paltiel, 209, 213
Ahmadiyya, 26, 33

Ahmad Shah Durrani, 126, 130
Air vent, 86
Aisha, 34
Ajyad, 17
Ajyad Fortress, 3, 15, 20
Akbar, 128
Akhenaten, 258
Akib ibn Usaid, 10
Alabaster, 83
Al Adl, 17
Al-Afdal ibn Salah ad-Din, 214
Al-Ahzab, 33
Al-Aqsa Mosque, 197, 202, 209, 221
Al-Baqi, 35
Al-Bilad (Saudi newspaper), 24
Albrecht of Mainz, 63
Al-Buraq mosque, 241
Al-Ekhbariya, 25
Alessandro Farnese (cardinal), 96
Alessandro Mattei, 97
Alexander Cunningham, 109, 117
Al Faisaliyyah, 17
Al-Fath, 4
Al-Fil, 8
Al Gemmezah, 17
Al Ghassalah, 17
Al-Hakim bi-Amr Allah, 193
Al Hindawiyyah, 17
Ali, 10, 39, 41
Al-i-Imran, 275
Al Imran, 4
Ali of Hejaz, 27, 42
Ali-Oraid, 15
Ali Pasha of Ioannina, 175
Al Iskan, 17
Al-Isra, 194, 241
Al-Khalidiya, Mecca, 17
Alluvial fan, 172
Al Maabda, 17
Al Madinah, 24
Al Madinah Region, 32
Al-Mamun, 191, 193
Al Mashaaer Al Mugaddassah Metro, 28
Al-Masjid an-Nabawi, 31, 32

295

Al Muaisem, 17
Al Nadwa, 24
Alnus glutinosa, 180
Al Nuzha, 18
Alpine Journal, 166
Alpine tundra, 174, 181
Al Rasaifah, 18
Al-Safa and Al-Marwah, 15
Al Shoqiyah, 18
Al Shubaikah, 18
Al Sulaimaniyyah, 18
Altar, 89
Altitude sickness, 163
Al Tundobawi, 18
Aluminium bronze, 198
Al Utaibiyyah, 18
Al-Wahda (Mecca), 25
Al-Walid I, 34, 191
Alypius of Antioch, 281
Alyssum handelii, 181
Al Zahir (Mecca neighborhood), 18
Al Zahra, 18
Amalek, 9
Ambrose, 83
Amidah, 237
Amin al-Husayni, 221
Ammianus Marcellinus, 281
Amphibian, 182
Amr ibn Hishām, 39
Amritsar, 126
Amun, 250
Amun-Re, 256
Anagarika Munindra, 120
Anat Hoffman, 239
Ancient Greek religion, 175
Ancient Rome, 67
Andrea Bolgi, 89
Andrea Sacchi, 83
André Thévet, 254
Andrew the Apostle, 81, 89
Angel, 39
Angelo Comastri, 52, 97
Angelo II Acciaioli, 96
Anglo-American Committee of Inquiry, 225
Annibaldo di Ceccano, 95
Annibale Albani, 97
Annibale Carracci, 79
Ansar (Islam), 37
Antonio Correr (cardinal), 96
Antonio da Sangallo the Younger, 52, 65
Antonio di Pietro Averlino, 77, 87
Apes, 27
Apophis, 259
Apostle Peter, 76
Apostles, 53
Apostolic succession, 58

Appurtenances, 218
April 2015 Nepal earthquake, 151
Arab, 33, 35, 116
Arabian mythology, 6
Arabian Peninsula, 4, 7
Arabian tribes that interacted with Muhammad, 35
Arabia Petraea, 6
Arabia Standard Time, 2
Arabic, 2, 3, 33, 41
Arabic language, 2, 3, 32, 33, 206
Arab Radio and Television Network, 25
Arafah, 16
Aramaic language, 41
Arbutus andrachne, 180
Arbutus unedo, 180
Archaeological Park of Dion, 176
Archangel, 9
Archangel Michael, 56
Archbasilica of St. John Lateran, 53, 57, 58
Architect, 52
Architectural style, 190
Architrave, 252
Archpriest, 52, 95
Ardās, 137
Arecaceae, 36
Ark of the Covenant, 284
Armatoloi, 175
Armed Police Force Nepal, 149
Armistice of Moudros, 42
Arnold Resnicoff, 231, 232
Arnolfo di Cambio, 88, 94
Ashkenazi Jews, 206
Ashlar, 210
Ashlars, 210
Ashoka, 105, 107
Asoka, 104, 107
Asprerula muscosa, 181
Assassination of Indira Gandhi, 139
Association football, 25
Aswan, 254
Athanasius, 83
Atrium (architecture), 61
Attic, 76
Attic style, 75
Aubrieta thessala, 181
Augustine, 83
Augustinian, 63
Aurelio Sabattani, 97
Australia, 175
Austria, 79
Avalokiteśvara, 120
Avignon Papacy, 62
Avrohom Bornsztain, 284
Awqaf, 199
Axis mundi, 163

Ayah, 35
Aziziyah, 18

Baba Buddha, 129
Babylonia, 212
Baghdad, 10
Bagmati River, 142, 153
Bagmati Zone, 141
Bahrain, 46
Baisakhi, 138
Bakkah, 4, 9, 273
Baklava, 25
Balcony, 81
Baldachin, 57, 58, 79, 80, 89
Baldassare Peruzzi, 65
Balkans, 181
Bal-Sagoth, 259
Baluster, 78
Banister Fletcher, 99
Banu Hudhayl, 7
Banu Khuzaa, 8
Banu Kinanah, 7
Banu Nadir, 35
Banu Qaynuqa, 35
Banu Qurayza, 35
Banu Tamim, 8
Baptistery, 56
Barack Obama, 245
Barclays Gate, 209, 241
Bar Kokhba revolt, 191, 213
Bar mitzvah, 228
Baroque, 52, 79, 83, 92
Baroque architecture, 72
Barque, 253
Basalt, 44
Basic Law of Saudi Arabia, 26
Basilica, 53
Basilica of Our Lady of Licheń, 79
Basilica of Our Lady of Peace of Yamoussoukro, 79
Basilica of St. Peter, 99
Bastet, 258
Battle of Badr, 9
Battle of Buath, 37
Battle of Jerusalem (1917), 218
Battle of Mecca (1916), 12
Battle of Mecca (1924), 15
Battle of the Trench, 10
Battle of Uhud, 10
Bear, 182
Bedouin, 8
Beech, 180
Beech marten, 182
Beer, 258
Beit Shean, 192
Bema, 61

Benedict XVI, 276
Bengal, 120
Benito Mussolini, 85
Benjamin of Tudela, 213, 237
Benyamin Netanyahu, 244
Berel Wein, 284
Bernardo Rossellino, 62
Bethlehem, 190
Bharhut, 108, 109
Bhatkal, 148
Bibliography, 30
Biblioteca Nazionale Centrale di Firenze, 254
Bibliotheca historica, 6
Bihar, 104, 121
Binding of Isaac, 190, 201
Bishop of Antioch, 57
Bishop of Rome, 57
Black Death, 11
Bodh Gaya, 103, 104
Bodhi, 105
Bodhi tree, 107, 108, 117, 121
Bologna, 26
Bon, 160
Bön, 160, 162, 163
Book of Zephaniah, 213
Booted eagle, 182
Borghese Palace, 74
Botany, 179
Brady Haran, 204
Brahmaputra, 160
Brahmaputra River, 160
Brick, 104, 119
Brickwork, 119
British India, 134
British Mandate for Palestine, 207
British people, 43
Bronze, 77
Brooklyn Museum, 251
Budapest, 202
Buddha, 108
Buddhahood, 162
Buddhism, 104, 160
Buddhist, 107, 119
Buddhist architecture, 104
Bugle, 177
Bunleua Sulilat, 117
Buraidah, 47
Buraq, 206, 209, 241
Byzantine, 211
Byzantine Empire, 6, 7, 191, 207

Cairo, 12, 42, 46
Cakrasaṃvara Tantra, 162
Calcutta, 111, 112
Caliph, 42, 200
Caliphate, 10, 41

297

Callixtus II, 61
Cambridge University Press, 30
Camel train, 7
Camillo Rusconi, 91
Campanula oreadum, 181
Canova, 88, 92
Capital city, 142
Cardinal (Catholicism), 78
Carlo Barberini, 97
Carlo Fontana, 52, 92
Carlo Maderno, 52, 53, 67, 74
Carum adamovicii, 181
Castel SantAngelo, 54, 70, 98
Castle, 20
Category:Hinduism, 142
Category:Islam, 2
Category:Mahabodhi Temple, 123
Category:Shaivism, 161
Cathedra, 53, 58
Cathedral, 53
Cathedra Petri, 82
Catholic Church, 51, 53, 58
Catholic Encyclopedia, 99
Catholicism, 87
Cedrus, 180
Cenozoic, 165
Centaurea incompleta, 181
Centaurea litochorea, 181
Centaurea transiens, 181
Central Asia, 26
Cerastrium theophrasti, 181
Cercis siliquastrum, 180
Chacham Bashi, 217, 220
Chaim Herzog, 227
Chaim Hirschensohn, 216
Chaim ibn Attar, 240
Chaim Weizmann, 218
Chair of Saint Peter, 56, 58, 79, 80
Chancel, 63, 67
Chaparral, 171
Chapel, 78
Chapelle Rouge, 253
Charity (virtue), 92
Charlemagne, 77, 87
Charles Allen (writer), 161, 167
Charles Clermont-Ganneau, 203
Charles Edward Stuart, 85, 92
Charles-Nicolas-Sigisbert Sonnini de Manoncourt, 256
Charles the Bald, 58
Charles William Wilson, 241
Cherry plum, 180
Cherub, 78, 88
China, 159, 160
Cholera, 12
Cholera outbreaks and pandemics, 12

Christ, 75
Christendom, 53, 57, 67
Christian, 7, 10, 254
Christian denomination, 51
Christian Era, 7
Christianity, 60
Christian pilgrimage, 191
Christian tradition, 52
Christian world, 53
Christina of Sweden, 87
Christopher Wren, 79
Chronicle of Ahimaaz, 237
Church architecture, 79
Church (building), 7, 53
Church of St. Giacomo, 202
Church of the Holy Sepulchre, 190–193, 242
Church of the Seat of Mary (Kathisma), 190
Ciborium (architecture), 79
Cinereous vulture, 182
Circumambulation, 36
Circus of Nero, 60, 84
Cistern, 17
CITEREFArvind-Pal Singh Mandair2013, 279
CITEREFChristopher ShackleArvind Mandair2013, 279
CITEREFClermont-Ganneau1899, 281
CITEREFHenry Walker2002, 279
CITEREFLouis E. FenechW. H. McLeod2014, 279
CITEREFNecipo.C4.9Flu2008, 281
CITEREFPardeep Singh Arshi1989, 279
CITEREFPashaura SinghLouis E. Fenech2014, 279
CITEREFSingh2011, 279
CITEREFThe Editors of Encyclopaedia Britannica2014, 279
CITEREFTrudy RingNoelle WatsonPaul Schellinger2012, 279
CITEREFVog.C3.BC.C3.A91864, 281
CITEREFW. Owen Cole2004, 279
Classicism, 72
Claude-Étienne Savary, 256
Claude Sicard, 256
Clement VIII, 72
Closed city, 3, 33
Coffering, 68
Colonnade, 54, 211
Colosseum, 62
Colossi of Memnon, 254
Commando, 15
Commandos 2: Men of Courage, 151
Committee, 74
Common Era, 213
Commons:Category:Karnak temple complex, 271
Commons:Category:Medina, 49

Commons:Category:Mount Kailash, 168
Commons:Category:Mount Olympus, 188
Commons:Category:Pashupatinath temple, 156
Commons:Category:Western Wall, 247
Commons:Harmandir Sahib, 140
Commons:Mahabodhi Temple, 123
Commons:Medina, 49
Concrete, 68
Conquest of Mecca, 41
Consecration, 52
Conservative Judaism, 228
Constantine I, 213, 254
Constantine the Great, 53, 61, 74, 77, 80, 87
Constantinople, 42
Constantius II, 254
Constitution of Medina, 37
Coptic language, 254
Corinthian order, 81
Cornice, 75
Cornus mas, 180
Cotinus coggygria, 180
Counter-reformation, 53, 74
Countess, 87
Course (architecture), 207
Cremation, 153
Crepuscular rays, 60
Crescent, 194
Cretaceous, 165
Crucifixion, 60, 84
Cruciform, 54
Crusades, 193
Crust (geology), 165
Crypt, 87
Crystal, 161
Cubit, 235
Curia, 74
Czech Republic, 79

Daily Telegraph, 274
Damascus, 10
Dammam, 29
Daniel Jones (phonetician), 281
Darchen, 164
Dates and numbers, 200, 201, 235
Dates (fruit), 46
David ben Gurion, 226
David Roberts (painter), 261
Day of Arafa, 27
Death, 92
Death on the Nile, 259
Decline of Buddhism in India, 116
Dedication, 52
Deer, 182
Defecation, 7
Deity, 6

Desert of Paran, 4
Destruction of early Islamic heritage sites in Saudi Arabia, 34
Destruction of historic buildings, 15
Destruction of Meccas historic and religious sites, 20
Deusdedit of San Pietro in Vincoli, 95
Deutscher Wetterdienst, 19
Dharam Yudh Morcha, 138
Dhikr, 221
Dhu al-Hijjah, 3
Dhu al-Qidah, 25
Diamond throne, 107, 108
Die Welt, 245
Digital object identifier, 99, 100, 203
Diocese, 52
Diocese of Rome, 52, 53
Diodorus Siculus, 6
Dion, Pieria, 171
Dionysus, 177
Disputed statement, 193, 214, 226
Diwali, 139
DMOZ, 140
Doctors of the Church, 58, 83
Doha, 46
Dome, 54, 70, 190
Domenico Fontana, 70, 74, 84
Domenico Tardini, 97
Dome of the Chain, 193
Dome of the Prophet, 194
Dome of the Rock, **189**, 204, 209, 235, 284
Domestic yak, 164
Dominican Order, 63
Donald Trump, 246
Donato Bramante, 52, 53, 63, 91
Door of the Dead in St. Peters Basilica, 87
Dorcas, 56
Douglas Valder Duff, 220
D:Q4513, 104
Drum, 162
Drum (architecture), 68, 192
Dubai, 46
Ducats, 97
Dung Gate, 211
Duomo, 67
Dusk, 25

Early Christian Church, 53
Ecosystem, 180
Edah HaChareidis, 220
Edfu, 254
Edmond James de Rothschild, 216
Edmund Allenby, 1st Viscount Allenby, 218
Edoardo Borromeo, 97
Edward Henry Howard, 97
Edward Keith-Roach, 220

Edwin Arnold, 119
Egypt, 33, 249
Egyptian temple, 250
Eighteenth dynasty of Egypt, 253
Ekrima Said Sabri, 245
Elasson, 184
Elassona, 177
Electric locomotive, 28
Eleventh dynasty of Egypt, 252
Elm, 180
Emir, 42
Emperor, 61
Emperor Charles V, 65
Encarta, 274
Enclave, 53
Encyclopædia Britannica, 31
Encyclopædia Britannica Eleventh Edition, 188, 271
Encyclopaedia Judaica, 275
Encyclopaedia of Islam, 30, 275
Encyclopedia Americana, 275
Endemism, 179
End time, 202
England, 79, 92
English, 2, 32, 170, 250
Enipeas (Pieria), 171
Enlightenment (Buddhism), 104
Entablature, 85
Ernest Richmond, 204
Erysimum olympicum, 181
Esna, 254
Ethiopia, 7
Ethnic group, 26
ETH Zurich, 30
Etymology, 3
Etz Chaim Yeshiva, 220
Eucharist, 79
Eugenio Pacelli, 97
Euphrates, 6
Europe, 26, 170
European robin, 182
European Union, 183
Everard des Barres, 194
Exodus Rabbah, 284
Eyal Weizman, 227

Facade, 75
Fahd of Saudi Arabia, 15
Faience, 194
Faisal bin Salman bin Abdulaziz Al Saud, 32
Faisal of Saudi Arabia, 244
Fakhri Pasha, 42
Fathers of the Church, 58
Fatimah, 34
Faulting, 165
Feast of Saints Peter and Paul, 82

Federico Tedeschini, 97
Feldheim Publishers, 284
Fellowship Church, 202
Ferdinando Marinelli Artistic Foundry, 87
Festival Hall of Thutmose III, 254
Festuca olympica, 181
File:He-Kotel.ogg, 206
File:Karnakfrieze1.jpg, 256
File:Karnakpanorama.jpg, 256
File:Pashupati dec 20 2009.jpg, 145
File:San Pietro in Vaticano 001.JPG, 277
File:Vatican StPeter Square.jpg, 57
Filippo Brunelleschi, 67, 68
Finial, 71
Firman (decree), 215
First ascent, 170
First Court (Cachette Court), 253
First Crusade, 214
First Jewish-Roman War, 213
First Saudi State, 11
First Temple, 232
Five Pillars of Islam, 10
Flag carrier, 20
Flora (plants), 170
Florence, 69, 87
Florence Cathedral, 63, 67, 68
Foteina, 184
Foundation Stone, 190, 200, 201, 206, 213, 235
Fountain, 84
Four sights, 105
France, 79
Francesco Barberini (seniore), 97
Francesco Cornaro (cardinal), 96
Francesco Marchisano, 97
Francesco Mochi, 89
Francis Bedford (photographer), 195
Francis Edwards Peters, 247
Francois Duquesnoy, 89
Fraxinus ornus, 180
Frederic Boissonnas, 170
Frédéric Boissonnas, 176
Frederick Catherwood, 192
Frederick Hartt, 100
Frederick Louis Norden, 256
Frieze, 75, 201
Ful medames, 25

Gabbai, 221
Gabriel, 9, 39, 200
Galasso Alghisi, 71
Galilee, 60
Gallipoli Campaign, 12
Gangdise Shan, 160
Ganges, 160
Garbhagriha, 142, 146, 148, 149

Garuda, 120
Gauri Kund, 165
Gautama Buddha, 104, 107
Gaya district, 104
Gaya, India, 105
Gazza (Mecca neighborhood), 18
Gebel el-Silsila, 256
Genísta sakellariadis, 181
Geographic coordinate system, 1, 32, 51, 103, 126, 141, 159, 169, 190, 206, 250
Geography (Ptolemy), 254
Geological, 171
Geological period, 44
Georgina Masson, 276
Georg Rosen (1821–1891), 242
Gershom Gorenberg, 283
Ghaghara, 160
Ghaghara River, 160
Ghassanids, 6
Giacomo Barozzi da Vignola, 52
Giacomo della Porta, 52, 70, 71
Giacomo Giustiniani, 97
Giacomo Manzù, 87
Gian Lorenzo Bernini, 52, 53, 57, 79
Giant order, 54, 67
Gilding, 78
Giordano Orsini (died 1438), 96
Giorgakis Olympios, 175
Giorgio Vasari, 70
Giotto, 87
Giovanni Battista Zeno, 96
Giovanni Giocondo, 65
Giovanni Pierluigi da Palestrina, 85
Giuliano Cesarini, 96
Giuliano da Sangallo, 65
Giulio Romano, 66
Giza pyramid complex, 250
Glossary of Hinduism terms, 142
God in Islam, 9, 200
God the Son, 201
Gold, 136, 161
Golden eagle, 182
Golden Gate (Jerusalem), 213
Golden Temple, **125**
Gold leaf, 198
Gompa, 165
Goose, 252
Grand Mosque Seizure, 15
Granger (Tourtechot), 256
Granite, 109, 119, 165
Granitic, 165
Granthi, 129
Great Depression, 20
Great Fire of Rome, 60
Great Hypostyle Hall, Karnak, 249, 252, 253
Great Mosque of Mecca, 1

Greece, 170
Greek, 170
Greek Civil War, 175
Greek cross, 63, 67, 74
Greek language, 60, 170
Greek mythology, 170, 175
Greek Resistance, 175
Green Dome, 33
Gregory of Nazianzus, 213
Gregory the Great, 56
Gregory XIV, 72
Grotto, 88
Groundbreaking, 52
Groupe dIntervention de la Gendarmerie Nationale, 15
Guercino, 91
Guhyeshwari Temple, 143, 146
Guide dogs, 211
Gupta Empire, 116, 119
Gurdwara, 126
Gurkha, 151
Gurla Mandhata, 166
Guru Amar Das, 127
Guru Arjan, 126, 128, 133
Guru Gobind Singh, 129
Guru Granth Sahib, 128, 132
Guru Hargobind, 129, 133
Guru Nanak, 26, 139
Guru Ram Das, 126, 139
Guru Teg Bahadur, 139
Gustav Bauernfeind, 214

Haaretz, 281, 283
Habayit Hayehudi, 202
Habesha people, 8
Hadith, 35, 39, 200
Hadrian, 92
Hagia Sophia, 67
Hagiography, 128
Haj Amin al-Husseini, 197
Haj Amin Al Husseinni, 223
Hajj, 3, 12, 15, 16, 22, 35, 41, 43
Halachic, 234
Hamza ibn 'Abd al-Muttalib, 39
Hanuman, 145
Haram, 35
Haramain High Speed Rail Project, 28, 47
Haram esh-Sharif, 207
Haredi, 243
Haredim, 228
Haridwar, 148
Harrat Rahat, 42
Hasan ibn Ali, 34
Hashemite, 42
Hashemites, 9
Hasidic, 243

Hasidic Judaism, 215
Hathor, 258
Hatikva, 223
Hatikvah, 227
Hatshepsut, 253, 258
Havatzelet, 234
Hazel, 180
Heaven, 39
Hebrew Bible, 212
Hebrew language, 206
Hebrew University, 192
Heinrich Barth, 176
Hejaz, 4, 43
Hejazi Arabic, 32
Helena (empress), 81, 89
Helen Gardner (art historian), 99
Henry Benedict Stuart, 85, 92, 97
Henry Cattan, 283
Heraclius, 192
Herbert Tichy, 166
Herodotus, 254
Herods Temple, 191, 213
Herod the Great, 191, 206, 210, 212
Highway 15 (Saudi Arabia), 29, 47
Highway 40 (Saudi Arabia), 29
Highway 60 (Saudi Arabia), 47
Hijra (Islam), 9, 32, 37, 41
Hijri year, 38, 191
Hillel Halkin, 246
Hilton Hotels & Resorts, 15
Himyarite Kingdom, 8, 36
Hindu, 142
Hinduism, 119, 142, 160, 161
Hindu temple, 104, 142
Hira, 3, 9, 20
His Shem ha-Gedolim, 284
History of Hinduism, 142
History of Iran, 35
Holiest sites in Islam, 3
Holly, 180
Holy city, 3
Holy Door, 54
Holy Lance, 81, 89
Holyland Model of Jerusalem, 191
Holy of Holies, 201, 207
Holy Sacrament, 56
Holy See, 51, 276
Holy Spirit, 58
Holy Trinity, 91
Holy water, 78
Homage (feudal), 79
Hoopoe, 182
Hot desert climate, 18, 44
Hourglass, 92
House of Muhammed, 48
Hubal, 6

Hugh Ruttledge, 166
Huna people, 116
Hussein bin Ali, Sharif of Mecca, 12, 43
Hussein of Jordan, 198
Hyksos, 253

IAST, 160
Ibn Furkah, 214
Ibn Hisham, 37
Ibn Ishaq, 7, 36, 37
Ibn Khaldun, 30
Ibn Khordadbeh, 35
Ibn Saud, 3, 43
Ibn Saud of Saudi Arabia, 27
Ibrahim Pasha of Egypt, 215, 217
Ice age, 179
Idolatry in Islam, 34
Ignatius of Antioch, 85
Igneous rock, 165
Immaculate Conception, 92
Immaculate Heart of Mary in Pittsburgh, 79
Immortals, 170
India, 104
Indian Mujahideen, 122
Indian Museum, 109, 111, 112
Indian Plate, 165
Indian subcontinent, 131
Indira Gandhi, 126, 138
Indulgences, 63
Indus, 160
Indus River, 160
Infidel, 40
International Air Transport Association airport code, 27, 46
International Civil Aviation Organization airport code, 27, 46
International school, 26
International Standard Book Number, 30, 99, 100, 122, 123, 139, 140, 167, 168, 203, 246, 247, 271, 281
International Standard Serial Number, 99, 100
Intruded, 165
Investiture Controversy, 87
Ippolito dEste, 96
Ippolito Rosellini, 255
Iranian rial, 198
Iraq, 8, 42
Iron Gate, 210
Isaac Luria, 233
Isaline Blew Horner, 123
Ishmael, 6
Ishmael in Islam, 2, 9
Islam, 2, 3, 7, 32, 190, 209
Islamic architecture, 190
Islamic invasions of India, 116
Islamic Movement in Israel, 244

Islamic schools and branches, 11
Islamic terrorist, 122
Islamic University of Madinah, 46
Islamic view of Abraham, 9
Islamism, 15
Islamization, 10
Ismailism, 11
Isra and Miraj, 190, 200
Israel, 246
Israel Antiquities Authority, 282
Israel Defense Forces, 228
Israeli Arabs, 199
Israeli flag, 198, 244
Israels Supreme Court, 228, 239
Israels unilateral disengagement plan, 238
Istanbul, 29, 42, 46, 202
Italian language, 51, 53
Italian Renaissance, 53
Italy, 276
Itinerarium Burdigalense, 213
Iw, 273

İznik, 47

Jabal al-Nour, 1, 5, 9, 20
Jabal Al Nour, 18
Jacob Ettlinger, 237
Jacopo Barozzi da Vignola, 70
Jacopo Sansovino, 66
Jaffa Gate, 211
Jahangir, 129
Jainism, 160, 161
Jallianwala Bagh, 138
Jamaraat Bridge, 1
Jambhala, 120
James Bruce, 256
James Francis Edward Stuart, 85, 87
James Lees-Milne, 69, 100
Janiculum, 54
Jankaea heldreichii, 181
Jannat al-Baqi, 34
Jannat al-Baqi cemetery, 48
Jarnail Singh Bhindranwale, 138
Jarwal (Mecca neighborhood), 18
Jataka, 107
Jeddah, 3, 4, 27, 29
Jerome, 213
Jerusalem, 35, 81, 190, 206, 283
Jerusalem Center for Public Affairs, 247
Jerusalem Islamic Waqf, 198, 225
Jerusalem Post, 226
Jesus, 53, 57, 200
Jet aircraft, 22
Jewish Agency, 239
Jewish Agency for Israel, 229
Jewish Encyclopedia, 36, 275

Jewish Legion, 219
Jibreel, 20
Jizya, 38
Joel Teitelbaum, 243
Johann Michael Vansleb, 254
Johann Tetzel, 63, 276
John Chancellor (British administrator), 220, 223
John Chrysostom, 83
John the Apostle, 277
John the Baptist, 75, 277
Jonathan Eybeschutz, 233
Joos van Ghistele, 254
Jordan, 8, 198
Jordanian occupation of the West Bank, 226
Joseph David Beglar, 117
Joseph Gikatilla, 237
Josephus Flavius, 212
J.R. Macduff, 282
JSTOR, 99, 100, 203, 204
Juan López (cardinal), 96
Jubilee (Christian), 87
Jubilee (Christianity), 54
Judaism, 36
Judeo-Spanish, 238
Juhayman al-Otaibi, 15
Jujube, 135
Julian the Apostate, 191
Jurhum (Mecca neighborhood), 18
Jyotirlinga, 143

Kaaba, 1, 3, 7, 9, 20, 41, 200
Kaab al-Ahbar, 200
Kaba, 36
Kabsa, 25
K. A. C. Creswell, 202
Kaddish, 227
Kafir, 40
Kairouan, 275
Kallipefki, Larissa, 184
Kalpa (aeon), 107
Kamandalu, 147
Kanalon Monastery, 177
Kareth, 235
Karlskirche, 79
Karma, 131
Karnak, **249**, 271
Karya, Larissa, 171
Kashi Math, 148
Kashyapa, 148
Katerini, 184
Kathmandu, 141, 142, 145, 148, 164
Kathmandu Valley, 142, 143, 148
Kav ha-Yashar, 284
Kebab, 25
Khadijah, 15

Khalid bin Faisal Al Saud, 2, 4
Khalsa, 129, 139
Khamis Mushait, 47
Khedive, 11
Khosrau I, 6
King Abdulaziz International Airport, 27, 28, 47
King Abdul Aziz Stadium, 25
King Abdullah Economic City, 28, 47
Kingdom of Aksum, 7
Kingdom of Axum, 6
Kingdom of Hejaz, 12
King Solomon, 232
Kiratpur, 127
Kirtan, 137
Kitzur Shulchan Aruch, 284
Klepht, 175, 176
Knesset, 228
Knights Templar, 193
Knights Templar Seal, 193
Knowledge Economic City, Medina, 46
Kodesh Hakodashim, 235
Kofta, 25
Kohen, 231
Kolkata, 109
Kolkota, 109
Kom Ombo, 254
Koninklijke Brill, 30
Köppen climate classification, 44
Kshatriya, 148
Kufa, 10, 41
Kuwait, 46
Kvitelach, 240

Lahore, 126, 129
Lake Manasarovar, 160, 165, 167
Lake Rakshastal, 160, 165
Lakhmids, 6
Lakshmi, 119
Lamb of God, 92
Lamentations Rabbah, 232, 284
Langar (Sikhism), 127, 137
Lanner falcon, 182
Lao Buddhist sculpture, 117
Lapidus, 273
Lapis lazuli, 161
Lara Croft, 259
Larissa (regional unit), 170
Late Antiquity, 232
Lateran Treaties, 85
Latin cross, 54, 62, 67, 74
Latin language, 51, 53
Latin Rite, 52
Laurus nobilis, 180
Lead, 198
League of Nations, 224

Lebanese cuisine, 25
Leivithra, 177
Leone Battista Alberti, 62
Leon Heuzey, 176
Leptokarya, 184
Leuke Kome, 6
Lever, 252
Lhasa, 164
Library of Congress Country Studies, 274
Ligusticum olympicum, 181
Limestone, 165, 210
Lingam, 145
Lion, 182
List of countries by highest point, 169
List of efforts to move and install stones, 252
List of largest buildings in the world, 3
List of largest church buildings in the world, 53, 59
List of largest domes, 59, 101
List of mountain lists, 169
List of obelisks in Rome, 78
List of religions and spiritual traditions, 190
List of rulers of Egypt, 35
List of tallest buildings in Rome, 59, 101
List of the longest Asian rivers, 160
List of World Heritage Sites in Europe, 53
List of World Heritage Sites in the Arab States, 250
Litochoro, 170, 171, 176
Little Western Wall, 207, 210
Liturgy, 53
Liwa (Arabic), 218
Lizard, 182
Loan word, 160
Loggia, 79
London, 79
Louis Hahge, 261
Louloudies, 177
Lower Egypt, 254, 256
Lucido Conti, 96
Ludovico di Varthema, 26
Luxor, 250
Luxor Governorate, 249
Luxor Temple, 251, 253

Macedonia (Greece), 170
Madain Saleh, 4
Madonna (art), 78
Madrassa, 227
Maha Bodhi Society, 120
Mahabodhi Temple, **103**
Mahabodhi Temple, Bagan, 117
Mahant, 116
Maha Shivaratri, 143
Mahayana Buddhism, 116
Mahmud II, 194

Major basilica, 52, 53, 57, 58
Makkah Region, 2
Mamluk, 211
Mamluk Sultanate (Cairo), 42, 194, 214
Man and the Biosphere Programme, 170
Mandi (food), 25
Mangaluru, 148
Maple, 180
Maquis shrubland, 180
Marble, 74, 194
Maria Klementyna Sobieska, 87, 92
Mariano Rampolla del Tindaro, 97
Marici (Buddhism), 120
Mario Mattei, 97
Marriage of the Virgin (Perugino), 202
Martin Luther, 63
Martyrdom, 60
Maryam (sura), 201
Mary, Queen of the World Cathedral, 79
Masjid al-Haram, 5, 15, 16, 20, 21, 200
Masjid al-Qiblatain, 35
Masjid al-Qiblatayn, 33
Mass (liturgy), 95
Matilda of Tuscany, 87
Maurya Empire, 107
Mayor, 4, 32
Mecca, **1**, 32, 35, 36, 43, 47, 48, 202
Mecca Gate, 20
Mecca Metro, 28
Meccan sura, 33
Mechitza, 220, 221
Media:He-Kotel.ogg, 206
Medina, 3, 28, 29, **31**, 49
Medina Metro, 47
Medinan sura, 33, 35
Mediterranean climate, 177
Meir Ben-Dov, 209
Melampyrum ciliatum, 181
Melchior de Vogüé, 191, 203
Melchisédech Thévenot, 254
Melee, 39
Meleke, 210
Memphis, Egypt, 254
Menhit, 258
Mercaz HaRav, 244
Merneptah, 253
Merv, 29
Mesorah Publications, 246
Messianic era, 202
Metamorphosed, 165
Metasedimentary, 165
Michelangelo, 52, 53, 57, 62, 66, 69, 73, 77, 91, 94
Michelozzo, 63
Microclimate, 179
Middle East, 24, 26

Middle Kingdom of Egypt, 250, 251
Middot (Talmud), 215
Midrash, 6, 232
Mikveh, 212
Milarepa, 162
Milia, Pieria, 175
Millenarianism, 11
Milwaukee, 79
Mimar Sinan, 215
Mina (Mecca neighborhood), 18
Minaret, 190
Mina, Saudi Arabia, 1, 16, 17, 28
Minor basilica, 57
Minyan, 215
Misfalah, 18
Mishpatim, 284
MIT Press, 99, 100
Mizrah, 237
Mnemosyne, 175
Modus vivendi, 220
Moed Katan, 284
Mohammed Tahir Husseini, 216
Moishe Sternbuch, 284
Moksha (Jainism), 161
Monier-Williams, 280
Monotheism, 9
Montreal, 79
Montu, 252, 258
Monument to the Royal Stuarts, 92
Moorish Revival, 202
Mordechai Gur, 227
Moroccan Quarter, 207, 208, 215, 227
Moroccans Gate, 241
Mosaic, 78, 194, 201
Moses, 200
Moshe Dayan, 198, 226
Mosque, 15
Mosque of abu-Qubais, 15
Mother church, 53, 58
Mother goddess, 257
Mountain, 170
Mountain range, 160, 170
Mount Arafat, 28
Mount Kailash, **159**
Mount Meru, 161
Mount of Olives, 202
Mount Olympus, **169**
Mount Uhud, 31, 34, 40
Mount Zion, 226
Muawiyah I, 192
Mucalinda, 117
Muezzin, 221
Mufti of Jerusalem, 245
Muhajirun, 9, 37
Muhammad, 3, 4, 7, 32, 35, 37, 190, 200, 209
Muhammad al-Bukhari, 35

305

Muhammad Ali of Egypt, 11
Muhammad bin Qasim, 116
Muhammad in Medina, 10
Muhammads first revelation, 3, 20
Mukhalinga, 147
Murex, 61
Muse, 175
Muslim, 3, 34, 116
Muslim Quarter, 207, 210
Muslim world, 10
Mut, 252, 253, 257, 258
Muzdalifah, 28

Nabataean Kingdom, 6
Nachshon Wachsman, 238
Nahmanides, 213
Nail (relic), 89
Najd, 24
Nakhawila, 46
Napoleon, 88
Napoleone Orsini Frangipani, 95
Narthex, 54, 74, 77
Natan Sharansky, 229
Nathan Straus, 220
National Geographic Society, 100
National government, 33
National Investigation Agency, 122
National Library of Israel, 219
National Park, 170
Natura 2000, 183
Nave, 52, 54, 75
Navicella (mosaic), 56
Nebaioth, 6
Nectanebo I, 254
Negative and positive rights, 218
Negus, 7
Nekhbet, 258
Neoclassical architecture, 92
Neos Panteleimonas, 184
Nepal, 141, 142, 145
Nepal Army, 145
Nepali language, 142
Nepal Police, 145
Nero, 60
Ner Tamid, 230
New International Encyclopedia, 49
New Kingdom, 250
New Synagogue, Berlin, 202
New Zealand, 175
Niccola Clarelli Parracciani, 97
Nikolaus Pevsner, 100
Nile, 254
Normandy landings, 238
Nubia, 254

Oak, 180

Obadiah ben Abraham, 214, 284
Obelisk, 84, 253
Obelisks of Rome, 60
Obverse and reverse, 198
OCLC, 99, 100, 202
Octagon, 190
Okaz, 24
Old City (Jerusalem), 190, 206
Old City of Jerusalem, 210
Old South Arabian, 4
Old St. Peters Basilica, 53, 61, 62
Old World, 59
Old World monkey, 27
Oleg Grabar, 203
Olympus, 188
Operation Blue Star, 138
Orach Chaim, 284
Order of Friars Minor Capuchin, 254
Oriental studies, 242
Origen, 60
Orpheus, 177
Orphism (religion), 177
Orthodox Judaism, 199
Osman Nuri Pasha, 24
Otto II, 85
Ottoman architecture, 190
Ottoman Caliphate, 11
Ottoman Dynasty, 42
Ottoman Empire, 5, 42, 175, 214
Ottoman return of Mecca 1813, 11
Ozymandias (comics), 259

Paadal Petra Sthalam, 143
Padmasambhava, 162
Pagan, 254
Paganism, 6
Pagoda, 104, 142, 146
Pakistani Armed Forces, 15
Pala Empire, 116
Palazzo Pubblico, 84
Paleontology, 27
Paleozoic, 44
Palestinian National Authority, 245
Palimpsest, 57
Pali Text Society, 123
Palm Sunday, 75, 84
Palmyra, 6
Pandemic, 11
Pantheon, Paris, 79
Pantheon, Rome, 63, 67, 68
Paolo Marella, 97
Papal Basilicas, 52, 57, 276
Papal conclave, 95
Paris, 79
Pārvatī, 161
Pashupati, 142

Pashupatinath Temple, **141**
Patna, 104, 127
Patriarch of the West, 276
Patricia Crone, 4
Paul Lucas (traveller), 254
Pausanias (geographer), 182
Peepul, 105
Peregrine falcon, 182
Peristyle, 68, 69
Persian Gulf, 6
Perugino, 202
Perushim, 215
Petra, 6
Petra, Pieria, 171
Phalgu, 105
Philae, 254
Phillyrea, 180
Pieria (regional unit), 170, 175
Pietà (Michelangelo), 56, 57, 91, 94
Pietro da Cortona, 91
Pietro Francesco Galleffi, 97
Pilaster, 78, 211
Pilgrim, 163
Pilgrimage, 3, 53, 104, 163, 207
Pillars of Islam, 3
Pinedjem I, 256
Pinus heldreichii, 180
Pinus nigra, 180
Piracy, 6
Pirke De-Rabbi Eliezer, 284
Pir (Sufism), 126
Pistacia terebinthus, 180
Plain, 33
Plaster, 110
Platamon Castle, 177
Platanus orientalis, 180
Poa thessala, 181
Politics of Saudi Arabia, 4
Ponte SantAngelo, 55
Pony, 164
Pope, 53, 57, 58
Pope Alexander VII, 83, 92
Pope Benedict XIII, 88
Pope Benedict XIV, 88
Pope Benedict XV, 92
Pope Benedict XVI, 242
Pope Clement I, 56
Pope Clement VII, 63
Pope Clement VIII, 63
Pope Clement XI, 87
Pope Francis, 96
Pope Gregory I, 61
Pope Gregory XIII, 63, 91
Pope Gregory XIV, 63, 91
Pope Gregory XV, 63
Pope Hadrian VI, 63

Pope Innocent IX, 63
Pope Innocent VIII, 92
Pope Innocent X, 63
Pope Innocent XI, 91
Pope Innocent XII, 92
Pope John Paul II, 87, 91, 242
Pope John XXIII, 92
Pope Julius II, 62
Pope Julius III, 63
Pope Leo X, 63
Pope Leo XI, 63
Pope Marcellus II, 63
Pope Nicholas III, 95
Pope Nicholas V, 62
Pope Paul II, 96
Pope Paul III, 63
Pope Paul IV, 63
Pope Paul V, 63, 74, 76
Pope Pius IV, 63
Pope Pius V, 63
Pope Pius VI, 88
Pope Pius VIII, 92
Pope Pius X, 92
Pope Pius XI, 91
Pope Pius XII, 61, 91
Pope Sixtus V, 63, 84
Pope Sylvester I, 74
Pope Urban VII, 63
Pope Urban VIII, 58, 63, 79
Porphyry (geology), 92
Portal:Hinduism, 142, 161
Portal:Islam, 2
Poskim, 233, 236
Post-Modernism, 79
Potentilla deorum, 182
PowerSlave, 259
Prague, 79
Precinct of Amun-Re, 249, 259
Precinct of Montu, 250
Precinct of Mut, 250, 253
Precipitation, 19, 45
Prefect, 92
Presentation of the Virgin, 56
Priestly blessing, 226, 231
Primary, secondary and tertiary sources, 234
Primate, 27
Prince Mohammad Bin Abdulaziz Airport, 46
Printers mark, 200
Private school, 26
Procopius, 4
Prophets and messengers in Islam, 32
Prophets in Islam, 2
Prostration, 163
Protestantism, 63
Protestant reformation, 53, 63
Psalm 84, 6

307

Ptolemaic dynasty, 251
Ptolemaic Kingdom, 250
Ptolemaic period, 250
Ptolemy, 6, 254
Ptolemy III Euergetes, 256
Ptolemy IV Philopator, 256
Punjabi, 127
Punjab, India, 126
Pydna (Ancient Site), 177
Pylon (architecture), 260
Pythion, 171

Q35484, 49
Qadiriyyah, 26
Qaitbay, 35
Qarmatians, 11
Qibla, 3, 33, 35
Quba Mosque, 31, 33
Queen Christina of Sweden, 91
Quercus coccifera, 180
Quercus pubescens, 180
Quran, 3, 8, 26, 33, 39, 200
Quraysh tribe, 7, 9
Quraysh (tribe), 6, 36, 39

Rabbi, 36
Rabbinic traditions, 282
Rabigh, 28, 47
Radbaz, 284
Radvaz, 233, 284
Raed Salah, 244
Rafael Merry del Val, 97
Raja ibn Haywah, 192
Rajat ash-Shams Mosque, 48
Rajbhandari, 148
Ralph Waldo Emerson, 57
Rama, 143
Ramadan (calendar month), 25
Ramat Gan, 284
Ramat Shlomo, 210
Ramesses II, 253
Ramses II, 262
Ranjit Singh, 126–128, 130
Raphael, 65, 202
Rapid transit, 28
Rashidun Caliphate, 10, 33
Ratnachakrama, 106
Ravi River, 130
Red fox, 182
Red Sea, 6, 33
Reform Judaism, 228
Reginald Dyer, 138
Regions of Saudi Arabia, 2, 32
Reinhold Messner, 166
Relative humidity, 19, 45
Relics of Muhammad, 42

Religion, 3
Renaissance architecture, 52, 53, 67
Renaud de Vichiers, 194
Reptile, 182
Responsa, 234, 284
Retaining wall, 210
Revelation, 9
Richard Francis Burton, 26
Richard Pococke, 256
Rigveda, 148
Rinpoche, 160
Rishabhanatha, 161
River source, 160
Riyadh, 27
Robert Thurman, 167
Robinsons Arch, 212, 229
Rock dove, 182
Rock partridge, 182
Roe deer, 182
Roman Curia, 63
Roman emperor, 53, 60
Roman Empire, 213, 232
Romanesque architecture, 77
Roman–Persian Wars, 6
Rome, 53
Romualdo Braschi-Onesti, 97
Roof lantern, 63
Roof pendant, 165
Round church, 194
Rowlatt Act, 138
Royal Stoa (Jerusalem), 212
Ruby, 161
Rudraksha, 147
Rumbach Street Synagogue, 202
Rynchosinapis nivalis, 182

Saadanius, 27
Sacrament, 79
Sacred architecture, 52
Sacred Fig, 105
Sacred Heart, 56
Sacristy, 56, 75, 92
Sadhus, 153
Sad ibn Muadh, 41
Sahih Bukhari, 35
Saint Basil, 56
Saint Erasmus, 56
Saint Joseph, 56, 92
Saint Longinus, 89
Saint Paul, 54
Saint Peter, 52–54, 61, 75, 92
Saint Peters Square, 83
Saint Peters tomb, 53, 61
Saint Petronilla, 91
Saint Sebastian, 56, 91
Saint Veronica, 89

Saiva, 145
Saladin, 194, 214, 227
Salafi, 11
Sala Keoku, 117
Salamander, 182
Salat, 20
Salman al-Farsi Mosque, 48
Saltire, 89
Samaveda, 148
Samosa, 25
Sanaa, 7
San Carlo ai Catinari, 79
Sanchi, 107–109
Sanchi Stupa No.2, 109
Sanctuary, 57
Sandra Mackey, 275
Sandstone, 119
San Pietro in Montorio, 91
Sanremo, 84
Sanskrit, 160
SantAgnese in Agone, 79
Santa Maria Maggiore, 57
Santa Maria Novella, 277
SantAndrea della Valle, 79
Sarcophagus, 92
Sasanian Empire, 211
Sassanid Empire, 6
Satavahana, 107
Satmar (Hasidic dynasty), 243
Saudia, 20
Saudi Arabia, 1, 2, 20, 29, 32, 43
Saudi Aramco, 275
Saudi Gazette, 24
Saudi T.V. Channel 1, 25
Saudi T.V. Channel II, 25
Saudi TV Sports, 25
Scipione Caffarelli-Borghese, 97
Scrambling, 176
Sculpture, 78
Sea Peoples, 253
Second Coming, 202
Second Fitna, 190
Second Islamic Civil War, 11
Second Jewish Temple, 206
Second language, 26
Second Saudi State, 11
Second Temple, 190, 191, 207, 210, 212, 243
Second Vatican Council, 58
Sedimentary rock, 171
Sedimentary rocks, 165
Segula (Kabbalah), 237
Sekhmet, 258
Selection criteria, 103
Sena dynasty, 116
Senusret I, 250
Sephardic, 238

Sephardi Jews, 215
Serious Sam, 259
Seti I, 253
Shah, 35
Shaivism, 161
Shallow sea, 171
Shalosh regalim, 226
Shangri-La, 167
Sharif, 42
Sharif of Mecca, 3, 11, 42
Shar Mansur, 18
Shavuot, 227
Shawarma, 25
Sheep, 252
Shekhinah, 232
Shelomo Dov Goitein, 192
Shikhara, 104
Shimon Peres, 226
Shir ha-Shirim Rabbah, 282
Shirk (Islam), 48
Shiromani Gurdwara Parbandhak Committee, 134
Shiva, 120, 142, 160, 161
Shiva Purana, 143
Shivaratri, 142, 154
Shlomo Goren, 226, 243
Shlomo Zalman Aurbach, 284
Shmuel Rabinovitch, 230, 246
Shmuel Rabinowitz, 232
Shofar, 225
Short-toed snake eagle, 182
Short tons, 210
Shunga Empire, 108
Sibt ibn al-Jawzi, 191
Siddhartha Gautama, 105
Siege of Jerusalem (1099), 193
Siege of Jerusalem (1187), 214
Siege of Jerusalem (70), 276
Siege of Jerusalem (AD 70), 190
Siege of Kut, 12
Siege of Mecca (683), 11
Siege of Mecca (692), 11
Siege of Medina, 42
Siena, 84
Sikhism, 126
Silene dionysii, 182
Silene oligantha, 182
Silhouette, 98
Simon the Zealot, 277
Simplified Chinese characters, 160
Singh Sabha movement, 126, 138
Sino-Indian border dispute, 164
Sir Ronald Storrs, 218
Sirsi, Karnataka, 148
Sistine Madonna, 78
Six-Day War, 198, 207, 208, 226, 240

Sixtus V, 72
Smallpox, 8
Snake, 182
Solar deity, 258
Solomonic columns, 80
Solomons temple, 210, 212
South Asia, 26
Southeast Asia, 26
Spain, 28
Sparrowhawk, 182
Sphere, 70
Spice trade, 6
Square mile, 44
Sringeri, 148
St. Andrew, 72
Stargate SG-1, 259
State school, 26
Status quo (Holy Land sites), 220
Status Quo of the Holy Places, 207
Stefano Bianca, 30
St. Josaphats Basilica, 79
St. Marks Basilica, 67
St. Mary of the Angels in Chicago, 79
St. Nicholas Church (Malá Strana), 79
Stonework, 207
St. Paul outside the Walls, 57
St Pauls Cathedral, 79
St. Peter, 57
St. Peters Baldachin, 79
St. Peters Basilica, **51**
St. Peters Square, 53, 54, 60
Strabo, 254
Stucco, 75, 104
Stupa, 105, 164
Subduction, 165
Succession to Muhammad, 3
Sufism, 26
Sukhmani Sahib, 128
Suleiman the Magnificent, 194, 202, 214, 217
Sultan, 214
Summit, 159, 169
Sunga, 109
Sungas, 108
Sunlight, 162
Sunshine duration, 19
Supreme Court of Nepal, 150
Supreme Muslim Council, 220
Suq Al Lail, 18
Sura, 8, 26, 33
Sura 17, 200
Surah, 194
Surya, 119, 120, 145
Sutlej, 160
Swastika, 163
Sykaminea, 171
Syria, 8, 38

Syrian cuisine, 25

Table of World Heritage Sites by country, 103
Tabuk, Saudi Arabia, 47
Tagzig Olmo Lung Ring, 163
Taibah University, 46
Taif, 29
Tallit, 228
Tantra, 161, 162
Tara (Buddhism), 120
Tau cross, 61
Tax collector, 35
Taxus baccata, 180
Teej, 142
Tefillin, 240
T. E. Lawrence, 12
Telephone numbering plan, 2
Tempietto, 83
Template:Hinduism, 142
Template:Islam, 2
Template:Saivism, 161
Template talk:Hinduism, 142
Template talk:Islam, 2
Template talk:Saivism, 161
Temple in Jerusalem, 80, 200–202, 206, 209, 235, 237
Temple Mount, 190, 202, 206, 209
Temple Mount and Eretz Yisrael Faithful Movement, 202
Temple Mount entry restrictions, 206
Temple of Amenhotep IV, 250
Temple of Solomon, 191, 193
Templum Domini, 193
Tenakh, 4
Terminating vista, 85
Termite, 143
Tethys Ocean, 165
Thamudic, 8
Thangka, 163
The 95 Theses, 63
Theban Triad, 250, 256
Thebes, Egypt, 250, 252, 258
The Economist, 273
The Marriage of the Virgin (Raphael), 202
The Mummy Returns, 259
The New York Times, 24, 273
The Qishla of Mecca, 20
The Sims 3: World Adventures, 259
The Spy Who Loved Me (film), 259
Thessaloniki, 170
Thessaly, 170
Third Temple, 202
Thomas the Apostle, 56, 92
Thutmose I, 253
Tiber, 54, 55, 85
Tibetan alphabet, 160

Tibetan languages, 160
Tibet Autonomous Region, 159, 160
Tigris, 6
Tihamah, 2, 4, 7, 20
Time (magazine), 246
Time zone, 2, 32
Tirthankara, 161
Tisha BAv, 207, 213, 223, 228, 236, 238
Tishrei, 238
Titan (mythology), 175
Titanomachy, 187
Titus, 276
Toleration, 218
Tomb, 85
Tomb of the Julii, 87
Tomb Raider: The Last Revelation, 259
Tom Holland (author), 4, 273
Tonnes, 210
Topographic isolation, 169
Topographic prominence, 159, 169, 170
Torah ark, 230
Torah scroll, 230
Torre Eurosky, 101
Town square, 85
Trade route, 6
Transept, 56, 61
Transformers: Revenge of the Fallen, 259
Transhimalaya, 160
Translation, 206
Transliteration, 170, 206
Trapezoid, 85
Travertine, 75
Treaty of Hudaybiyyah, 10
Tribes of Arabia, 7
True Cross, 72, 81, 89
Truth, 92
Tsaritsani, 177
Tufa, 68
Tung, Sikkim, 128
Turkey, 29, 47
Turkic peoples, 116
Turkish cuisine, 25
Turkmenistan, 29
Turpin Bannister, 99
Turtle, 182
Tuscan order, 85
Tutelary deity, 252
Twelve Apostles, 57, 75
Twelve Olympians, 175

Ubaydah ibn al-Harith, 39
UCLA, 252
Udupi, 148
Uffizi Gallery, 62
Ultra prominent peak, 169
Umar, 10, 33, 41

Umar ibn Al-Khattab, 200
Umayyad, 211
Umayyad architecture, 190
Umayyad Caliphate, 10, 34, 190, 191, 207
Umayyah ibn Khalaf, 39
Ummah, 10
Umm Al-Qura University, 26
Umrah, 16, 25, 35
UNESCO, 59, 121, 183
UNESCO World Heritage Site, 104
UNESCO World Heritage Sites, 142
Unfinished obelisk, 254
United Kingdom of Great Britain and Ireland, 42
University of Baghdad, 8
University of Nottingham, 204
Upper Egypt, 250, 254
Urban area, 32
UTC+3, 2, 32
Uthman, 41
Uthman ibn Affan, 10, 38

Vaad Leumi, 220, 221
Vaisakhi, 139
Vaishnav, 145
Vajrapani, 120
Vajravārāhī, 120
Vajrayana, 162
Valley of Baca, 6
Vatican City, 51, 53, 57, 61, 276
Vatican Hill, 61
Vatican State, 67
Vayeira, 4
Vegetable, 46
Veil of Veronica, 81, 89
Venice, 66
Veronica thessalica, 182
Vespasian, 276
Vestry, 67, 75
Via Cornelia, 61
Via della Conciliazione, 55, 85
Vico Consorti, 87
Vienna, 79
Viola striis - notata, 182
Virgilio Noè, 97
Vishnu, 120
Vishnu Purana, 161
Vivant Denon, 256
Vlachs, 171
Voice of Palestine, 284
Vrontou, Pieria, 171
Vulgate, 73

Wadjet, 258
Wahhabist, 20
Wāli, 24

Walid ibn Utba, 39
Waqf, 207, 214
War elephant, 7
Warrens Gate, 207
Washington Institute for Near East Policy, 281
Watchmen, 259
Weather station, 178
Weligama Sri Sumangala, 119
Wenceslaus I, Duke of Bohemia, 56
Western Christianity, 79
Western Stone, 210
Western Wall, 190, **205**
Western Wall Heritage Foundation, 230
Western Wall Tunnel, 207
White stork, 182
Wikimedia Commons, 123
Wikipedia:Citation needed, 4, 25, 26, 105, 122, 139, 150, 174, 175, 187, 193, 194, 198, 200, 202, 209, 227, 237, 238, 243, 250
Wikipedia:Citing sources, 117
Wikipedia:Media help, 206
Wikipedia:Please clarify, 3, 25, 58, 99
Wikisource, 271
Wiktionary:alp, 160
Wikt:مكة, 2
Wild boar, 182
Wildcat, 182
William George Browne, 256
William Montgomery Watt, 36
Willow, 180
Wilsons Arch (Jerusalem), 210, 230
W:International Space Station, 21
With Jordan, 226
Women of the Wall, 228, 239
Works, 284
World Agudath Israel, 220
World Heritage Committee, 52, 103, 250
World Heritage Site, 52, 59, 103, 121, 250
World Union for Progressive Judaism, 228, 238
World War I, 12, 42
Wylie transliteration, 160

Yaakov Chaim Sofer, 284
Yalkut Yosef, 234
Yamantaka, 120
Yaqub al-Ghusayn, 197
Yaqut al-Hamawi, 4
Yarlung Tsangpo, 160
Ya Sin, 194
Year of the Elephant, 7
Yehuda Meir Getz, 232, 240
Yemen, 7, 25, 35, 36
Yeshivah, 244
Yisroel Yaakov Fisher, 237
Yitzhak Rabin, 226

Yoel Sirkis, 236
Yom Kippur, 220
Yom Yerushalayim, 228, 244
Yoni, 147
Yoreh Deah, 284
Yosef Chaim Sonnenfeld, 220, 225
Yosemite Decimal System, 176

Zamzam Well, 7, 20
Zedekiahs Cave, 210
Zeus, 175
Zhang-Zhung language, 160
Zionism, 208
Zionist Organisation, 220
Zohar, 232, 284
Zvi Hirsch Kaindenover, 233

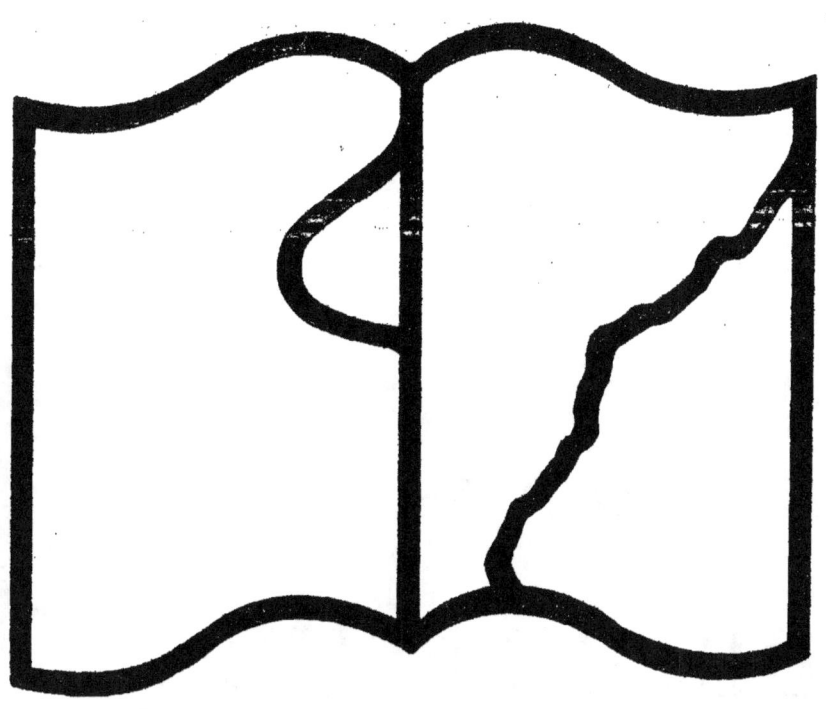

**Symbole applicable
pour tout, ou partie
des documents microfilmés**

Texte détérioré — reliure défectueuse

NF Z 43-120-11

ŒUVRES

DE GOETHE

III

PARIS. — IMPRIMERIE DE CH. LAHURE ET Cie
Rues de Fleurus, 9, et de l'Ouest, 21

THÉATRE
DE GOETHE

TRADUCTION NOUVELLE

PAR JACQUES PORCHAT

TOME DEUXIÈME

PARIS
LIBRAIRIE DE L. HACHETTE ET Cie
RUE PIERRE-SARRAZIN, N° 14

1860